RUBÁIYÁT OF OMAR KHAYYÁM

EDWARD FITZGERALD was born in 1809 at Bredfield, Suffolk, to a wealthy Anglo-Irish family. He was educated at King Edward VI Grammar School in Bury St Edmunds and at Trinity College, Cambridge. He married Lucy Barton in 1856 but they separated the following year. FitzGerald followed no profession; his lifelong interest was in friendship. He was close to Thackeray, Tennyson, and Carlyle, but never thought of himself as a writer; his own publications were occasional, almost all anonymous, and paid for by himself. His first book was *Euphranor* (1851), a prose dialogue on the education of young men; his first translations were *Six Dramas of Calderón* (1853). FitzGerald's interest in Persian was sparked by his friendship with a young scholar, Edward Cowell. When Cowell left Britain for India in 1856, he gave FitzGerald a copy of a Persian manuscript containing poems attributed to Omar Khayyám. FitzGerald's *Rubáiyát of Omar Khayyám* appeared in 1859. It sold no copies and was relegated to the 'penny box' outside the shop of its (nominal) publisher, Bernard Quaritch; there, in 1861, it was 'discovered' by members of the Pre-Raphaelite circle including D. G. Rossetti and Swinburne, and its fame was assured. Three further editions appeared in FitzGerald's lifetime. Besides the *Rubáiyát*, FitzGerald's letters are his most sustained literary achievement. He died in 1883.

OMAR IBN IBRAHIM AL-KHAYYÁM (1048–1131) was born in Nishapur, in north-east Persia (now Iran). He achieved fame as a mathematician, astronomer, and philosopher; the first allusion to him as a poet comes over forty years after his death, and only in the following century was he identified as a composer of the short, epigrammatic poems known in Persian as *ruba'iyat*. The question of their authorship remains unsettled; FitzGerald certainly believed in the authenticity of the ones he translated.

DANIEL KARLIN is Winterstoke Professor of English at the University of Bristol and has previously taught at University College London, Boston University, and the University of Sheffield. His books include *Browning's Hatreds* and *Proust's English*, as well as editions of Robert Browning and Rudyard Kipling.

OXFORD WORLD'S CLASSICS

*For over 100 years Oxford World's Classics have brought
readers closer to the world's great literature. Now with over 700
titles—from the 4,000-year-old myths of Mesopotamia to the
twentieth century's greatest novels—the series makes available
lesser-known as well as celebrated writing.*

*The pocket-sized hardbacks of the early years contained
introductions by Virginia Woolf, T. S. Eliot, Graham Greene,
and other literary figures which enriched the experience of reading.
Today the series is recognized for its fine scholarship and
reliability in texts that span world literature, drama and poetry,
religion, philosophy and politics. Each edition includes perceptive
commentary and essential background information to meet the
changing needs of readers.*

OXFORD WORLD'S CLASSICS

EDWARD FITZGERALD

Rubáiyát of Omar Khayyám

The Astronomer–Poet of Persia

Edited with an Introduction and Notes by
DANIEL KARLIN

OXFORD
UNIVERSITY PRESS

OXFORD

UNIVERSITY PRESS

Great Clarendon Street, Oxford OX2 6DP

Oxford University Press is a department of the University of Oxford.
It furthers the University's objective of excellence in research, scholarship,
and education by publishing worldwide in

Oxford New York

Auckland Cape Town Dar es Salaam Hong Kong Karachi
Kuala Lumpur Madrid Melbourne Mexico City Nairobi
New Delhi Shanghai Taipei Toronto

With offices in

Argentina Austria Brazil Chile Czech Republic France Greece
Guatemala Hungary Italy Japan Poland Portugal Singapore
South Korea Switzerland Thailand Turkey Ukraine Vietnam

Oxford is a registered trade mark of Oxford University Press
in the UK and in certain other countries

Published in the United States
by Oxford University Press Inc., New York

British Library Cataloguing in Publication Data

Data available

Library of Congress Cataloging-in-Publication Data

Data available

Typeset by Cepha Imaging Private Ltd., Bangalore, India
Printed in Great Britain
on acid-free paper by
Clays Ltd, Elcograf S.p.A.

ISBN 978–0–19–958050–7

17

ACKNOWLEDGEMENTS

THE focus of this edition is on the poem that Edward FitzGerald called *Rubáiyát of Omar Khayyám*, not on the authentic original *ruba'iyat* (plural of *ruba'i*, a short epigrammatic poem) of Omar ibn Ibrahim al-Khayyam (1048–1131)—assuming these could be identified. I have not commented on questions of attribution at all, and cannot comment on questions of accuracy, except at second-hand. Nevertheless it is essential to have some knowledge of FitzGerald's Persian texts; here I have relied mainly on the versions of A. J. Arberry, whose flavour is a bit archaic to modern taste but who is (as far as I can judge) properly 'literal' in that he does not introduce figures of speech which are not in the original, or at least does not do so without explanation. I have also consulted the older versions of Edward Heron-Allen (about whom Arberry is sometimes unnecessarily sharp) and I have looked at other modern versions, of which the best (to my layman's mind) is that by Peter Avery and John Heath-Stubbs, which repeats in some measure the collaboration between a scholar of Persian and an English poet from which our *Rubáiyát* was born. I have benefited from the work of other editors, critics, and biographers, even where I have disagreed with their conclusions or emphases. I owe a particular debt to work by Peter Avery, Dick Davis, Christopher Decker, Erik Gray, Robert Bernard Martin, and Alfred McKinley Terhune, FitzGerald's biographer and (with Annabelle Burdick Terhune) the editor of his letters.

I am grateful to staff at the British Library, Cambridge University Library, and the Library of Trinity College, Cambridge, and to Professor Adrian Poole, for facilitating my research. Samantha Matthews compiled the Chronology and gave me, as always, invaluable help and advice at every stage.

My work in this book is dedicated to my son, Ben Karlin, and my daughter, Katie O'Shea.

his tenderness, his puckish wit, who binds the poem together and, so to speak, convinces us of its integrity, of its giving utterance to something inevitable, and therefore permanent.

FitzGerald's creation of the figure of Omar can be understood in a number of different, but overlapping 'frames' of interpretation. Biography and history define the poem's personal and cultural 'moment', its origins in FitzGerald's own life and character, and its responsiveness to contemporary events and ideas. The 'Victorian' aspect of the poem seems especially attuned to the malaise of religious orthodoxy in the mid-nineteenth century, and to the growing popularity of an 'aesthetic' reaction against the forces of respectability; at the same time we must acknowledge that the poem did not originate as an intellectual project, but was set in motion by circumstances in FitzGerald's life which he would have done almost anything to avoid, and of which his introduction to the poetry of Omar Khayyám was in some ways an accidental by-product. His 'Orientalism', though it shares some of the characteristics of a well-established tradition in English, and indeed European literature, is distinctive in that it began as a linguistic exercise, not a literary choice. FitzGerald's method as a translator comes into play here, as does his profound living sense of his own literary tradition: these are the sources of what he called the poem's 'English music', without which its bleak vision could not have been so powerfully or movingly conveyed.

Edward FitzGerald: Life and Contacts

To Edmund Gosse there was something exasperating and pitiable in the spectacle of Edward FitzGerald's 'career'. 'He was a man of taste in easy circumstances,' Gosse remarked, 'and until he was forty years of age he was nothing else whatever.'[12] Biographers have done what they can to disperse the atmosphere of drift and dilettantism that suffuses his life, but Gosse's judgement, that of a man who had worked for his living and was subject to the discipline of a professional writer and 'man of letters', is more clear-sighted. FitzGerald was born in 1809 to a wealthy Anglo-Irish family—so wealthy that

---

[12] *Variorum*, I. xi.

what remained, after multiple financial reverses (the most serious being his father's disastrous speculation in coal-mining in the grounds of one of his own estates), was more than enough to support him throughout his life. His father was a squirearchical cipher; his mother was a Thackerayan grotesque of social pretension and emotional nullity. Recalling his small child's view of the world from the nursery at Bredfield Hall, he wrote many years later: 'My Mother used to come up sometimes, and we Children were not much comforted.'[13] For years FitzGerald's only 'occupation', after his parents separated, was to accompany his mother, as nominal male companion, to society dinners and the theatre in London and Brighton. He writhed, but until her death in 1855 could not escape. His education, at the King Edward VI Grammar School in Bury St Edmunds and Trinity College, Cambridge, was benign and productive of close friendships and wide, unsystematic learning (mostly outside the formal curriculum); but it led to no profession, indeed to no activity. He had no fixed idea of what to do; there was no need for him to make what Samuel Johnson, in *Rasselas*, calls 'the choice of life'. It may be said that not to choose itself constitutes a choice, but it is hardly a vocation.

FitzGerald's way of life became an odd blend of transience and tenacity, and a paradoxical emblem of his social origins and standing. He did not have a house of his own until he bought Little Grange on the outskirts of Woodbridge in 1864—and he did not actually move in until he was evicted from his lodgings in 1873. (He then took to signing himself 'Littlegrange' or 'The Laird of Little Grange'.) Yet he was rooted in Suffolk; his *Sea Words and Phrases along the Suffolk Coast* (1869) is evidence of intense attachment, and of his hostility to the landowners who bought up the coastline, blocked up footpaths, and persecuted poachers. No one but a gentleman completely assured of his own breeding could have excoriated one of his neighbours as a 'bull-dog-named Potentate, on whose large slice of Suffolk birds do accumulate and men decay; cottages left to ruin lest they should harbour a dog, or a gun, or a poor man'.[14] No one but a gentleman could have got away with dressing as FitzGerald dressed, or behaving as he behaved in public, while reserving the privileges of his rank. His slovenliness was not an affectation, and neither was his occasional

---

[13] *Letters*, iii. 331.   [14] *Variorum*, vi. 239–40.

and startling rudeness.[15] He was not disreputable, but he was not respectable either; he was not 'alienated', not a *poète maudit* like Baudelaire (*Les Fleurs du mal* was published in 1857, two years before the *Rubáiyát*); he was not urban enough for that. Yet he was unassimilated, except to the grand tradition of English eccentricity. Nowhere is this more evident than in his life as a writer, which may be described as a kind of anti-career, devoid of professional or financial ambition, haphazard, miscellaneous, and undeveloped: for although the *Rubáiyát* belongs to a group of translations, the group itself has no intellectual or stylistic coherence, and nothing but chronological sequence links FitzGerald's first composition to his last.

FitzGerald was capable of hard and devoted intellectual work, as we shall see; but the impetus for this work had to come from a personal, not an intellectual source. From his schooldays onward, what mattered to him most were friendships, almost all with men. Into these relationships he poured his capacity for both emotional and intellectual exchange; physical desire was almost certainly sublimated. His homoerotic feelings, clear as they seem to modern biographers and critics such as Robert Bernard Martin and Dick Davis, were probably unclear to him, at least in the form conveyed by our word 'gay'; but it is clear enough that friendship in itself mattered more to him than any other form of relationship, including family.

We owe the *Rubáiyát* to the loss, or threatened loss, of one such friendship, and to FitzGerald's single disastrous experiment in social conformity, his marriage to Lucy Barton. Both these events took place in 1856. In February of that year, FitzGerald learned that his close friend, and mentor in Persian, Edward Cowell, had accepted an appointment as Professor of English History at the Presidency College in Calcutta. FitzGerald was approaching his 47th birthday; Cowell had just turned 30. They had met in 1844, when Cowell was only 18. He was the son of an Ipswich merchant, a self-made scholar with a passion for both European and Oriental languages; he taught himself Persian at the age of 14, but had to work in the family business until he was 23, when he finally matriculated at Oxford. It was there, on a 'wet Sunday' in December 1852, that he suggested to FitzGerald

---

[15] On FitzGerald's cultivated slovenliness, see Martin, p. 231. Anecdotes of his eccentricities, abruptnesses, and put-downs are legion; they were already being collected and disseminated at the time of his centenary (in e.g. *Edward FitzGerald 1809–1909: Centenary Celebrations Souvenir*, Ipswich, 1909).

the study of Persian as an intellectual pastime, 'and guaranteed to teach the grammar in a day'.[16] FitzGerald was slow to enthuse: 'I am not *greatly* impressed with the desire to poke out even a smatter of Persian', he wrote to Cowell in October 1853, and in December he told Frederick Tennyson that he was persevering only 'because it is a point in common with [Cowell], and enables us to study a little together'. A month later he had the bug: he was 'Persian mad'.[17] But Cowell himself, though he never abandoned Persian, was always more interested in Sanskrit; when he graduated in 1854 he found few academic openings in England, whereas India offered both a career and an opportunity to develop his scholarship on native ground.

FitzGerald tried hard to persuade Cowell not to go to Calcutta. 'What is to become of my Stupendous Learning when you go?' he wrote. 'I scarce see my old Friends, and make no new ones. I shall die starved of human regard. . . . I want you to do Work in England, as well as help to keep me alive in it.'[18] But Cowell's mind was made up; the irony is that his parting gift to FitzGerald was to stimulate his friend's 'Stupendous Learning' to its highest pitch.

In April 1856 Cowell came across a fifteenth-century manuscript compilation of poems by Omar Khayyám, in Sir William Ouseley's collection of Oriental manuscripts, purchased by the Bodleian Library in 1843. Cowell transcribed the Ouseley MS, and then made a copy of his transcript for FitzGerald, which he finished in FitzGerald's company and gave to him on 11 July, when FitzGerald was staying with him at Rushmere, near Oxford. A week or so later FitzGerald wrote to him with what seems almost like brusqueness. 'Thanks for Omar. I have looked over most of him since I left you. Here are Queries etc.' But the brusqueness covers pain that can't quite be suppressed, for Cowell's departure for India was imminent. A list of dry queries about vocabulary and idiom is followed by this: 'Well—all this I have written; but my Thoughts are often upon other Things in which you are concerned: of which I less care to speak.'[19] His farewell letter of 28 July takes stock of his diminished expectations: 'I shall very soon write to you; and hope to keep up something of Communion by such meagre Intercourse.'[20]

Yet Cowell's gift to FitzGerald of the Ouseley MS did more than FitzGerald could have hoped to establish 'something of Communion'

---

[16] Terhune, p. 170.   [17] *Letters*, ii. 110, 117, 119.   [18] Ibid. 214.
[19] Ibid. 234–5.   [20] Ibid. 236.

between them—much more than a 'meagre Intercourse' of letters could have done on its own. With unconscious tact and perfect timing, Cowell had presented FitzGerald with a kind of magic mirror, in which he could see himself—'savage against Destiny', as he put it, but also given to 'Epicurean pathos'—and also conjure the image of his absent friend.[21] But Cowell's departure, though it might have prompted FitzGerald to read and relish Omar's 'curious Infidel and Epicurean Tetrastichs', would probably not have been enough for them to claim him, body and soul, as they did over the next two years. For that daemonic possession we have to thank the un-daemonic figure of Lucy Barton.

FitzGerald's marriage remains an enigma. However he defined his sexual nature he had never tried to live against it. Yet on 4 November 1856, just over two months after the Cowells left for India, he married Lucy Barton, the 48-year-old daughter of an old Suffolk friend, Bernard Barton, the 'Quaker Poet'. Why did he do it?

The explanation refers rather to the engagement than the marriage itself. Bernard Barton's death in 1849 left Lucy impoverished and dependent. He may have asked FitzGerald to look after Lucy, and each may have interpreted this request in a different sense. FitzGerald either said something, or allowed something to be inferred by Lucy, which he later found impossible to disavow. His own financial affairs were embroiled at the time, in the aftermath of his father's bankruptcy, and it seems that Lucy understood that the marriage would have to be delayed. She accepted a position as governess and companion in a wealthy family who were friends of her father, and sat down to wait. FitzGerald, on the other hand, seems to have hoped the whole arrangement would quietly dissolve in time. He maintained no contact with Lucy. He spoke to no one of his being 'engaged', and only the shadow of a rumour flitted here and there among his friends.

The catastrophe was precipitated by the death of FitzGerald's mother in January 1855. Released from filial bondage, he was free to enter wedlock; in the summer of 1856, when the estate was settled, he found himself comparatively wealthy. The timing was

---

[21] These phrases (and the one in the following sentence) come from a letter to Tennyson of 15 July 1856, written just after FitzGerald returned from his last visit to the Cowells (ibid. 234). See note to st. LXXIV (p. 166).

fortuitous—better say fatal. FitzGerald became aware that Lucy expected him to fulfil a promise he had not intended to make; his circumstances no longer gave him an excuse for further delay; at the same time he understood that Cowell did really intend to go to India. It is likely that he made up his mind to marry Lucy on the rebound from Cowell's abandonment of him.

FitzGerald was rarely mean-minded, and even more rarely mean in his behaviour; but his own suffering, and shame at his folly, hardened him to treat Lucy with intolerance and contempt. He thought the daughter of his old Quaker friend had acquired airs and graces and expected him to lead a life of fashion. He began by refusing to dress for the wedding itself, which he attended in his usual shabby clothes, looking 'like a victim being led to his doom'.[22] The sexual side of the marriage is undocumented, but cannot have been happy. FitzGerald seems to have set himself systematically to thwart Lucy's desire to live elegantly, or even respectably. Anecdotes of their brief time together as husband and wife make painful reading, and include a rare glimpse of FitzGerald drunk—and not in the happy manner of Omar Khayyám.[23] By May 1857 he and Lucy were spending more time apart than together, and in August their separation was formally agreed. As though cured of toothache, FitzGerald regained his generosity and composure. Lucy had an allowance of £300 a year and agreed not to live in Woodbridge. The arrangement was amicable, and, so to speak, well founded. If Lucy had shown blundering insensitivity in holding FitzGerald to his 'promise', she let him off with good grace, and more lightly than he deserved.

The period of FitzGerald's greatest misery in his marriage was the winter of 1856–7. During this time he wrote regularly to Cowell, and these letters are filled with Persian, though Omar is by no means an exclusive concern. But in the spring and early summer, as his separation from Lucy became a de facto reality, Omar began more and more to preoccupy his thoughts. Although Cowell had, so to speak, left him to Lucy, he had also left him this trace of himself, a manuscript that was a labour of love. On 5 June 1857 he wrote to Cowell from the Bedfordshire estate of one of his closest friends, William Browne, telling him of his reading of Omar Khayyám 'in a Paddock covered with Buttercups and brushed by a delicious Breeze', offering

---

[22] *Letters*, ii. 242 n. 1.
[23] Terhune, p. 199.

the first of his verse translations—not into English, but what he called 'Monkish Latin' (i.e. medieval Latin, which ignores the quantitative scansion of classical Latin prosody and puts Latin phrases into 'English' metrical patterns); he told Cowell that the stanza was one of a number he had composed. He knew that Cowell 'would be sorry . . . to think that Omar breathes a sort of Consolation to me!'—but he told him all the same.[24]

Cowell had not forgotten either FitzGerald or Omar. Soon after his arrival at Calcutta towards the end of November 1856, he found, in the library of the Asiatic Institute, a manuscript of Omar made by an Indian scribe, later in date and considerably longer than the Ouseley MS. He arranged for it to be copied by a local scribe, and sent the copy to FitzGerald, who received it on 14 June 1857, along with a present for Lucy, a box made of aromatic wood. Lucy was away, and FitzGerald sent thanks for both gifts:

My Letter will not have to be posted for a few days yet, so as my Wife may yet return in time to inclose her thanks for the beautiful Box which came forth [from] its Coffin breathing a veritable باد صبا which has also perfumed my MS. . . . And the human Interest which all MSS have beyond Printed Books—written by a living hand at the end of which was a living Soul like my own—under a darker skin—some 'dark Indian face with white Turban wreathed' and under an Indian Sun. And you spoke to him those thousands of miles away, and he spoke to you, and this MS. was put into your hands when done; and then deposited in that little box, made also by some dark hand, along with its aromatic Companion: you and your dear Wife saw them after they were nailed down; and directed the Box; and so they have crossed the Atlantic, and after some durance in London have reached my hands at last.[25]

Images of imprisonment and death are 'perfumed' with divine creativity, as FitzGerald continues the metaphor of Omar 'breathing consolation' to him. The phrase 'a living Soul' echoes Genesis 2: 7: 'And the Lord God formed man of the dust of the ground, and breathed into his nostrils the breath of life; and man became a living soul'. The 'human Interest' which FitzGerald sees in 'all MSS' means more than that such things arouse our curiosity; we all have an *interest* in each other, are joined by our common humanity, however differentiated by

---

[24] *Letters*, ii. 273. The Latin stanza contributed to st. IV.

[25] *Letters*, ii. 274. Terhune translates the Persian phrase as 'morning breeze' (p. 275 n. 8).

'a darker skin'. Yet this affirmation of union has to battle against the fact of distance ('thousands of miles away'), and the intimation that the MS is itself like an embalmed corpse, 'deposited in that little box' and 'nailed down'; or that its 'aromatic Companion', an empty box, is like a satire on his marriage. No wonder FitzGerald placed Omar, from the first, in a garden; no wonder he has him, in a line absent from the Persian original, accuse God of devising both Eden and the snake.[26] Perhaps, as one of few Victorian readers to know and love the poetry of Andrew Marvell, he remembered the stanza of 'The Garden' in which Marvell evokes 'that happy garden-state | While man there walked without a mate', and which concludes: 'Two paradises 'twere in one | To live in paradise alone'.[27]

The Victorian 'Moment'

The early reviewers of the *Rubáiyát* sensed that it was in tune with the zeitgeist, though they could not be sure whether the affinity was Omar Khayyám's or the translator's. Charles Eliot Norton, for example, writing in 1869, begins by announcing that 'The prevailing traits of the genius of Omar Khayyám are so coincident with certain characteristics of the spiritual temper of our own generation, that it is hardly surprising that his poetry, of which hitherto the Western world knew nothing, is beginning to excite the interest it deserves', but he later acknowledges that some of these 'traits' have been 're-enforced by the English [translation]', and that 'every now and then a note of the nineteenth century seems to mingle its tone with those of the twelfth'. His scruple does not amount to unease, but it registers a difficulty, so that when he again emphasizes 'how close the thought and the sentiment of the Persian poet often are to the thought and sentiment of our own day', he immediately qualifies the point: 'So that in its English dress it reads like the latest and freshest expression of the perplexity and of the doubt of the generation to which we ourselves belong'.[28]

Thomas W. Hinchliff, who cites Norton's essay in his own article of 1870, was less concerned about whether this 'expression' belonged

---

[26] See st. LVIII, and Explanatory Notes, p. 162.

[27] 'The Garden', ll. 57–8, 63–4. FitzGerald wrote of Marvell as 'an old favourite of mine' in 1872 (*Letters*, iii. 322).

[28] Extracts from Norton's review (and from Hinchliff's, quoted in the following paragraph) are reprinted in App. 1.

to Omar or to his translator. He was also less inclined to see it as a peculiarly modern phenomenon: 'The scepticism of Omar is but the "old old story" clad in a more than usually poetical dress . . . it has flowed down to us from the days of *Vanitas vanitatum*, in a continued succession till the day when our own Laureate set the great battle of the human soul before us in his poem of *The Two Voices*'. The double analogy, with the Old Testament book of Ecclesiastes ('Vanity of vanities, saith the Preacher; all is vanity') and with Tennyson, repos-itions the poem in a tradition of metaphysical scepticism, so that its spirit appears not so much 'Victorian' as universal and recurrent. Yet it might be objected that Hinchliff's phrase 'more than usually poetical dress' begs the question. The appeal made by the poem to Victorian 'aestheticism' can be made to sound frivolous (Swinburne rushing off to compose 'Laus Veneris' in the 'Rubáiyát stanza' form), but it may be taken to imply something with a very broad cultural scope. Robert Bernard Martin, for example, argues that the poem spoke to those who advocated 'the warm-blooded worship of beauty', not for its own sake but as part of a conscious stance against both religious and scientific dogma; what FitzGerald meant in persistently calling the poem 'Epicurean' was a philosophy

in which man recognises that sense perception is his only guide to knowledge, that his mode in distinguishing choices is by the enlightened pleasure of the senses, and that the best life is a retired one where marriage, the begetting of children, and civic responsibility are no longer paramount or even desirable. It was a doctrine of withdrawal that seemed increasingly attractive in the face of the inhumane society caused by the combination of the Industrial Revolution, intolerant Calvinism, and the theory of evolution.[29]

The broad-brush sweep of generalization with which Martin con-cludes assumes too readily the co-operation of different kinds of social and cultural forces and the uniformity of their impact. A different interpretation of the 'aesthetic' of the poem leads Erik Gray to see Housman's *A Shropshire Lad* as the poem's 'true immediate heir', because of its 'mingling of indifference with pathos and regret'.[30] According to this view, the 'Victorian' aspect of the work reaches its most precise, but also its narrowest definition.

---

[29] Martin, p. 221.
[30] Gray, p. 135; as he notes, the influence of the *Rubáiyát* on Housman is mentioned by Davis (p. 1).

Hinchliff's reading of the poem as 'the old old story' may be incomplete, but it has the merit of staying within the boundaries of the text; Norton's positive assertion that the poem articulates 'the thought and sentiment of our own day' overstates the case, and has led to claims which cannot be justified. For example, the coincidence of the date of publication of the first edition of the *Rubáiyát*, 1859, with that of Darwin's *On the Origin of Species by Natural Selection*, has been made the basis for affirming that the *Rubáiyát* mounts an equivalent challenge to the certainties and pieties of imperial Britain. Leaving aside the disproportion of scale, and the lack of understanding of Darwin's achievement and influence that this comparison implies, it is a problematic parallel on its own account. Darwin was a Victorian progressive optimist, and *Origin of Species* ends on a note of expansive speculative delight, filled with hope for future discoveries, future triumphs of our race, even though natural selection means that 'we' will have changed beyond recognition when these triumphs occur. Almost all the anxieties that *Origin of Species* is said to have caused, including those concerning the existence of God, the finality of death, the prospect of extinction, existed in British society long before its publication; in the long run, what Darwin accomplished was a tremendous act of consolation. FitzGerald was genuinely baffled when he was told

that Mr. Leslie Stephen, who lately lost his Wife, who was Thackeray's youngest Daughter, positively found Consolation in Wordsworth's Excursion, and—Omar K.! And he who told me—an American Professor—said the same thing had happened to him. This is a little Mystery . . .[31]

The false consciousness which FitzGerald detects in such readings is captured in his pun on the word 'positively'. The idiomatic usage ('really and truly!') signals the absurdity of reading the poem *positively*, as though it said Yes to the universe. The word *yes* occurs once in the poem, in stanza XLVII, where it is exposed at the end of a line—apparently by FitzGerald's need for a rhyme, but actually by his scorn of evasion:

> And if the Wine you drink, the Lip you press,
> End in the Nothing all Things end in—Yes—
>   Then fancy while Thou art, Thou art but what
> Thou shalt be—Nothing—Thou shalt not be less.

[31] To Anna Biddell, 15 [for 13] Sept. 1876, *Letters*, iii. 704.

The *Rubáiyát* says Yes to Nothing: look how the two words are sin-gled out. The word *nothing* is central to the poem, and if that is true then the kind of consolation FitzGerald thought he was offering, and which he himself took from his study of Omar, could not be further removed from Darwin.

Nevertheless, the *Rubáiyát* is not a work detached from the real world, seeking to escape Victorian fog and gloom on a Persian magic carpet. The opening paragraph of the Preface links Omar's life with that of a great statesman who served a dynasty of ruthless conquer-ors, and a religious fanatic—a terrorist, we would call him today—'whose very Name has lengthen'd down to us as a terrible Synonym for Murder'. Omar's own choice of a life of contemplation and study is not represented as an idyll: he was 'regarded askance in his own Time and Country', and 'especially hated and dreaded' by the hypo-crites whom he scorned; even the scribes who compiled the manu-script collections of his poems felt they had to preface them with a stanza of 'Apology' or 'Execration'. The poem itself is filled with images of threatened or broken power: the biblical King David, the heroes of Persian myth, historical rulers such as Mahmud of Ghazni, 'buried Caesar', all emblems of 'mortal sovranty'; the 'Saints and Sages', the rulers of the intellectual world; Omar himself, whose prowess as mathematician and astronomer is not spared. The social world—the world of the tavern, of good fellowship, of carousing and defiant jokes ('Indeed, indeed, Repentance oft before | I swore—but was I sober when I swore?')—is as vivid as the idealized eroticism of 'Thou | Beside me singing in the Wilderness'. The imagery of the poem is concrete and drawn from human actions, pastimes, artefacts, social forms: a caravan travelling at night, a potter 'thumping his wet clay' in the marketplace, a game of chess, a polo match, a magic lantern, the Muezzin's call to prayer. This is not to say that the *Rubáiyát* is a 'realist' work, only that it is rooted in reality. Here again the relation between its verse and prose parts is significant. Take that image of the caravan, one of the most consciously 'sublime' moments in the poem:

> The Stars are setting and the Caravan
> Starts for the Dawn of Nothing[15]—Oh, make haste!

How odd the superscript numeral looks! It brings you back down to earth; the endnote explains that the ground of the metaphor is 'The Caravan travelling by Night (after their New Year's Day of the

Vernal Equinox)', in other words a mundane custom to avoid the heat of the day.

It is true that the poem advocates withdrawal from the public world, and the cultivation of a form of quietism: 'The Quarrel of the Universe let be' (st. XLV). It is an attitude that chimes with FitzGerald's own abjuration of interest in political events at home or abroad. The friend on whose Persian scholarship he relied, Edward Cowell, had arrived in Calcutta in late 1856, a few months before the outbreak of the Indian Mutiny. FitzGerald continued to write long, detailed letters about Persian poetry to him, and his comments on the calamitous events in India are sparse and numb:

I say nothing about these Indian Army Revolts, because I know nothing. The Daily News reported Calcutta in a State of Siege. You will believe I think of you and *her*. Meantime, as I can neither do nor say anything of service in the matter, I will go on with my first Survey of Omar . . .[32]

Later in the same month:

I can say nothing of all these Affairs of which I know so little. Only that wiser men seem to have been nearly as useless and ignorant as myself. I must go back quietly to old Omar, whom in the main I do comprehend.[33]

The public world of the poem, too, is one of savagery and clamour, a 'hubbub' best endured in an inconspicuous corner (st. XLV). But it would be wrong to assume from this that the poem turns its face away from its own times. It seeks rather to engage with ideas, not events, with the assumptions that underlie social forms—what we mean by 'ideology'. In a poem remarkable for its indifference to that great Victorian theme, social class (the crowd of drinkers outside the tavern in stanza III, for example, cannot be coloured in as rustics, or slum-dwellers, or young men-about-town), there is a constant reminder of the abiding structures of human society, and their pressure on the individual to conform. The poem yearns for a space which is defined by in-betweenness, a 'Strip of Herbage strown | That just divides the desert from the sown', a space whose social correlate is a kind of utopian ignorance, 'Where name of Slave and Sultán scarce is known' (st. X). *Scarce* seems to acknowledge that this is a fantasy; we must accept that the primary form of social relationship is that of ruler and subject. The power of the ruler extends

---

[32] 3–14 July 1857, *Letters*, ii. 287.   [33] Ibid. 294.

into the metaphysical realm, where it is denominated 'God' or 'Law', and the obedience of the subject is articulated not just in outward obedience but in inward conformity, an act of assent which entails a large measure of hypocrisy and cant. The poem refuses this act of assent; that is what makes it a radical, a daring work. FitzGerald was conscious of this: in December 1867, when he was in the midst of preparing the second edition of the *Rubáiyát*, his friend Mowbray Donne asked him if he would like to see one of the Latin comedies by Plautus or Terence performed annually by the pupils of Westminster School. FitzGerald replied that he 'never could care for Terence' because he had 'no Devil'. 'Talking of Devil,' he went on,

I am really reprinting that old Persian . . . It is the only one of all my Great Works that ever has been asked for: I am persuaded, *because* of the Wickedness, which is now at the heart of so much—Goodness! Not that the Persian has anything at all new: but he has dared to *say* it, as Lucretius did: and now it is put into tolerable English Music. That is all.[34]

The need for a spirit of denial, of dissent from orthodox forms of thought and expression, is felt in all periods, but the 'moment' of the *Rubáiyát*—roughly the half-century between its 'discovery' and the outbreak of the First World War—was especially conducive to its 'devil'. By opposing its slight, but unbending reed to the gale of progress, the poem took the measure, for many of its late Victorian readers, of the idols that their existence as social beings required them to worship.

East and West in the Rubáiyát

As far as we can tell FitzGerald never met a Persian person, or indeed any Muslim. He did not know either Persian or Arabic as a living language; it is as though a modern Iranian scholar learned English in order to translate Chaucer. At the same time his study of the language was intensive, and his scrutiny of Omar's texts, in the manuscripts available to him, was laborious and exacting. His correspondence with Edward Cowell is filled with queries about words, phrases, idioms. Considering that he was in his mid-forties when he began to learn a language written in a different alphabet, and that within four years he was able to read its poetry in defective copies of medieval manuscripts, we can dismiss as a travesty the image of the self-amusing amateur, skimming the surface of Persian culture in order to throw off an Orientalist fantasia.

The personal and intimate communion that FitzGerald held with Omar Khayyám, to the point where he spoke of him as 'my Omar', was founded on perusal of manuscripts, which, even though they were copies of copies of copies in a series whose originals had long since been lost, had for FitzGerald the emotional charge of human contact. It contrasts with the knowledge he had of Persia itself, and of Islam, all of which was second-hand and from printed books. When he began studying Persian with Cowell FitzGerald had what one might call an average set of prejudices for an Englishman of his class as to the characteristics of 'the East'. In October 1855 he took a break from his work on the Persian allegorical poem *Salámán and Absál* and read some Schiller: 'It is something to get out of the Sweetmeat, Childish, Oriental World back to the vigorous North!' he wrote to Cowell.[35] He made a similar remark to Tennyson in January 1856: 'It is a comfort to get to masculine Thought after the effeminate Persian.'[36] Such attitudes would have been in part challenged, and in part confirmed, by his extensive scholarly reading— works such as Bathélemy d'Herbelot's magisterial *Bibliothèque orientale ou Dictionaire universel contenant généralement tout ce qui regarde la connaissance des peuples de l'Orient* (Paris: Compagnie des Libraires, 1697), or Sir William Ouseley's *Travels in various countries of the East; more particularly Persia. A work wherein the Author has described, as far as his own Observations extended, the State of those Countries in 1810, 1811, and 1812; and has endeavoured to illustrate many subjects of Antiquarian Research, History, Geography, Philology and Miscellaneous Literature, with extracts from rare and valuable Oriental Manuscripts*, a work published in three volumes between 1819 and 1823, and which does everything the title page promises and more. FitzGerald accepted without question the right of the West to take what it wanted from the East. A small remark in the Preface is revealing in part because it is so casual: manuscripts of Omar are rare in the West, FitzGerald observes, 'in spite of all that Arms and Science have brought us'.

---

[35] Ibid. ii. 184.   [36] Ibid. 190.

Alongside antiquarian works, FitzGerald also read books written much closer in time to his own study of Persian; a good deal of the information he gives in his endnotes derives from Robert Binning's *A Journal of Two Years' Travel in Persia, Ceylon, etc.*, published in two volumes in 1857, when he had already begun his study of Omar. Binning offered FitzGerald a convenient package of attitudes (some prejudiced, some not) about everything from Persian history to Muslim religious observances. Islam comes out badly in this picture; Persian 'effeminacy', it turns out, is not innate but the result of a historical process. FitzGerald adopts and repeats a long-standing cliché of cultural history when he says in the Preface that Omar belonged in spirit to 'that older Time and stouter Temper, before the native Soul of Persia was quite broke by a foreign Creed as well as foreign Conquest'; when he read in Ouseley that spoken Persian tended 'to *smooth away* sounds', he commented to Cowell that while this might be true of 'all colloquial talk', it would be even truer 'as a people declines in vigour; and would naturally be more than usually so with the Persians'.[37] He casually remarks in an endnote that the fasting month of Ramadan 'makes the Musulman unhealthy and unamiable', generalizing from a local observation made by Binning in Ispahan. The backwardness of Persia, viewed from the standpoint of the 'enlightened' West, was commonly attributed to the oppressive influence of Islam, which fostered despotism in the ruling class and craven superstition among the people; resistance to 'civilization and improvement' would take centuries to overcome, Binning says, 'unless it may please Providence to interpose in some signal manner, such as we cannot anticipate, to dispel the Cimmerian darkness that attends *Islâm*, and overshadows wheresoever this false faith obtains, by the Gospel light of Truth'.[38] But FitzGerald, though he enjoyed and recommended Binning's book,[39] did not read it uncritically. The passage just quoted comes at the end, in the course of Binning's sour summing-up of his time in Persia (his advice to travellers is 'Go somewhere else, or stay at home'). He describes the country as a 'beggarly wilderness'—a word which is somewhat differently deployed in FitzGerald's stanza XI—and states that its physical aspect is 'particularly ugly and uninteresting', consisting of 'a vast dreary desert intersected with huge chains of bare, sterile mountains',

[37] 18 Sept. 1854, ibid. 147.   [38] Binning, ii. 380.   [39] *Letters*, ii. 325.

whose green places were few and far between.[40] Perhaps FitzGerald saw that Binning had contradicted himself; at any rate, the extract he used in one of his endnotes comes from earlier in the book, and sketches a landscape whose flowers and birds connect Persia to 'a North-country spring'.[41] In another and profounder respect FitzGerald dissented from Binning's assertion that there can be no 'amalgamation of ideas and sympathies between Eastern and Western nations'.[42] The Preface to the *Rubáiyát* is evidence that FitzGerald thought (or came to think) precisely the opposite; but it would also be true to say that he did not write the poem in order to advocate this view.

By FitzGerald's time literary Orientalism had a long history and had developed in complex and sometimes contradictory directions. The particular appeal made by the *Rubáiyát* needs to be distinguished from that of the *Arabian Nights*, for example, and from the 'Eastern tale' which had flourished in prose and verse since the mid-eighteenth century: the designation of Omar Khayyám in the title as 'the Astronomer-Poet of Persia' is like a warning not to expect caliphs and harems, genii and giaours, magic carpets or Circassian beauties. It also connotes a respect for what is historically and culturally distinctive, as opposed to 'Oriental' in a vague, generalized sense, or consciously artificial, as in Tennyson's 'Recollections of the Arabian Nights' (1830), where the speaker's declaration 'True Mussulman was I and sworn' (l. 9) refers indulgently to a fantasy of childhood reading. However, it must be acknowledged that the poem has stuggled to escape its generic label. The very first notice was dismissive not just in its brevity (and sloppiness) but in its taking for granted the category to which the work 'naturally' belonged:

Naturally there is an abundance of gorgeous imagery in *Rubuitjat of Omar Khayyam, the Astronomer-Poet of Persia*, translated into English Verse (Quaritch), with an excellent biographical introduction.—Another worshipper of the Star of the East is L. A. D., who publishes a piece of excessive light and fragile Orientalism, entitled *Prince Ahmed and The Fair of Pari-Banon* (Saunders & Otley).[43]

---

[40] Binning, ii. 374.
[41] See endnote 3, pp. 54–5, and Explanatory Notes, pp. 148–9.
[42] Binning, ii. 380.
[43] *Athenaeum*, 1650 (11 June 1859), 776 (in a round-up of recent publications called 'Our Literary Table').

The history of the poem's illustration alone confirms how determinedly FitzGerald has been construed as a 'worshipper of the Star of the East'.[44] It is a question whether any work of art draws down its own fate; but we can be fairly sure that when he wrote the poem FitzGerald both knew what 'light and fragile Orientalism' was, and thought of himself as doing something pointedly different.

The adoption of an Oriental 'mask' as a way of reflecting on one's own society is another matter, however, and here the *Rubáiyát* is deeply indebted to a genre that goes back to Montesquieu's *Lettres persanes* (1721) and Samuel Johnson's *Rasselas* (1759). This applies especially to the critique of religion: Omar's indignant or satirical reflections on Islamic dogma, or on pious hypocrites, may 'veil' an attack on Christianity, but the veil is virtually transparent in stanzas such as LVII and LVIII. Although it presents itself as a translation and not a work of fiction, the *Rubáiyát* 'invents' its Oriental speaker as much as it discovers him; indeed this is an inevitable consequence of FitzGerald's method of translation, in which equivalence of feeling and idiom matters more than literal accuracy. Yet the fact of translation also offers a counterweight to invention, and to certain kinds of adaptation or appropriation of an Oriental persona. Goethe's great Oriental poetic cycle, for example, the *West-östlicher Divan* (1819), was inspired by his reading of Háfiz, not directly but in German translation; it is 'variation' on an Oriental theme. If Goethe saw himself 'as' Háfiz, he nevertheless takes priority, just as 'West' does in the title. Goethe allows himself a licence not greater, arguably, than FitzGerald took with Omar, but different, because Háfiz was for him a means to an end, enabling a release of imaginative energy that took flight *from* the original rather than turning towards it. The same might be said of a closer contemporary to FitzGerald, Matthew Arnold, whose *Sohrab and Rustum* (1853) filters an episode from Firdúsi's *Shah-Nameh*, which Arnold knew only in French translation, through his transmutation into English of the diction of Homeric Greek.[45] No reader of the poem would be impelled to return to the

---

[44] See William H. Martin and Sandra Mason, *The Art of Omar Khayyam: Illustrating FitzGerald's* Rubaiyat (London and New York: I. B. Tauris, 2007). I am sorry not to be able to agree with the authors of this book, one of the most informative and enjoyable to be published on the *Rubáiyát*, on the quality of the art they document.

[45] Line 3 of st. IX mentions Rustum with disrespect, and may be a sly rejoinder to Arnold's epic *afflatus*. But there is no evidence that FitzGerald knew the poem.

'original', or rather the original is not an ancient Persian, but an ancient Greek text.

FitzGerald's status as a translator brings into play another dimension of Orientalism, the growth of scholarly and what we would now call academic interest in the languages and literatures of the East. The dominating figure here is that of Sir William Jones (1746–94), whose scholarship encompassed Sanscrit, Arabic, and Persian, and who laid the foundations for the study of comparative philology in Britain. It was Jones's Persian grammar that Cowell had studied in his precocious teens; he subsequently recommended it to FitzGerald, in part because its precepts were illustrated by quotations from Háfiz. 'As to Jones' Grammar,' FitzGerald wrote to Cowell in January 1854, 'I have a sort of *Love* for it! Instead of such Dry as dust Scholars as usually make Grammars, how more than ever necessary is it to have men of Poetic Taste to do it, so as to make the thing as delightful as possible to learners.'[46] But FitzGerald did not follow Jones's 'Poetic Taste' in the matter of translation. Jones's versions of Persian lyric poetry, including Háfiz, are stilted eighteenth-century confections, and facilitated a rapid turn to cliché in later imitators; FitzGerald referred disparagingly to his first attempt at an English version of Omar as 'a poor Sir W. Jones sort of Parody'.[47] It was Jones's scholarship, transmitted and reinforced by Cowell, that mattered to FitzGerald; the gateway to his 'Orientalism' is that of a language encountered at first hand, whose contours imposed themselves on his imagination in ways that second-hand reading, however profound, could never have done. Behind the 'abundance of gorgeous imagery' in the *Rubáiyát* is something missing from most literary Orientalism of the period: the hard outline of a dictionary.

The Genesis of the English Rubáiyát

The fact that FitzGerald began by translating Omar into 'Monkish Latin' has significance for an interpretation of the poem, both because the analogy between Omar's scepticism and that of classical 'Epicurean' writers such as Lucretius helped form FitzGerald's conception of him, and because some of the English phrasing in the poem was filtered through the earlier Latin. But the Latin venture in itself was

---

[46] *Letters*, ii. 118.   [47] See below, p. xxxv.

a dead end. The affinity that FitzGerald increasingly sensed between Omar and himself rested on a refusal to conform to the religious orthodoxy and received ideas of his time and place. It was, so to speak, a family row, and could only be voiced in his native tongue.

We can pinpoint the moment at which FitzGerald took his first step towards an English verse translation. His enthusiasm had grown through the summer of 1857: in March Omar had been on a par with Háfiz, by late June he was 'the best Persian I have seen'.[48] Finally, on 14 July (which FitzGerald sorrowfully recalled as 'the Anniversary of our Adieu at Rushmere') he closed his letter to Cowell as follows:

Have I previously asked you to observe 486 پی فرخ صنم صبوح هنگام of which I send a poor Sir W. Jones sort of Parody which came into my mind walking in the Garden here; where the Rose is blowing as in Persia? And with this poor little Envoy my letter shall end. I will not stop to make the Verse better.

> I long for Wine! oh Sáki of my Soul,
> Prepare thy Song and fill the morning Bowl;
> For this first Summer Month that brings the Rose
> Takes many a Sultan with it as it goes.[49]

The stanza concludes the letter, and unusually for FitzGerald the letter is not signed. The anonymity of the *Rubáiyát* begins here: FitzGerald stubbornly refused to put his name to his verse, even when his authorship became known and had made him famous. As a gesture of diffidence it goes with the others: even the statement that he has made an English translation of a single quatrain is conveyed in a relative clause ('of which') in a sentence whose main syntactical structure ('Have I previously asked you to observe 486 . . . ?') concerns a question about the Persian text. It is a 'poor . . . sort of Parody', a 'poor little Envoy', not worth making better. But leaving aside its relation to the *Rubáiyát* (line 3 found its way almost unchanged into stanza VIII) this is a strong and artful poem. Strength comes from the poise of the metrical balance, in which the caesura shifts in the third line and disappears altogether in the fourth, which is charged with time's irresistible force. Artfulness comes from the

---

[48] The first remark is in a letter to Cowell of 4–20 Mar.: 'Háfiz, and old Omar Khayyám ring like true Metal'; the second in a letter to George Borrow of 24 June (*Letters*, ii. 262, 284).

[49] Ibid. 289. Terhune translates the Persian as: 'In the morning, oh sweetheart of good fortune' (p. 290 n. 44). FitzGerald's numbering of the Calcutta MS is wrong; '486' should be 497 (Arberry, p. 145).

ordering of sounds, in which words beginning with the same letter recur in an intricate pattern of echo and variation ('Sáki . . . Soul . . . Song . . . Summer . . . Sultan'; 'my . . . morning . . . month . . . many'), or are linked by internal rhyme ('I long . . . thy Song'); the long 'o' binds the couplet rhymes together ('soul . . . bowl . . . rose . . . goes') so that this lyric which begins with a personal cry and ends with a generalized maxim seems to spring from a single pulse of thought.

The path to the English *Rubáiyát* lay clear to FitzGerald from this point, with the exception of the stanza form, which he had already imitated in some of his Latin versions and which was therefore only waiting to be adopted. He must gradually have accumulated more English versions over the next four or five months, and the design for the poem must have occurred to him in the same period, though he gave Cowell only one oblique hint, in a letter written in early August, that he had anything like such a project in mind.[50] Then, in a letter of 8 December, he revealed that he had advanced further than Cowell could have anticipated:

And now about old Omar. You talked of sending a Paper about him to Fraser . . . I suppose you have not had time to do what you proposed, or are you overcome with the Flood of bad Latin I poured upon you? Well: don't be surprised (*vext*, you won't be) if *I* solicit Fraser for room for a few Quatrains in English Verse, however—with only such an Introduction as you and Sprenger give me—very short—so as to leave you say all that is Scholarly if you will. . . . I don't know what you will say to all this. However I dare say it won't matter whether I do the Paper or not, for I don't believe they'll put it in.[51]

FitzGerald's parenthesis '(*vext* you won't be)' sounds a little nervous, but he need not have worried. Cowell had not, in fact, abandoned his intention to write an article on Omar; but when he received this letter he redirected his piece to the *Calcutta Review*: it appeared in March 1858. In fact, FitzGerald was able to quote a sizeable amount of it in his Preface to the first edition of the *Rubáiyát* a year later, for he was quite right to predict that *Fraser's Magazine* would not publish what he sent them, even though the publisher, John Parker, had agreed to take it. His piece consisted of translations of thirty-five quatrains, with a short introduction; knowing that *Fraser's* had a mainstream Tory and

[50] 'I see how a very pretty *Eclogue* might be tessellated out of his scattered Quatrains: but you would not like the Moral of it. Alas!' (*Letters*, ii. 294; FitzGerald's emphasis).

[51] Ibid. 305. 'Sprenger' is A. Sprenger, *Catalogue of the Arabic, Persian, and Hindustani Manuscripts of the Library of the Kings of Oudh*, vol. i (Calcutta, 1854).

Anglican readership, he deliberately left out some of the more provoca-
tive material, but even so it proved too strong; and since FitzGerald was
(in metropolitan terms) a nobody, Parker simply sat on the piece from
January 1858, when FitzGerald sent it to him, until November, when
the unworldly author finally asked for it back.

We do not have FitzGerald's manuscript of the *Fraser's* piece and
cannot say for certain what stanzas it contained and in what form.
He announced his decision to withdraw it in a letter to Cowell of
2 November, and on 13 January he wrote that he wanted 'to enlarge
it to near as much again, of such matter as he [Parker] would not dare
to put in Fraser'.[52] Some of this new material must already have been
drafted, but we have no way of telling how much; nor do we know
whether, or to what extent, the stanzas retrieved from *Fraser's* were
revised before the book appeared.

The manuscript which FitzGerald sent to *Fraser's* was a fair copy,
and he told Cowell that he had retained only 'a rough and imperfect
Copy'.[53] Since neither of these manuscripts is extant, FitzGerald's
method of composition of the English version has to be inferred by
analogy with his method in making his Latin translations. The Latin
manuscript (now in the library of Trinity College, Cambridge)
is itself a 'rough and imperfect' document. It contains drafts of
thirty-one quatrains, numbered up to 'XII'; most of these are in a
reasonably finished state (one has an incomplete line, two have alter-
native readings); of the remaining nineteen quatrains, eight are
incomplete, and all show evidence of drafting and revision.[54]
FitzGerald drafted lines and phrases in pencil, and then either traced
over them, or revised them, in ink; on a few occasions he added alter-
native phrases, again in pencil, producing an undecidable text. With
some allowance for the greater difficulty of composing in Latin verse
(though not in classical quantitative metre), we can speculate that
FitzGerald's 'rough and imperfect' English draft of the *Rubáiyát*
would have had a similar appearance.

There is, however, one major difference between the Latin and
English versions. Although twenty-two of the Latin quatrains have
some equivalent in the English *Rubáiyát* (not all in the first edition of

---

[52] *Letters*, ii. 322–3, 325.
[53] 3 Sept. 1858, ibid. 318.
[54] The Latin MS is reprinted in Arberry (pp. 58–64, with trans. and commentary on
pp. 110–31) and Decker (pp. 233–7, without trans.).

the poem; some of the quatrains added in the second edition had Latin precursors), the Latin quatrains are in no particular order. The first bears some relation to stanza LI, the second to stanza LX (part of the 'Kúza-Náma' or 'Book of Pots' section), the third to stanza XXV, and so on. Whatever he thought he was doing with his Latin versions, FitzGerald had clearly not arrived at the concept which shapes the English version into an ordered sequence, in violation of the principle of organization in the original Persian manuscripts. This concept, for which he used the classical term 'Eclogue', brings into focus the issue of what FitzGerald thought he was doing as a translator.

FitzGerald as Editor and Translator

The act of translation, for FitzGerald, was inseparable from that of editing. Besides poems by Omar Khayyám, he translated Spanish plays by Calderón, Greek dramas by Aeschylus and Sophocles, Persian allegorical poems by Jámi and Attar; all were subject to adaptation and reshaping. He cut, conflated, reordered, and rewrote. He had a theory of translation which allowed, indeed enjoined this method, but the theory itself sprang from something in him deeper than an intellectual opinion.

It is hard to give this something a name, but 'modesty' offers a starting point. Paradoxical though it seems, FitzGerald's presumption of authority over the texts he translates is simultaneously the sign of his lack of belief in his own creative, *originative* power. He wrote to Bernard Barton in 1842: 'I know that I could write volume after volume as well as others of the mob of gentlemen who write with ease: but I think unless a man can do better, he had best not do at all; I have not the strong inward call, nor cruel-sweet pangs of parturition, that prove the birth of anything bigger than a mouse.'[55] The frame of reference here is Augustan and classical: Pope's 'mob of gentlemen who wrote with ease' from 'The First Epistle of the Second Book of Horace, Imitated', Horace himself for the mountain that gives birth to a mouse in *De Arte Poetica*. But FitzGerald could change his instrument without changing his tune. 'I do not care about my own verses,' he wrote to Elizabeth Cowell in 1851:

They are not *original*—which is saying, they are not worth anything. They may possess sense, fancy etc.—but they always recall other and better poems.

[55] *Letters*, i. 308.

You see all *moulded* rather by Tennyson etc. than *growing* spontaneously from my own mind. No doubt there is original feeling, too; but it is not strong enough to grow up alone and whole of itself—it takes an alien form, and always gives evidence that it does so.[56]

The vocabulary here is that of Romanticism, with its emphasis on the organic link between the imagination and nature: Wordsworth's 'spontaneous overflow of powerful feelings', Keats's dictum that 'If poetry comes not as naturally as leaves to a tree it had better not come at all'. But whether he was appealing to Pope or Keats, FitzGerald maintained the same faith throughout his life: he insisted that he had no 'genius', that he possessed only the secondary powers of imagination, the powers of selection and arrangement; *tact* rather than *touch*; the ability, not to make something, but to see what could be made of it. His letters are filled with projects for furbishing up old classics, making them palatable to a modern audience, and he thought he was just the man to do this kind of work. 'I suppose you never read that aggravating Book, Clarissa Harlowe?' he wrote to a friend in 1865.

Now, with a pair of Scissors, I *could* make that a readable Book; and being a perfectly original Work of Genius, I should like to do that Service to my Country before I die. But I should only be abused, and unsold for my pains.[57]

The reference to the scissors has literal force: FitzGerald was nothing if not a hands-on editor, and he liked to 'customize' his own library: 'He cut down books to one half or one third of their original length and bound them with others which he had treated similarly. Works of two or three volumes he reduced to one. Sometimes he wrote in a paragraph to supply the context of a deletion. Here and there he added marginal notes'.[58] His bent was for reduction, for concentration, for distillation. It is a process epitomized in the generous, but also curiously self-pleasing labour he undertook after the death of Bernard Barton, in the compilation of a memorial volume of his verse:

I have now looked over *all* his Volumes with some care; and have selected what will fill about 200 pages of print—as I suppose—really all the best part out of *nine volumes*! Some of the poems I take entire—some half—some only a few stanzas, and these dovetailed together—with a change of a word, or even of a line here and there, to give them logic and fluency. It is wonderful when you come to look close into most of these poems to see the

[56] Ibid. ii. 14.   [57] Ibid. 548.   [58] Terhune, p. 148.

elements of repetition, indistinctness, etc. which go to make them diffuse and weary. I am sure I have distilled many pretty little poems out of long dull ones which the world has discarded. I do not pretend to be a poet: but I have faculty enough to mend some of B. B.'s dropped stitches, though I really could not make any whole poem so good as many of his. As a matter of _Art_, I have no doubt whatsoever I am right: whether I am right in _morals_ to use a dead man so I am not so certain.[59]

The method FitzGerald adopted for his translation of Omar Khayyám is foreshadowed here; what he says about Barton's 'repetition' and 'diffuseness' is applied in the Preface to Persian poetry in general; even Omar, who is supposedly an exception, has had to be pruned. According to his own figures, FitzGerald had 674 quatrains to work with in the Ouseley and Calcutta MSS (though the latter was 'swelled . . . by all kinds of Repetition and Corruption'), and ended up with 75 in the first edition. And as he told Cowell, 'Many Quatrains are mashed together'; the whole poem had been 'most ingeniously tessellated' out of discrete fragments.[60] The qualm FitzGerald feels as to whether he was 'right in _morals_ to use a dead man so' has been felt, of course, by every translator of works from the past. In Barton's case, FitzGerald could persuade himself that he 'only desire[d] to do a good little job for his memory, and make a presentable book for Miss B.'s profit'.[61] The case of the _Rubáiyát_ is more complicated. FitzGerald's sympathetic understanding of Omar—his grasp of him, we might say—had a possessive side to it. He wrote to Cowell in December 1857, when he was first thinking of sending his English translations to _Fraser's_: 'in truth I take old Omar rather more as my property than yours: he and I are more akin, are we not? You see all [his] Beauty, but you can't feel _with_ him in some respects as I do.'[62] Though FitzGerald was the least mercenary of authors, the context of this remark, which is after all to do with a plan of publication, can't but make 'old Omar' a literary 'property' whose exploitation rights FitzGerald is prepared to claim. And may a man not do as he likes with his own?

Controversy about the accuracy of FitzGerald's translations has focused on individual words and phrases, and on the general issue of 'literal' versus 'free' versions; but arguably FitzGerald's major

[59] Ibid. i. 633.   [60] _Letters_, ii. 318, 323.
[61] Ibid. i. 633.   [62] Ibid. ii. 305.

intervention was not as translator, but as editor. As he acknowledges in the Preface, the quatrains in the original MSS are 'independent Stanzas' which 'follow one another according to Alphabetic Rhyme'. FitzGerald's arrangement imposes an order on this 'strange Farrago of Grave and Gay', so that the poem becomes 'something of an Eclogue'; or, to use his more mellifluous phrase in his letter to Cowell, 'it is most ingeniously tessellated into a sort of Epicurean Eclogue in a Persian Garden'.[63] The narrative, according to FitzGerald's later account, occupies a single day: 'He [Omar] begins with Dawn pretty sober and contemplative: then as he thinks and drinks, grows savage, blasphemous, etc., and then again sobers down into melancholy at nightfall'.[64] It may be doubted whether this logical progression was in FitzGerald's mind from the start, but there is no doubt that the stanzas of the *Rubáiyát* are presented in a sequence that is foreign to the intention of the author, and arguably to the epigrammatic, 'occasional' spirit of the *ruba'i* as a poetic form.

The structure of the poem, in one sense, 'translates' nothing, because it has no counterpart in the original text. What, then, of the verse itself? FitzGerald's ideas about translation evolved in the late 1840s and 1850s, in dialogue with Cowell, who introduced him to Spanish and Persian and revived his interest in Greek. The two significant precursors of the *Rubáiyát* are *Six Dramas of Calderón* (1853) and FitzGerald's first Persian attempt, Jámi's *Salámán and Absál* (1856). And here we need to make a distinction between FitzGerald's treatment of the Spanish texts as opposed to the Persian. In his 'Advertisement' to the Calderón volume, FitzGerald speaks of the translator having to accept that language is a reflection of national temperament: 'an exact translation' of Calderón would fail because 'Spanish passion' would come out as 'bombast to English ears'; 'idioms that [are] true and intelligible to one nation, check the current of sympathy in others to which they are unfamiliar'. Many years later, writing about Calderón to James Russell Lowell, he repeated that translators must not 'hamper themselves with Forms of Verse—and Thought—irreconcilable with English Language and English Ways of Thinking'.[65] But with regard to Persian FitzGerald was not so sure. Not long after he began to learn the language, he

---

[63] Ibid. ii. 323.   [64] 31 Mar. 1872, ibid. iii. 339.
[65] 19 Dec. 1878, ibid. iv. 167.

wrote to Elizabeth Cowell about the deficiencies of current transla-
tions of Sadi:

Certainly Eastwick is *wretched* in the Verse: and both he and Ross . . . seem
to me on a wrong tack wholly in their *Style* of rendering the Prose. Because
it is elegant Persian they try to render it into *Elegant* English; but I think it
should be translated *something* as the Bible is translated, preserving the
Oriental Idiom. It should be kept as Oriental as possible, only using the
most idiomatic Saxon *words* to convey the Eastern Metaphor.[66]

'Preserving the Oriental Idiom' by reference to the Bible is even more
strongly argued over a year later, in a letter to Cowell urging him to
continue to translate Háfiz, and telling him how to go about it:

I am more and more convinced of the Necessity of keeping as much as
possible to the Oriental *Forms*, and carefully avoiding any that bring one
back to Europe and the 19th Century. It is better to be orientally obscure
than Europeanly clear. I always refer back to the Bible: which Selden says
is translated so strangely as no Book ever then was, keeping so close to
almost unintelligible idioms both of Country and Era. . . . I think you agree
with me; but I am sure it is *the* rule never to be lost sight of. Unlike as the
two Peoples may be, we English may yet translate, and read in translation,
from the Persian Poetry more literally than from Greek and Latin—partly
owing indeed to some affinity in the structure of our Languages.[67]

The date is significant, for by this time FitzGerald was already work-
ing on his translation of *Salámán and Absál*, which he mentions at the
end of the letter. And here the argument takes an unexpected turn:
'I advise what I don't practise: for my Salámán just fails in that [it]
loses its Oriental Flavor, and takes an English, if not a Modern
Dress. But I had to choose between being readably English, or
unreadably Oriental'.[68] True, FitzGerald goes on to suggest that
Háfiz is not as 'unreadably Oriental' as Jámi, but this sounds like a
rationalization and in any case would undermine the original argu-
ment that it is 'better to be orientally obscure than Europeanly clear'.
In the preface to *Salámán and Absál* itself he offers a variation on this
argument: if Jámi were a better poet it would be right to give a literal
prose version of him, 'such as any one should adopt who does not feel
himself so much a Poet as him he translates and some he translates
for—before whom it is best to lay the raw material as genuine as may

---

[66] 24 Jan. 1854, ibid. ii. 119.   [67] 7 May 1855, ibid. 164.
[68] Ibid. 164–5.

be, to work up to their own better Fancies'. FitzGerald clearly regarded Omar as a better poet than Jámi, yet when he came to translate him he did exactly the opposite of what he recommends here. Far from presenting readers with 'the raw material genuine as may be', he applied to Omar the same principle he had applied to Calderón. He turned his back on '*the* rule never to be lost sight of', and substituted another, with a proverbial quip that has become the rallying-cry of 'free' translation: 'at all Cost, a Thing must *live*: with a transfusion of one's own worse Life if one can't retain the Original's better. Better a live Sparrow than a stuffed Eagle'.[69]

'*Tolerable English Music*'

The 'Life' which FitzGerald brought to the *Rubáiyát* came from an eclectic range of reading and an idiosyncratic approach to poetic language. Although FitzGerald went to Cambridge, he found nothing of value there except friendship, and as far as English literature is concerned he was self-taught. In this he resembled poets such as Wordsworth and Tennyson, or novelists such as Thackeray, but unlike them he did not follow a vocation as a writer and had no need to test his ideas, prejudices, and stylistic mannerisms in the literary marketplace, just as he did not have to submit his spelling and orthography to the scrutiny of a publisher. Nor did he have to be systematic in the knowledge he acquired or the uses he made of it—unlike scholars such as Cowell, or his friend James Spedding, who devoted his life to editing the works of Francis Bacon. He read what he liked, when he liked, and if he wanted to follow up an enthusiasm to the point of publication, he was free to do so, as he did with all his translations; none were commissioned, or professionally edited (the *Rubáiyát* endnotes, uneven in length and tone, are enough to tell you that). Yet all FitzGerald's miscellaneous and undisciplined learning, all his lack of guidance, bore fruit in the *Rubáiyát*, where freedom from received ideas about literary value and literary decorum was as essential to success as a scholar's harness, or that of a 'recognized' poet, would have been fatal.

Nowhere is this more evident, or more important, than in the famous *Rubáiyát* stanza, a quatrain in which the first, second, and

[69] To Cowell, 27 Apr. 1859, ibid. 335.

fourth lines rhyme, but the third is unrhymed.[70] FitzGerald took this form from the Persian, but he had English precedents in mind for poems in quatrains that address the topic of mortality: at a distance Thomas Gray's *Elegy Written in a Country Churchyard*, and closer in time Tennyson's *In Memoriam*.

FitzGerald said of Gray that he 'made of his own few thoughts, and many of other men's, a something which we all love to keep ever about us'.[71] That might have been said of him, too; nevertheless the *Rubáiyát* tacitly rebukes the *Elegy* both for its gentility and for its self-regard. The *Elegy* is in part a great poem because its eloquence is so compromised: in speaking *of* one social class, but *to* another, it is driven to extremes of commonplace in order to find a ground where the two can meet. FitzGerald takes full advantage of the foreignness of his setting to disengage the *Rubáiyát* from the English class system; whatever else he may be, the speaker of the poem is not an English gentleman in Oriental costume. Gray's poem ends with an auto-elegy, in which the poet stages a double performance of 'future memory', first by the oral recollections of the 'hoary-headed swain' (l. 97), and second by the epitaph on the tomb. The *Rubáiyát*, too, ends with an auto-elegy, but the contrast could not be more pointed. Not only does FitzGerald's speaker nowhere allude to himself as a poet, but when he imagines his own death he does so without reference to any of his gifts other than that of his having been, once upon a time, a drunkard.

The case of *In Memoriam* is more deep-seated, because closer to home, and it also rests on a more technical distinction in the form of the quatrain. FitzGerald loved and admired Tennyson all his life, but as a poet he parted company with him after 1842. He fell asleep when Tennyson read him *The Princess*, and wrote of *In Memoriam* (to Tennyson's brother Frederick!) that though 'full of finest things . . . it is monotonous, and has that air of being evolved by a Poetical Machine of the highest order'.[72] FitzGerald's phrasing here points to the stanza form, the basic recurring feature that would carry the charge of 'monotony' and mechanical efficiency. Tennyson himself had referred to the 'sad mechanic exercise' of expressing grief in

[70] There are a handful of fully rhymed stanzas in the poem (x, xxvi, xxxii, xlix) and one which is all-but (lix).

[71] *Letters*, iv. 223.

[72] 31 Dec. 1850, ibid. i. 696.

'measured language' (st. v), but he meant to describe a form of psychological dissociation, whereas FitzGerald's 'Poetical Machine' is an image of artistic conformity to the spirit of the age. *In Memoriam*, according to this view, turns out one affordable luxury of sentiment after another, all to the same high standard of finish and reliability, and the stanza form—opening, expanding, pausing, closing—is the engine of this manufacturing process. By contrast, FitzGerald saw that the third, unrhymed, line was crucial to the Persian *ruba'i* and therefore to his own technique: its refusal to form a couplet, to *pair* with anything else, is an emblem of intellectual and spiritual solitariness. Both broken and free, the *Rubáiyát* stanza declares its independence from Tennyson in just the way that FitzGerald thought his own 'original' poetry could never do.

It is typical of FitzGerald's inspired anachronism that he should make the stanza form he found in the Persian 'allude' to Tennyson. His stroke of genius was not simply to translate 'freely'—he did that with Calderón and produced worthy stodge—but to steep Omar in English allusions and idioms which *already* had their own life, which were not in the position of borrowing from the Persian but of lending to it. The 'debate' with *In Memoriam* in this sense is part of the poem's intense literariness, which avoids self-consciousness by having a proper function, by being needed to make it work. Take, for example, the sequence of stanzas XXIII–XXV: XXIII and XXV are dense with allusions to the Bible and to Shakespeare, framing, in XXIV, the sublime and scornful cry of the 'Muezzín from the Tower of Darkness'. The pulse of thought here is neither 'exotic' nor 'English'; the imagining of one culture has become fused with that of another. FitzGerald can do this with a single phrase, as he does with the 'silken Tassel of my Purse' in stanza XIII, or the 'surly Tapster' of stanza LXIV, or the 'sorry Scheme of Things' in stanza LXIII. All of these have literary affiliations (ranging from Chaucer to the late eighteenth century) but FitzGerald also made use of English idioms which belong to colloquial speech and to the people, not the poets: exclamations ('Fools!' 'What!' 'Pish!'), popular wisdom ('take the Cash in hand'), familiar and proverbial expressions ('He's a Good Fellow', 'sold my Reputation for a Song'), native forms of address ('come with old Khayyám', 'You know, my Friends'), and words of deliberately unpoetic vintage (the potter 'thumping his wet Clay'). Erik Gray points out a particularly fine pun on the idiom 'neither Here nor There' in stanza XXIV.[73] These threads are woven into the poem's diction which is so far from being an Oriental tapestry that it contains only a handful, far fewer than you might expect, of actual Persian words.[74]

Above all FitzGerald escaped uniformity of tone. The sequence of stanzas may not reproduce the 'strange Farrago of Grave and Gay' which he found in the Persian manuscripts, with their arbitrary method of arrangement by alphabetical rhyme, but 'Grave and Gay' are both present, sometimes in alternating stanzas—VIII–XII, for example, or XXXIII–XXXIV, in which, following the grand and gloomy utterance of the 'rolling Heav'n', the 'earthen Bowl' gives the seeker of the 'Well of Life' a dusty answer. But this last example reminds us also that 'Grave and Gay' are not competing for mastery, but sharing the poem's burden.

The Dawn of Nothing

The vision of the *Rubáiyát*, despite the pleasures that it offers, is bleak. The nature of this bleakness can be illustrated by the phrase Tennyson thought FitzGerald had 'stolen' from one of his poems. In 'The Gardener's Daughter', one of the 'English Idylls' first published in Tennyson's *Poems* of 1842, the narrator speaks of his transient attraction to Juliet: she had been

> To me myself, for some three careless moons,
> The summer pilot of an empty heart
> Unto the shores of nothing!

(ll. 15–17)

The 'theft' that Tennyson spotted comes in stanza XXXVIII of the *Rubáiyát*:

> One Moment in Annihilation's Waste,
> One Moment, of the Well of Life to taste—
>   The Stars are setting and the Caravan
> Starts for the Dawn of Nothing—Oh, make haste!

Tennyson's image has light and shade, it is not frivolous, but it does not mean *nothing* as FitzGerald's means it. He had been 'at a loss for

---

[73] Gray, p. 111.

[74] 'Péhleví', 'Muezzín', 'Parwín and Mushtara' (astronomical names), 'Sufí', 'Kúza-Náma' (FitzGerald's coinage), 'Tamám shud'.

a word to express the "*no*-thing"', he told Tennyson; words like 'Nothingness', 'Non-existence', 'Non-entity' all seemed too clumsy; 'I remember often wanting a word like the French "*Néant*" to express what is so much the burden of the old Song'.[75] *So much*, for FitzGerald, lies in the word 'Nothing'.

To help him contemplate, and face the prospect of, this *nothing*, FitzGerald had the cold-comforting presence of the great Roman philosopher-poet Lucretius, whose *De Rerum Natura*, like Omar's poetry, had been introduced to him by Cowell. A strand of classical reference runs through the *Rubáiyát*—his dead king in stanza XVIII is a 'buried Caesar', even the stanza numerals are in Roman letters— but the presence of Lucretius is not so much in the texture of the work as in its conceptual frame. FitzGerald saw in Omar's poetry a lighter (but not more light-hearted) expression of Lucretius' uncompromising materialism, and of his perception of human life as an accident of circumstance, not something we own but part of a process to which we belong. Lucretius led back to his master, Epicurus, and to the original clarity and toughness of Epicurean thought, far removed from the hedonism with which it came to be identified. The exhortation to seek pleasure because life is short is intrinsically melancholy, and this melancholy governs the vocabulary, and above all the cadences, of the *Rubáiyát*, but it does so without the indulgence of self-pity. In this respect FitzGerald kept to a Lucretian standard which his *fin-de-siècle* admirers and imitators were unable to follow. Take, for example, stanza XV:

> And those who husbanded the Golden Grain,
> And those who flung it to the Winds like Rain,
>   Alike to no such aureate Earth are turn'd
> As, buried once, Men want dug up again.

The grave jest comes directly from Omar, but FitzGerald gives it a subtle shift of emphasis. Omar's comment is directed at a generalized 'you': 'You are not gold, O heedless, ignorant one, that they | should place you in the earth, and then bring you out again.'[76] It is FitzGerald who introduces the notion that misers and spendthrifts are *alike* in

---

[75] *Letters*, iii. 342. Tennyson's refusal to accept this as the last word can be seen in the lines he added to his poem 'To E. FitzGerald' after FitzGerald's death, in which he states that the 'deeper night' of death is 'A clearer day | Than our poor twilight dawn on earth': see App. II, p. 136.

[76] Arberry, p. 202.

this respect. This is a different thought, a Lucretian thought, and thus a colder one. It is driven home, as so often in the *Rubáiyát*, by syntax and rhythm. The first two lines, with their repetition ('And those . . . And those') and their regular iambic beat, have a simplicity that the last two lines disrupt: the syntactic inversion in the third line allows the stress to fall on 'turn'd' just as the line itself turns, only to come up against the strong stress on 'As'—in fact the sequence 'túrn'd | Ás, búried' places three strong stresses in a row, a violation of prosodic decorum like the heft of an axe before it comes down.

It may be that the immense late-Victorian and Edwardian popularity of the poem rested wholly on a shallow reading, fixed on its shimmering surface, its phrase-making lilt, its metaphysical glamour—everything that led to its being stigmatized as the kind of poetry you enjoy when you're an adolescent, or an immature person of any age. But FitzGerald thought differently. He said of Omar (not himself) that he 'sang, in an acceptable way it seems, of what all men feel in their hearts, but had not exprest in verse before'.[77] If he was right, then a different image takes shape. Perhaps the poem was popular precisely because readers sensed its intellectual and emotional integrity, and its courage. In return for the gift that we offer to a work of art, bringing it to life by our intelligent and passionate apprehension, we ask it to face life (some aspect of life) on our behalf, and we are never fooled for long when the work wriggles out of the bargain. It is hard even for new readers to approach the *Rubáiyát* today without some preconceived idea of its being little more than a decorative frieze of poses and gestures. On the contrary, it will take us as far as we care to go with one particular response to 'Human Death and Fate'. If this is so—if the poem keeps its word—then it should be recoverable; the spell under which it has lain can be broken, and its tongue untied.

[77] *Letters*, iv. 487.

PUBLICATION HISTORY

Publication

Rubáiyát of Omar Khayyám, the Astronomer-Poet of Persia was pub-
lished anonymously, as a pamphlet in paper covers, in late February or
early March 1859; the British Museum received its copy on 30 March,
the day before FitzGerald's fiftieth birthday. The print run was 250
copies, and the price was 1 shilling. The publisher was Bernard
Quaritch, a bookseller and only occasionally a publisher, whose firm,
founded in 1847, specialized in antiquarian and Oriental books and
manuscripts; FitzGerald was a regular customer, which may explain
why Quaritch took on what was a very small bit of business.

The terms 'published' and 'publisher' are not quite accurate.
FitzGerald paid for, and supervised, the printing of the edition; he
kept forty copies for himself, and Quaritch agreed to put his name on
the title page and distribute the book from his premises in Castle
Street, Leicester Square. In addition to the cost of printing,
FitzGerald paid for a modest amount of advertising in literary jour-
nals. There was no contract, no sale of copyright (meaning Quaritch
could not reprint the poem without FitzGerald's permission), and
no agreement to pay royalties or share profits. FitzGerald received
(and expected to receive) nothing; Quaritch stood to gain the sum of
£10. 10s., or 10 guineas—if he sold all 210 copies in his charge.

It seems likely that the *Rubáiyát* sold no copies at all. In an 1899
catalogue Quaritch noted that the sale fell 'absolutely dead at the
published price of 1s.'.[1] FitzGerald gave away just three of his forty
copies (and none to established literary friends such as Tennyson,
Thackeray, and Carlyle). There were only two reviews, or rather one
review and a brief mention in a 'books received' column.[2] In 1860
Quaritch moved his business office from Castle Street to Piccadilly,
though he retained the Castle Street premises; he later told FitzGerald
that the edition 'was as much lost as sold' in the course of this move.
In 1861 the remaining copies were placed in the 'penny box' on the
street outside the Castle Street shop. They were discovered in July

---

[1] Cited in *Letters*, ii. 417.
[2] For the review, see App. I, p. 95; the brief notice is cited above, p. xxxii.

of that year by two young Irishmen, both practising as barristers in London and both with literary leanings: Whitley Stokes (1830–1909), who was to become a distinguished jurist in India and was already a dedicated Celtic scholar, and John Ormsby (1829–95), who later translated the Spanish romance of the Cid. Stokes knew several members of the Pre-Raphaelite circle, including Dante Gabriel Rossetti, for whom he bought a copy. In turn, Rossetti showed the poem to Swinburne, and the two returned to Quaritch's shop for more copies. By the following day, according to Swinburne's famous account, the price had risen 'to the sinfully extravagant sum of twopence'. Rossetti and Swinburne began distributing the poem to friends and literary associates, among them Browning, Burne-Jones, Meredith, Morris, Ruskin, and Tennyson. By December 1861 the remains of the first edition had returned to the interior of Quaritch's shop, where one of FitzGerald's friends saw a copy and wrote to ask if he were the author.[3]

By the mid-1860s FitzGerald had thoughts of a second edition. Quaritch told Cowell that he thought 'a small edition would sell', and Cowell relayed this remark to FitzGerald; but when FitzGerald wrote to Quaritch, he 'replied that he had then just happened on some ten copies of Omar, which are quite enough for the present'.[4] Then, in 1867, FitzGerald became aware of the new, French translation of Omar, *Les Quatrains de Khèyam*, by J. B. [Louis Jean Baptiste] Nicolas, 'former Chief Dragoman of the French Embassy in Persia [and] French Consul at Rescht', as he is described on the title page. He noticed it in another of Quaritch's catalogues, just above an item which gave him an unpleasant shock:

Item 9245: The Rubáiyát of Omar Khayyám . Translated by Edward FitzGerald. sq.8vo.sd. RARE, 3s6d.[5]

Not only had Quaritch revealed FitzGerald's name, but he was selling the poem at what seemed to FitzGerald a shamefully high price. 'I blush to see it!' he told Quaritch; nevertheless it reminded him to ask, again, whether Quaritch would consider a second edition. 'I had always wished to add some twenty or thirty more Stanzas to it and some

---

[3] *Letters*, ii. 416. My sources are Terhune (pp. 206–7), Terhune's updated account in *Letters* (ii. 417–18), Martin (pp. 218–19), and Decker (pp. xxxii–xxxiv).

[4] *Letters*, ii. 572.

[5] *Catalogue of Oriental Literature* [etc.] (Bernard Quaritch, 1867).

additional matter: but it seemed absurd to reprint a thing for that alone.'[6] As he read through Nicolas's edition, FitzGerald's wish to revise his own translation was doubled by his wish to rebut the false account of Omar as a Sufi conveyed by Nicolas. He had a copy of Nicolas sent to Cowell, and bombarded him with anxious comments and queries on this subject. Meanwhile the additions and changes he was making to his own text increased the number of stanzas from 75 to 110, and he was uncertain about this, too. He asked Cowell to look at a separate proof of the poem text, and to tell him 'if there is now too much of it. For you know there may be too much of a *very* good thing: and still more easily of a *pretty* good. I know that one is very apt to go wrong in re-castings, additions, etc. "Leave well alone" is a safe rule.'[7]

Quaritch agreed to publish a new edition of 200 copies (still with no contract, and no transfer of copyright); it appeared in February 1868, and sold far more quickly than FitzGerald (and perhaps Quaritch) anticipated. The reason was that a new market had opened up, in America, stimulated by Charles Eliot Norton's article in the *North American Review*.[8] Quaritch probably realized that it would not be long before an American publisher pirated the book, and he was now the one who opened negotiations. In doing so, however, he also raised the question of *which* edition to reprint. FitzGerald asked Tennyson's advice; Quaritch had told him 'that he, and his Readers, like the First Edition best: so he would reprint that', whereas FitzGerald himself preferred the second. Tennyson could answer 'in two words', FitzGerald pleaded: 'And your words would be more than all the rest.'[9] The only consequence of this appeal was that Tennyson started a hare about FitzGerald's having 'stolen' a line of his from 'The Gardener's Daughter', an 'accusation' he made without the slightest ill will but which gave FitzGerald real pain.[10] Meanwhile Quaritch had come up with a compromise: why not reprint both editions, in a conflated text? FitzGerald was unconvinced, and thought the matter through to a compromise of his own:

on looking over the two Versions, and ready to adopt your plan of reconciling two in one, I considered that such a scheme, with brackets, etc., *would*

---

[6] 14 Oct. 1867, *Letters*, iii. 50.   [7] 2 Dec. 1867, ibid. 65.
[8] See App. I, p. 98.   [9] 25 Mar. 1872, *Letters*, iii. 336.
[10] See above, pp. xlvi–xlvii, and Variants, pp. 80–1.

be making too much of the thing: and you and I might both be laughed at for treating my Omar as if it were some precious fragment of Antiquity. . . .

I doubt therefore that, if Omar be republished, he must go forth in one Shape or another—in his first, or second, suit. And I certainly vote for Version 2, with some whole Stanzas which may be 'de trop' cut out, and some of the old readings replaced.[11]

Revision of the text along these lines, and reordering of the sequence of the stanzas, took FitzGerald the whole summer of 1872; the third edition appeared in late August. Cowell pressed him to tone down his attack on Nicolas's edition and to cut out, or moderate, some of the more inflammatory stanzas, but Quaritch argued forcefully on the other side and FitzGerald 'left it to him to settle the Business, and bear the blame'.[12] The reason may be that for this edition, unlike the first two, Quaritch acted much more as a conventional publisher, at least in terms of marketing the book. His greater sway is indicated in his setting the price for the edition at 7s. 6d., a fivefold increase on the price of the second edition. FitzGerald was baffled: 'I suppose it is that he expects to sell only a few; and those few to a few who do not mind giving for one hundred such Quatrains what they might buy all Tennyson for.'[13] Slowly but surely, the *Rubáiyát* was changing from an eccentric and individual enterprise to a commercial 'property' whose production and distribution lay in other hands than those of the author.

Competition from America duly appeared in the form of cheaper 'popular' editions, and in August 1877 Quaritch began pressing FitzGerald to allow him to reprint the *Rubáiyát* in a similar format. FitzGerald replied that he had 'never even *wished* for a "popular Edition" of Omar: but only for one of a price proportionable to his size and value'—a clear rebuke for the high price of the third edition. He also told Quaritch that he would like to publish the *Rubáiyát* paired with his first Persian translation, *Salámán and Absál*—'both, at a moderate price'.[14] Author and publisher were now at odds, but the pressure told more on Quaritch than FitzGerald. In January 1878 another cheap edition appeared, published by James R. Osgood in Boston. FitzGerald was sent a copy, and immediately wrote to Quaritch, blandly stating that he wished Osgood had let him know about it beforehand, 'as I have a few alterations, and an additional Note'.[15]

---

[11] 31 Mar. 1872, *Letters*, iii. 339.   [12] To Cowell, 18 July 1872, ibid. iii. 363.
[13] To Cowell, 9 Oct. 1872, ibid. iii. 377.   [14] 19 Aug. 1877, ibid. iv. 68–9.
[15] Ibid. iii. 92.

Still, he confided to Quaritch two days later, he was inclined to 'leave Omar for the present; there has been enough of him here, and now will be more in America'—as though the last point would make Quaritch feel better![16] Quaritch endured the torment until November, when he wrote FitzGerald a letter of expostulation and cajolement:

Dear Sir,
    Do let me reprint the Rubáiyát! I have so many inquiries for copies that it is painful to be unable to supply a want felt by that part of the public with which I desire to be in connexion, and which you, as the poet idolized by a small but choice circle, ought to be anxious to gratify personally, rather than throw into the hands of American pirates the opportunity of reprinting and *misprinting ad libitum*.
    Allow me to publish another edition, and pay you twenty-five guineas as the honorarium. You know it would be well done, and creditable to us both.
Your devoted servant,
Bernard Quaritch[17]

FitzGerald relented, but on his terms: Quaritch agreed to publish the *Rubáiyát* in conjunction with *Salámán*, and indeed never to reprint the *Rubáiyát* separately. FitzGerald also insisted on his anonymity, not just on the title page of the book but in advertisements for it. This was a symbolic victory, since his authorship was by now widely known, and he himself had already allowed his name to be cited in an article on his work by H. Schütz Wilson.[18] Quaritch secured only one concession, on the size of the print run, which he persuaded FitzGerald to raise from 500 to 1,000 copies, at 10s. 6d.—a price FitzGerald seems to have accepted as reasonable for a volume which added to the *Rubáiyát* the bulkier *Salámán*.[19] The edition was published in August 1879, and though FitzGerald made a few minor changes in his copy, which gave supposed authority to a posthumous 'fifth edition', the fourth was really his last word on the text as a whole. Whether it was his best is another matter.

Revision

FitzGerald's major revisions to the verse text of the *Rubáiyát* were for the second (*1868*) and third editions (*1872*); for the prose text (his Preface and endnotes) we may add the fourth (*1879*). In *1868*

---

[16] Ibid. 93.   [17] Ibid. 158–9.
[18] See App. I, p. 110.   [19] *Letters*, iv. 174–6 and n. 2.

a significant strategic change was made to the title page, which instead of stating that the *Rubáiyát* had been 'Translated into English Verse' substitutes the term 'Rendered'. The number of stanzas went up from 75 to 110, a very substantial addition was made to the Preface, and there were several new and expanded endnotes. In *1872* the number of stanzas was reduced to 101 and the added material in the Preface was considerably shortened. In *1879* the material added to the Preface in *1868*, and partially retained in *1872*, was completely omitted; the verse text is very close to *1872*, with the exception of one stanza which restored a complete stanza from *1868*, and a further addition was made to one of the endnotes.

The second edition has some fine things, which one would like to sneak into the first edition text:

> Whether at Naishápúr or Babylon,
> Whether the Cup with sweet or bitter run,
>   The Wine of Life keeps oozing drop by drop,
> The Leaves of Life keep falling one by one.

or

> Earth could not answer; nor the Seas that mourn
> In flowing Purple, of their Lord forlorn;
>   Nor Heaven, with those eternal Signs reveal'd
> And hidden by the sleeve of Night and Morn.

FitzGerald's addition to the Preface, with its vigorous defence of his view of Omar as a true materialist and literal wine-drinker, and not an allegorically minded Sufi, is also worth having, long French quotations and all. But these good things are overwhelmed by a series of catastrophic errors of judgement. The second edition is both bloated by addition and defaced by alteration. Naturally attention has focused on the opening stanza:

> Awake! for Morning in the Bowl of Night
> Has flung the Stone that puts the Stars to Flight:[1]
>   And Lo! the Hunter of the East has caught
> The Sultán's Turret in a Noose of Light.

This became:

> Wake! For the Sun behind yon Eastern height
> Has chased the Sessions of the Stars from Night;
>   And, to the field of Heav'n ascending, strikes
> The Sultán's Turret with a Shaft of Light.

We are spoilt for choice; but take another example, stanza XXXIII:

> Then to the rolling Heav'n itself I cried,
> Asking, 'What Lamp had Destiny to guide
>   Her little Children stumbling in the Dark?'
> And—'A blind Understanding!' Heav'n replied.

whose piercing and tender human question is dissipated in an abstruse philosophical formula and pompous diction:

> Then of the THEE IN ME who works behind
> The Veil of Universe I cried to find
>   A Lamp to guide me through the darkness; and
> Something then said—'An Understanding blind.'

These are examples of rewriting which suggest that FitzGerald had lost touch with his own poem; the added stanzas show him deliberately abandoning the concision and allusiveness which are so much a part of the *1859* text for the dubious pleasure of explaining himself. He omitted the excellent stanza XLV, with its game ending ('Make Game of that which makes as much of Thee'), and replaced it with three stanzas of flabby argument (see Variants, p. 82); he spoiled the taut sequence of stanzas LVI–LVII with three interpolated stanzas, including this gem of theological indignation, meant to underline Omar's prescient denunciation of Calvinism:

> What! out of senseless Nothing to provoke
> A conscious Something to resent the yoke
>   Of unpermitted Pleasure, under pain
> Of Everlasting Penalties, if broke!

In *1872* FitzGerald carried out some repairs on the mess he had made. But *1872* has its own problems. It is marked by Cowell's influence, both direct and indirect (that is, FitzGerald acted on his advice, and on what he knew Cowell would want). Cowell's opinion of Omar was changing; in his 1858 article for the *Calcutta Review* he denied that Omar was a Sufi, now he was not so sure; moreover, as a devout Christian he was alarmed at the popularity of FitzGerald's version of Omar's pagan scepticism. Accordingly, some of the changes in *1872* do not so much revise *1868* as reflect a new uncertainty of approach. The revision of the final sentences of the Preface is one example; so is the elimination of some (though not all) of the 'controversial' stanzas added in *1868*. Yet some of FitzGerald's other revisions were clearly motivated by his having thought better of things he had done in *1868*; unfortunately he did not simply revert to the *1859* readings. Take, for example, the last two lines of stanza XXX: 'Another and another Cup to drown | The Memory of this Impertinence!' In *1868* these lines read: 'Ah, contrite Heav'n endowed us with the Vine | To drug the memory of that insolence!' Pomposity displaces colloquial vigour in the first of these lines; the apposite and resounding 'drown' at the end of the line mutates into the feeble 'drug', and the splutter of indignation in 'this Impertinence' has become dulled and distanced into 'that insolence'. In *1872* it is better, but only because it is hard to see how it could have been worse: 'Oh, many a Cup of this forbidden Wine | Must drown the memory of that insolence!' Now we have a neat contrast between 'this' and 'that', and at least 'drown' has returned, though not in its rightful place. Such are the consequences of sticking half-heartedly to your guns.

In his 'critical edition' of the *Rubáiyát*, Christopher Decker claims that 'there is no best version of the text, but there are several best versions', meaning that each edition of the work is of equal authority, and the editor's task should not be to express a preference, but to reproduce each text as faithfully as possible.[20] It is certainly helpful to scholars to have all four texts available in a single volume, but it does not let the editor of a 'reader's edition' of the *Rubáiyát* off the hook. In his fine chapter on the poem in *The Poetry of Indifference*, Erik Gray argues with (to me) all-but-persuasive eloquence that the 'coexistence of different versions is an essential aspect of the *Rubáiyát*' and that the uncertainty generated by its competing texts 'enables it to remain a living presence in the mind far beyond the usual date'.[21] But I remain convinced that the first edition of the *Rubáiyát* is a masterpiece and that subsequent editions did little to make it better and a lot to make it worse. I hope that readers will take an interest in the revisions, but that they will do so always in relation to this primary text, presented here not as one phase of a textual continuum, but as a single, and beautiful, object of attention.

---

[20] Decker, p. lix.   [21] Gray, pp. 107–8.

NOTE ON THE TEXT

Copy-Text

THE copy-text for this edition is that of the first edition (*1859*). Selected variants are recorded from the three other editions published in FitzGerald's lifetime (*1868*, *1872*, and *1879*), together with some explanatory annotation regarding material which appears only in the revised text.

FitzGerald's notes, cued with superscripts in the text, follow immediately after the poem. The editor's further Explanatory Notes are not cued, and can be found at the back of the book.

Emendations

Besides a couple of missing quotation marks, the following emendations have been made to the copy-text (corrected reading followed by the reading in *1859*):

[Preface] p. 5, l. 24. A. D. 1090] A. B. 1090 [corrected in *1868*]

[Preface] p. 8, l. 15. Bibliothèque] Bibliothéque [FitzGerald noticed this error in the proofs for *1872*; d'Herbelot's original 1697 title page, as Decker points out, has no accent at all (p. lxiv). See next entry.]

[Preface] p. 12, l. 3. Bibliothèque Impériale] Bibliothèque Imperiále [The correct spelling of 'Bibliothèque' is in *1868*, though FitzGerald missed his previous error, which had to wait until *1872* to be put right. 'Imperiále', however, remained majestically wrong until the Bibliothèque itself became 'Nationale' in *1879*. It seems odd that FitzGerald never realized this error, and that no one pointed it out; nevertheless I have assumed that he would have corrected it had it been brought to his attention.]

[Preface] p. 12, l. 6. Rubáiyát] Rabáiyát [corrected in *1872*]

XIV.4 Lighting] Lightning [corrected in *1868* and by FitzGerald in a number of copies of *1859* (Decker, p. lxv)]

The endnote numerals 14, 15, 16 in the poem text of 1859 are out of sequence, running 15, 16, 14. I have put them in the correct order. See Explanatory Notes, p. 156.

Stanza LXVI lacks a numeral for endnote 22, which clearly belongs to it. I have placed this numeral at the end of the second line; this is where the equivalent numeral (25) is placed in *1868*.

Other Editorial Changes

Repeat quotation marks at the start of a new line (both in prose passages in the Preface, e.g. the extract from Nizám al Mulk's *Testament*, pp. 4–5, and in passages of speech in the poem, e.g. stanzas I and II) have been removed.

Where a prose quotation runs over several paragraphs, only the quotation marks at the beginning and end of the whole passage have been retained. The alternation between double and single quotation marks within quotations has been regularized, except in the Preface.

Titles and stanza numerals in *1859* are followed by a full stop. Stanza numerals are indented further right in *1859* than in this edition (e.g. in stanza I the numeral comes above 'the', in stanza II above 'Left', etc.).

FitzGerald's English Spelling and Orthography

Like most authors, FitzGerald had a number of idiosyncratic spellings (*Vizyr, coop't, Fansy*); and he continued, far into the nineteenth century, the outmoded Practice of spelling Nouns with initial Capitals. Unlike most authors of his period, however, he was not subject to the normalizing practices of Victorian printers and publishers; until the fourth edition of the *Rubáiyát* he paid for, and supervised, the printing of his own work. All editions published in his lifetime reflect his personal orthography in a way which is strikingly at variance with the trend of the period towards standardized forms. I have retained all of FitzGerald's spellings, with a note where needed. FitzGerald himself did become uneasy about his capitals, and offered to surrender his control over the text to a professional 'Critic' (i.e. a publisher's reader)—but not in respect of the *Rubáiyát*. The fourth edition of the poem (1879) was paired with a revised version of his first Persian translation, Jámi's *Salámán and Absál*. In a letter of 18 April 1879 to his publisher, Bernard Quaritch, he said that he intended 'to weed out a lot of *Capitals*, which some one said stuck up like thistles out of corn' (*Letters*, iv. 198); it is clear that he is referring only to *Salámán and Absál*. Two days later he wrote again, deprecating his 'habit of beginning Nouns with Capitals': 'it is contrary to the usage of far better men than myself, and looks ugly. Perhaps your Critic would be at the trouble of striking out those which he considers not emphatically wanted' (ibid. 199). But this permission applied, again, only to *Salámán and Absál*; the text of the *Rubáiyát* in 1879 left all the thistles standing.

NOTE ON THE PRONUNCIATION AND TRANSCRIPTION OF PERSIAN WORDS

MOST English-speaking readers of the poem know no Persian and have to get along with FitzGerald's idiosyncratic and inconsistent spelling and accentuation of Persian words as best they can. He himself took great interest in this issue (his correspondence with Cowell is filled with debate about it), but he did not explain his choices in any edition of the poem; though he did offer a single sentence in the preface to the first edition of *Salámán and Absál* (1856): 'The *accented* Vowels are to be pronounced long, as in Italian—Salámán—Absál—Shírín, &c' (p. viii). This would be of some help to an Italian reader. Decker (pp. 238–49) provides a comprehensive guide to the pronunciation of Persian words and proper names in the *Rubáiyát*, which takes account of FitzGerald's uncertainties and inconsistencies, but which is sometimes over-anxious about the need for readers to conform to a system that the author took twenty years to get not quite right. As Decker points out, FitzGerald created an additional difficulty by using the same accent (′) to indicate the pronunciation of vowels and (in the poem) to tell readers which syllable to stress; but there are only a few cases where he uses it for the latter purpose. He usually (though not always) treated quotations differently from his own text, respecting their spelling and orthography: for example, he spelt *Khorassán* in the first sentence of the Preface, but transcribed *Khorassan* from Cowell's article in the *Calcutta Review*, and he did not alter the article's inconsistency in spelling *Sabbáh* and *Sabbah* within a few lines. I offer the following guidance:

á	as in *father*, so *Khayyám* rhymes with *psalm*, not *jam*.
â	used in only one Persian word, *sâdhik* (endnote 2), probably taken from a dictionary or other source and inadvertently left unchanged; pronounced as *á*.
ai	as *eye* in *Rubáiyát*, *Hátim Tai*; as *day* in *Kaikobád*, *Kaikhosrú*. The case of *Naishápúr* (or *Naishápur*) is problematic: either *ee* or *ay* is possible.
é	used in only one Persian word, *Péhlevi*; the accent indicates that the stress falls on the first syllable; both the first and second *e* are pronounced as in *set*.

í, ý   as in *eel*; final 'i' is always so pronounced, whether accented or not (*Jamshýd, Sufí, Subhi*).

ú   as in *rude*, so *Mahmúd* rhymes with *food*, not *mud*.

The consonantal cluster *kh* should be pronounced as in Scottish *loch*, but I have always taken the 'h' in *Khayyám* to be silent and (to the best of my knowledge) this is the standard pronunciation for English-speaking readers. Proponents of *ch* can console themselves with *Khorassán*. On the other hand I have always slightly roughened the intermediate *h* (*Bahrám, Mahmúd, Péhlevi*) without really knowing why. I suspect that most readers of the poem come to similar personal accommodations.

The different sources I have consulted in preparing this edition all use different transcription systems. I have respected these in direct quotations, but in my own text I have conformed to FitzGerald's usage, with one or two exceptions, the most important of which is the spelling *ruba'i, ruba'iyat* to refer to the original Persian form.

SELECT BIBLIOGRAPHY

The place of publication is London unless otherwise specified. Asterisked works have useful bibliographies either of primary sources or criticism.

Editions of the Rubáiyát in FitzGerald's Lifetime

Rubáiyát of Omar Khayyám, the Astronomer-Poet of Persia. Translated into English Verse (Bernard Quaritch, 1859).
Rubáiyát of Omar Khayyám, the Astronomer-Poet of Persia. Rendered into English Verse (Bernard Quaritch, 1868).
Rubáiyát of Omar Khayyám, the Astronomer-Poet of Persia. Rendered into English Verse (Bernard Quaritch, 1872).
Rubáiyát of Omar Khayyám; and the Salámán and Ábsál of Jámí; rendered into English Verse (Bernard Quaritch, 1879). [The separate title page for the Rubáiyát has the tag 'the Astronomer-Poet of Persia'.]

Collected Editions of FitzGerald's Work

Michael Kerney (ed.), Works of Edward FitzGerald, 2 vols. (Bernard Quaritch, 1887).
W. Aldis Wright (ed.), Letters and Literary Remains of Edward FitzGerald, 7 vols. (Macmillan, 1902–3). [Originally published in 3 vols. in 1889; incorporates further volumes of letters and miscellaneous writings.]
George Bentham (ed.), The Variorum and Definitive Edition of the Poetical and Prose Writings of Edward FitzGerald, 7 vols. (New York: Doubleday, Page, 1902–3).

Separate Editions of the Rubáiyát

*Edward Heron-Allen (ed.), Edward FitzGerald's Rubá'iyât of Omar Khayyâm, with their Original Persian Sources (Bernard Quaritch, 1899).
*A. J. Arberry (ed.), The Romance of the Rubaiyat: Edward FitzGerald's First Edition Reprinted with Introduction and Notes (George Allen & Unwin, 1959).
Carl J. Weber (ed.), FitzGerald's Rubáiyát: Centennial Edition (Waterville, Me: Colby College Press, 1959).
Dick Davis (ed.), Rubáiyát of Omar Khayyám (Harmondsworth: Penguin Books, 1989) [Penguin Poetry Bookshelf].
*Christopher Decker (ed.), Edward FitzGerald, Rubáiyát of Omar Khayyám: A Critical Edition (Charlottesville: University Press of Virginia, 1997).

Richard Brodie (ed.), *Rubáiyát of Omar Khayyám*: online texts of 1st, 2nd, 3rd, and 4th editions. http://www.therubaiyat.com

Other Translations of Poems by, or Attributed to, Omar Khayyám

E. H. Whinfield, *The Quatrains of Omar Khayyam: The Persian Text with an English Verse Translation* (Trübner, 1883).

Justin McCarthy, *Rubaiyat of Omar Khayyam* (David Nutt, 1889).

Richard Le Gallienne, *Rubáiyát of Omar Khayyám: A Paraphrase from Several Literal Translations* (Grant Richards, 1897).

Edward Heron-Allen, *The Ruba'iyat of Omar Khayyām: A Facsimile of the MS in the Bodleian Library* (H. S. Nichols, 1898).

Nathan Haskell Dole (ed.), *Rubáiyát of Omar Khayyám: English, French, German, Italian, and Danish Translations Comparatively Arranged in Accordance with the Text of Edward FitzGerald's Version*, 2 vols. (Boston: L. C. Page, 1898).

*Peter Avery and John Heath-Stubbs, *The Ruba'iyat of Omar Khayyám* (Allen Lane, 1979).

Letters

W. Aldis Wright (ed.), *Letters and Literary Remains*: see 'Collected Editions'.

F. R. Barton (ed.), *Some New Letters of Edward FitzGerald to Bernard Barton* (Williams & Norgate, 1923).

C. Quaritch Wrentmore (ed.), *Letters from Edward FitzGerald to Bernard Quaritch 1853 to 1883* (Bernard Quaritch, 1926).

Catharine Bodham Johnson and Neilson Campbell Hannay (eds.), *A FitzGerald Friendship: Being Letters from Edward FitzGerald to William Bodham Donne* (New York: William Rudge, 1932).

Alfred McKinley Terhune and Annabelle Burdick Terhune (eds.), *The Letters of Edward FitzGerald*, 4 vols. (Princeton: Princeton University Press, 1980).

Biography, Criticism, and Reference

A. C. Benson, *Edward FitzGerald* (New York: Macmillan, 1905).

*Alfred McKinley Terhune, *The Life of Edward FitzGerald* (Oxford University Press, 1947).

*Iran B. Hassani Jewett, *Edward FitzGerald* (Boston: Twayne, 1977).

Daniel Schenker, 'Fugitive Articulation: An Introduction to *The Rubáiyát of Omar Khayyám*', *Victorian Poetry*, 19 (1981), 49–64.

*Robert Bernard Martin, *With Friends Possessed: A Life of Edward FitzGerald* (New York: Atheneum, 1985).

Robert Douglas-Fairhurst, *Victorian Afterlives: The Shaping of Influence in Nineteenth-Century Literature* (Oxford: Oxford University Press, 2002).

Christopher Decker, 'Edward FitzGerald and Other Men's Flowers: Allusion in the *Rubáiyát of Omar Khayyám*', *Literary Imagination*, 6/2 (2004), 213–39.

Erik Gray, *The Poetry of Indifference: From the Romantics to the Rubáiyát* (Amherst: University of Massachusetts Press, 2005).

David G. Riede, *Allegories of One's Own Mind: Melancholy in Victorian Poetry* (Columbus: Ohio State University Press, 2005).

William H. Martin and Sandra Mason, *The Art of Omar Khayyam: Illustrating FitzGerald's Rubaiyat* (I. B. Tauris, 2007).

*Victorian Poetry, 46/1 (Spring 2008) [Special FitzGerald issue edited with an introductory essay by Erik Gray; five essays, by Giuseppe Albano, Anna Jane Barton, Annmarie Drury, Daniel Karlin, and Herbert F. Tucker; bibliography of FitzGerald criticism since 1959].

A CHRONOLOGY OF
EDWARD FITZGERALD

1809   (31 Mar.) Born Edward Purcell at Bredfield, Suffolk, seventh of eight children of John and Mary Frances FitzGerald Purcell.

1816–18   Family lives in France, at Saint-Germain-en-Laye and Paris.

1818   Adopts the surname FitzGerald on death of his maternal grandfather.

1818–25   Attends King Edward VI Grammar School, Bury St Edmunds, Suffolk, where he forms lasting friendships with William Airy, W. B. Donne, John M. Kemble, and James Spedding.

1826   FitzGerald family moves to Wherstead, near Ipswich.

1826–30   Studies at Trinity College, Cambridge, occupying rooms at 19 King's Parade. Forms lasting friendships with John Allen, Robert Hindes Groome, Charles Merivale, W. M. Thackeray, and W. H. Thompson.

1830   (Feb.) Graduates with a pass degree. Alfred Tennyson publishes *Poems, Chiefly Lyrical*.

1830–7   Lives as a 'genteel gypsy' (Terhune) on £300 annual allowance, moving between the family home, London lodgings, his sister Eleanor Kerrich's home at Geldestone Hall, Norfolk, and Cambridge; and travels with and visits to friends.

1831   One of EFG's few original poems, 'Meadows in Spring', published in *Hone's Year Book* (Apr.) and the *Athenaeum* (July).

1832   Forms close friendship with W. K. Browne of Bedford. Around this time, meets the 'Quaker poet' Bernard Barton at his mother's house, and they become friends. Tennyson publishes *Poems*.

1833   (Autumn) Begins friendship with Tennyson.

1835   (Aug.) FitzGerald family moves into Boulge Hall, near Woodbridge, Suffolk. Forms important friendship with George Crabbe, vicar of Bredfield, son of the poet.

1837   EFG moves into Boulge Cottage, outside the gates of Boulge Hall park, his home for the next sixteen years. He becomes increasingly disenchanted with London life.

1837–9   Forms friendships with Samuel Laurence, Savile Morton, Frederick Pollock, and Frederick Tennyson on visits to London.

1841   'Chronomoros' published in *Fulcher's Sudbury Pocketbook* for 1841.

1842   EFG persuades Alfred Tennyson to publish *Poems* with Edward Moxon, and helps prepare the volume, the last work by Tennyson of which he wholeheartedly approves.

1842–7   Assists Thomas Carlyle with research on Oliver Cromwell.

1844   Begins an important friendship with Edward Byles Cowell of Ipswich.

1846   (Oct.) Starts writing *Euphranor*.

1847   Cowell marries Elizabeth Charlesworth of Bramford, near Ipswich, with whom EFG claimed to be in love in the late 1830s.

1848   EFG's father is declared bankrupt. EFG in London trying to resolve his father's business affairs.

1849   (Feb.) Bernard Barton dies. A misunderstanding between FitzGerald and Barton's daughter Lucy leads to an 'engagement' which he seems not to have intended or wanted, but which he would eventually honour. (May) EFG's parents separate. (Oct.) *Selections from the poems and letters of Bernard Barton* published. Although Lucy Barton's name appears on the title page, EFG edited and in some cases rewrote the selections, as well as writing the 'Memoir'.

1850   Begins to study Spanish. Tennyson publishes *In Memoriam*.

1851   *Euphranor: a dialogue on youth* published.

1852   *Polonius: a collection of wise saws and modern instances* published. (18 Mar.) EFG's father dies. (Autumn) Translating Calderón plays. (Dec.) Starts studying Persian with Cowell at Oxford.

1853   *Six Dramas of Calderón Freely Translated* published, the only book published under EFG's name in his lifetime. (Nov.) Forced to leave Boulge Cottage. Moves to lodgings at Farlingay Hall, Job Smith's farm near Woodbridge. Translates his first Persian poem, 'The Gardener and the Nightingale', from Sádi's *Gulistán*.

1854   (Spring) Revising *Euphranor* and reading Jámi's *Sáláman and Absál*. (July) Begins to study German.

1855   (30 Jan.) EFG's mother dies. (Apr.) Submits *Sálámán and Absál* to *Fraser's Magazine*; rejected (May). (June) *Euphranor: a dialogue on youth* (2nd edn.) published.

1856   (Feb.) Cowell appointed Professor of Modern History and Political Economy, Presidency College, Calcutta. (Apr.) *Sálámán and Absál: an allegory translated from the Persian of Jámi* published. Cowell sends EFG transcriptions of parts of the recently discovered Ouseley MS of Omar Khayyám's poems in the Bodleian Library, Oxford. (June) Travels to the Continent with W. K. Browne and George Crabbe. (14 July) Cowell gives EFG a complete transcription of Ouseley MS. (1 Aug.) The Cowells leave for India. (4 Nov.) EFG marries Lucy Barton (1808–98) at Chichester.

1857   The FitzGeralds spend Christmas apart, take London lodgings for two months, but live together only at intervals. EFG begins studying the Persian poet Attár's *Mantic-ut-Tair* ('Parliament of Birds'), and works on a translation of Aeschylus' *Agamemnon*. (May) Outbreak of Indian Mutiny. (15 June) Receives Cowell's transcript of the Calcutta MS of Omar Khayyám's poems from India. (Aug.) The FitzGeralds agree on a separation. (16 Sept.) George Crabbe of Bredfield dies.

1858   (Spring) Submits partial translation of *Omar* (35 stanzas) to *Fraser's Magazine*.

1859   (Jan.) Withdraws *Omar* from *Fraser's Magazine*. (Feb.) W. K. Browne seriously injured in a horse-riding accident. (Mar.) *Rubáiyát of Omar Khayyám, the astronomer-poet of Persia, translated into English verse* published anonymously, printed by EFG and with Bernard Quaritch as nominal publisher; few, if any, copies are sold at the published price of 1*s.*; only one review of any substance appears, in the *Literary Gazette*. (30 Mar.) Browne dies.

1860   Quaritch moves offices and some copies of the *Rubáiyát* are lost in the move; the remainder are deposited in the 'penny box' outside his shop. (Dec.) EFG moves from Farlingay Hall to lodgings on Market Hill, Woodbridge.

1860–1   Occasional contributions to *Notes and Queries* signed 'Parathina'.

1861   (July) Whitley Stokes and John Ormsby 'discover' the *Rubáiyát* in the 'penny box' and buy copies for friends including D. G. Rossetti and Swinburne, who in turn enthusiastically distribute copies among their circle.

1860–70   Occasional contributions to *East Anglian Notes and Queries*
           signed 'F' or 'E. F. G.'.

1860–76   (June–Nov.) EFG sails regularly, mostly on the River Deben
           and along the east coast, but also to Holland (1863) and the
           south coast (1866).

1861   (Apr.) EFG names his new boat the *Waveney*.

1862   (Summer) Unauthorized edition of FitzGerald's *Rubáiyát* pri-
           vately printed in Madras, India, almost certainly by Whitley
           Stokes.

1863   (June) EFG's schooner, the *Scandal*, launched. (24 Dec.)
           Thackeray dies.

1864   (May) Buys cottage and 6 acres of land in Woodbridge, later
           named Little Grange.

1865   *The Mighty Magician* and *Such Stuff as Dreams are Made Of*,
           two plays translated from Calderón, privately printed.

1866   (Jan.) Discusses second edition of *Rubáiyát* with Quaritch, and
           considers possible revisions. Begins friendship with Lowestoft
           fisherman Joseph ('Posh') Fletcher. Swinburne publishes
           Poems and Ballads, one of the most famous (and scandalous) of
           which, 'Laus Veneris', is written in the 'Rubáiyát stanza'.

1867   (June) Cowell elected as Professor of Sanskrit at Cambridge.
           (July) EFG lets out Little Grange rather than live in it himself.
           (Aug.) Agrees with Quaritch to prepare a second edition of the
           Rubáiyát. (Oct.) Receives J. B. Nicolas's French translation of
           Omar Khayyám and restarts discussions with Quaritch about a
           second edition of the *Rubáiyát*. (Dec.) Begins friendship with
           W. Aldis Wright.

1867–70   In herring-fishing partnership with Posh Fletcher. Fletcher
           captains the *Meum and Tuum*, a herring-lugger that EFG pays
           to be built at Lowestoft, but proves financially unreliable.

1868   (Feb.) *Rubáiyát of Omar Khayyám* (2nd edn.) published.

1868–70   Occasional contributions to *East Anglian . . . Notes and Queries*
           on Suffolk sea slang.

1869   (Spring) *Agamemnon: a tragedy taken from Aeschylus* privately
           printed. EFG consults an oculist in London about his impaired
           eyesight. For the rest of his life EFG is increasingly reliant on
           hiring boys to read to him. (Oct.) Charles Eliot Norton reviews
           Rubáiyát in the *North American Review*.

1870   (Summer) Pirated edition of the *Rubáiyát* (2nd edn.) printed by James Watson in Ohio, US.

1871   *Sáláman and Absál* (2nd edn.) privately printed.

1872   (Spring) *Rubáiyát* (2nd edn.) is sold out; EFG agrees to a third edition. (Aug.) *Rubáiyát* (3rd edn.) published.

1874   (Jan.) EFG forced to move out of Market Hill lodgings, moves into Little Grange.

1875   (Feb.) First published identification of EFG as author (apart from *Six Dramas of Calderón*) in FitzEdward Hall's essay in *Lippincott's Magazine*.

1876   *Agamemnon* (2nd edn.) published.

1877   Friendship with *Punch* artist Charles Keene begins.

1877–8 Occasional contributions to 'Suffolk Notes and Queries' column in *Ipswich Journal*

1879   (Spring) *Readings in Crabbe. Tales of the Hall* privately printed. (Aug.) *Rubáiyát* (4th edn.) published in combined edition with *Sáláman and Absál* (3rd edn).

1880–1 *The downfall and death of King Oedipus: a drama in two parts, chiefly taken from the Oedipus Tyrranus and Colonæus of Sophocles* privately printed in two parts as 'Oedipus in Thebes' and 'Oedipus at Athens'.

1881   Revising *Euphranor* again. (Mar.) James Spedding dies after being struck by a cab in London. (Dec.) Spanish Royal Academy awards EFG a medal in recognition of his translations.

1882   (May) *Euphranor: a May-Day conversation at Cambridge, '´Tis forty years since'* (3rd edn.) privately printed. (June) W. B. Donne dies.

1883   (Mar.) Revises introduction to *Readings in Crabbe*. (Apr.) Draws up his will. (May) Entrusts copies of his works with final corrections to W. Aldis Wright. (14 June) EFG dies while staying at Merton Rectory with George Crabbe, son of Crabbe of Bredfield. (19 June) Burial in Boulge churchyard.

1889   So-called '5th edition' of *Rubáiyát* published, with some MS corrections by EFG incorporated in text.

1892   Formation of the Omar Khayyám Club.

RUBÁIYÁT

OF OMAR
KHAYYÁM

OMAR KHAYYÁM,

THE ASTRONOMER-POET OF PERSIA

OMAR KHAYYÁM was born at Naishápúr in Khorassán in the latter half of our Eleventh, and died within the First Quarter of our Twelfth, Century. The slender Story of his Life is curiously twined about that of two others very considerable Figures in their Time and Country: one of them, Hasan al Sabbáh, whose very Name has lengthen'd down to us as a terrible Synonym for Murder: and the other (who also tells the Story of all Three) Nizám al Mulk, Vizyr to Alp the Lion and Malik Shah, Son and Grandson of Toghrul Beg the Tartar, who had wrested Persia from the feeble Successor of Mahmúd the Great, and founded that Seljukian Dynasty which finally roused Europe into the Crusades. This Nizám al Mulk, in his *Wasýat*—or *Testament*—which he wrote and left as a Memorial for future Statesmen—relates the following, as quoted in the Calcutta Review, No. 59, from Mirkhond's History of the Assassins.

"'One of the greatest of the wise men of Khorassan was

[*Preface*]

the Imám Mowaffak of Naishápur, a man highly hon-
oured and reverenced,—may God rejoice his soul; his
illustrious years exceeded eighty-five, and it was the uni-
versal belief that every boy who read the Koran or studied
the traditions in his presence, would assuredly attain to
honour and happiness. For this cause did my father send
me from Tús to Naishápúr with Abd-u-samad, the doctor
of law, that I might employ myself in study and learning
under the guidance of that illustrious teacher. Towards me
he ever turned an eye of favour and kindness, and as his
pupil I felt for him extreme affection and devotion, so that
I passed four years in his service. When I first came there,
I found two other pupils of mine own age newly arrived,
Hakim Omar Khayyám, and the ill-fated Ben Sabbáh.
Both were endowed with sharpness of wit and the highest
natural powers; and we three formed a close friendship
together. When the Imám rose from his lectures, they
used to join me, and we repeated to each other the lessons
we had heard. Now Omar was a native of Naishápur,
while Hasan Ben Sabbah's father was one Ali, a man of
austere life and practice, but heretical in his creed and
doctrine. One day Hasan said to me and to Khayyám, "It
is a universal belief that the pupils of the Imám Mowaffak
will attain to fortune. Now, even if we *all* do not attain
thereto, without doubt one of us will; what then shall be

[*Preface*]

our mutual pledge and bond?" We answered "Be it what you please." "Well," he said, "let us make a vow, that to whomsoever this fortune falls, he shall share it equally with the rest, and reserve no pre-eminence for himself." "Be it so," we both replied, and on these terms we mutually pledged our words. Years rolled on, and I went from Khorassan to Transoxiana, and wandered to Ghazni and Cabul; and when I returned, I was invested with office, and rose to be administrator of affairs during the Sultanate of Sultan Alp Arslán.'

He goes on to state, that years passed by, and both his old school-friends found him out, and came and claimed a share in his good fortune, according to the school-day vow. The Vizier was generous and kept his word. Hasan demanded a place in the government, which the Sultan granted at the Vizier's request; but discontented with a gradual rise, he plunged into the maze of intrigue of an oriental court, and, failing in a base attempt to supplant his benefactor, he was disgraced and fell. After many mishaps and wanderings, Hasan became the head of the Persian sect of the *Ismailians*,—a party of fanatics who had long murmured in obscurity, but rose to an evil eminence under the guidance of his strong and evil will. In A. D. 1090, he seized the castle of Alamút, in the province of Rúdbar, which lies in the mountainous tract, south of the Caspian

5

sea; and it was from this mountain home he obtained that evil celebrity among the Crusaders as the OLD MAN OF THE MOUNTAINS, and spread terror through the Mohammedan world; and it is yet disputed whether the word *Assassin*, which they have left in the language of modern Europe as their dark memorial, is derived from the *hashish*, or opiate of hemp-leaves (the Indian *bhang*,) with which they maddened themselves to the sullen pitch of oriental desperation, or from the name of the founder of the dynasty, whom we have seen in his quiet collegiate days, at Naishápur. One of the countless victims of the Assassin's dagger was Nizám-ul-Mulk himself, the old school-boy friend.

Omar Khayyám also came to the Vizier to claim his share; but not to ask for title or office. 'The greatest boon you can confer on me,' he said, 'is to let me live in a corner under the shadow of your fortune, to spread wide the advantages of Science, and pray for your long life and prosperity.' The Vizier tells us, that, when he found Omar was really sincere in his refusal, he pressed him no further, but granted him a yearly pension of 1,200 *mithkáls* of gold, from the treasury of Naishápur.

At Naishápur thus lived and died Omar Khayyám, 'busied,' adds the Vizier, 'in winning knowledge of every kind, and especially in Astronomy, wherein he attained to a very high pre-eminence. Under the Sultanate of Malik

Shah, he came to Merv, and obtained great praise for his proficiency in science, and the Sultan showered favours upon him.'

When Malik Shah determined to reform the calendar, Omar was one of the eight learned men employed to do it; the result was the *Jaláli* era, (so called from *Jalal-ul-din*, one of the king's names,)—'a computation of time,' says Gibbon, 'which surpasses the Julian, and approaches the accuracy of the Gregorian style.' He is also the author of some astronomical tables, entitled Zíji-Maliksháhí," and the French have lately republished and translated an Arabic Treatise of his on Algebra.

These severer Studies, and his Verses, which, though happily fewer than any Persian Poet's, and, though perhaps fugitively composed, the Result of no fugitive Emotion or Thought, are probably the Work and Event of his Life, leaving little else to record. Perhaps he liked a little Farming too, so often as he speaks of the "Edge of the Tilth" on which he loved to rest with his Diwán of Verse, his Loaf—and his Wine.

"His Takhallus or poetical name (Khayyám) signifies a Tent-maker, and he is said to have at one time exercised that trade, perhaps before Nizám-ul-Mulk's generosity raised him to independence. Many Persian poets similarly derive their names from their occupations; thus we have

[*Preface*]

Attár, 'a druggist,' Assar, 'an oil presser,' &c." (Though all these, like our Smiths, Archers, Millers, Fletchers, &c. may simply retain the Sirname of an hereditary calling.) "Omar himself alludes to his name in the following whimsical lines:—

> 'Khayyám, who stitched the tents of science,
> Has fallen in grief's furnace and been suddenly burned;
> The shears of Fate have cut the tent ropes of his life,
> And the broker of Hope has sold him for nothing!'

We have only one more anecdote to give of his Life, and that relates to the close; related in the anonymous preface which is sometimes prefixed to his poems; it has been printed in the Persian in the appendix to Hyde's *Veterum Persarum Religio*, p. 499; and D'Herbelot alludes to it in his Bibliothèque, under *Khiam:*—*

'It is written in the chronicles of the ancients that this King of the Wise, Omar Khayyám, died at Naishápur in the year of the Hegira, 517 (A.D. 1123); in science he was

---

* Though *he* attributes the story to a Khiam, "Philosophe Musulman qui a vécu en Odeur de Sainteté dans la Fin du premier et le Commencement du second Siècle," no part of which, except the "Philosophe," can apply to *our* Khayyám, who, however, may claim the Story as *his*, on the Score of Rubáiyát, 77 and 78 of the present Version. The Rashness of the Words, according to D'Herbelot, consisted in being so opposed to those in the Korán: "No Man knows where he shall die."

[*Preface*]

unrivalled,—the very paragon of his age. Khwájah Nizámi of Samarcand, who was one of his pupils, relates the following story: "I often used to hold conversations with my teacher, Omar Khayyám, in a garden; and one day he said to me, 'my tomb shall be in a spot, where the north wind may scatter roses over it.' I wondered at the words he spake, but I knew that his were no idle words. Years after, when I chanced to revisit Naishápur, I went to his final resting place, and lo! it was just outside a garden, and trees laden with fruit stretched their boughs over the garden wall, and dropped their flowers upon his tomb, so as the stone was hidden under them."'"

Thus far—without fear of Trespass—from the Calcutta Review.

Though the Sultan "shower'd Favours upon him," Omar's Epicurean Audacity of Thought and Speech caused him to be regarded askance in his own Time and Country. He is said to have been especially hated and dreaded by the Súfis, whose Practice he ridiculed, and whose Faith amounts to little more than his own when stript of the Mysticism and formal Compliment to Islamism which Omar would not hide under. Their Poets, including Háfiz, who are (with the exception of Firdúsi) the most considerable in Persia, borrowed largely, indeed, of Omar's material, but turning it to a mystical Use more

[*Preface*]

convenient to Themselves and the People they address'd; a People quite as quick of Doubt as of Belief; quite as keen of the Bodily Senses as of the Intellectual; and delighting in a cloudy Element compounded of all, in which they could float luxuriously between Heaven and Earth, and this World and the Next, on the wings of a poetical expression, that could be recited indifferently whether at the Mosque or the Tavern. Omar was too honest of Heart as well as of Head for this. Having failed (however mistakenly) of finding any Providence but Destiny, and any World but This, he set about making the most of it; preferring rather to soothe the Soul through the Senses into Acquiescence with Things as they were, than to perplex it with vain mortifications after what they *might be*. It has been seen that his Worldly Desires, however, were not exorbitant; and he very likely takes a humourous pleasure in exaggerating them above that Intellect in whose exercise he must have found great pleasure, though not in a Theological direction. However this may be, his Worldly Pleasures are what they profess to be without any Pretence at divine Allegory: his Wine is the veritable Juice of the Grape: his Tavern, where it was to be had: his Sáki, the Flesh and Blood that poured it out for him: all which, and where the Roses were in Bloom, was all he profess'd to want of this World or to expect of Paradise.

[*Preface*]

The Mathematic Faculty, too, which regulated his Fansy, and condensed his Verse to a Quality and Quantity unknown in Persian, perhaps in Oriental, Poetry, help'd by its very virtue perhaps to render him less popular with his countrymen. If the Greeks were Children in Gossip, what does Persian Literature imply but a *Second Childishness* of Garrulity? And certainly if no *ungeometric* Greek was to enter Plato's School of Philosophy, no so unchastised a Persian should enter on the Race of Persian Verse, with its "fatal Facility" of running on long after Thought is winded! But Omar was not only the single Mathematician of his Country's Poets; he was also of that older Time and stouter Temper, before the native Soul of Persia was quite broke by a foreign Creed as well as foreign Conquest. Like his great Predecessor Firdúsi, who was as little of a *Mystic*; who scorned to use even a *Word* of the very language in which the New Faith came clothed; and who was suspected, not of Omar's Irreligion indeed, but of secretly clinging to the ancient Fire-Religion of Zerdusht, of which so many of the Kings he sang were Worshippers.

For whatever Reason, however, Omar, as before said, has never been popular in his own Country, and therefore has been but charily transmitted abroad. The MSS. of his Poems, mutilated beyond the average Casualties of Oriental Transcription, are so rare in the East as scarce to have reacht Westward at all, in spite of all that Arms and Science have brought us. There is none at the India House, none at the Bibliothèque Impériale of Paris. We know but of one in England; No. 140 of the Ouseley MSS. at the Bodleian, written at Shiraz, A.D. 1460. This contains but 158 Rubáiyát. One in the Asiatic Society's Library of Calcutta, (of which we have a Copy) contains (and yet incomplete) 516, though swelled to that by all kinds of Repetition and Corruption. So Von Hammer speaks of *his* Copy as containing about 200, while Dr. Sprenger catalogues the Lucknow MS. at double that Number. The Scribes, too, of the Oxford and Calcutta MSS. seem to do their Work under a sort of Protest; each beginning with a Tetrastich (whether genuine or not) taken out of its alphabetic order; the Oxford with one of Apology; the Calcutta with one of Execration too stupid for Omar's, even had Omar been stupid enough to execrate himself.*

The Reviewer, who translates the foregoing Particulars of Omar's Life, and some of his Verse into Prose, concludes by comparing him with Lucretius, both in natural Temper and Genius, and as acted upon by the

---

* "Since this Paper was written" (adds the Reviewer in a note) "we have met with a Copy of a very rare Edition, printed at Calcutta in 1836. This contains 438 Tetrastichs, with an Appendix containing 54 others not found in some MSS."

[*Preface*]

Circumstances in which he lived. Both indeed men of subtle Intellect and high Imagination, instructed in Learning beyond their day, and of Hearts passionate for Truth and Justice; who justly revolted from their Country's false Religion, and false, or foolish, Devotion to it; but who yet fell short of replacing what they subverted by any such better *Hope* as others, upon whom no better *Faith* had dawned, had yet made a Law to themselves. Lucretius, indeed, with such material as Epicurus furnished, consoled himself with the construction of a Machine that needed no Constructor, and acting by a Law that implied no Lawgiver; and so composing himself into a Stoical rather than Epicurean severity of Attitude, sat down to contemplate the mechanical Drama of the Universe of which he was part Actor; himself and all about him, (as in his own sublime Description of the Roman Theatre,) coloured with the lurid reflex of the Curtain that was suspended between them and the outer Sun. Omar, more desperate, or more careless, of any such laborious System as resulted in nothing more than hopeless Necessity, flung his own Genius and Learning with a bitter jest into the general Ruin which their insufficient glimpses only served to reveal; and, yielding his Senses to the actual Rose and Vine, only *diverted* his thoughts by balancing ideal possibilities of Fate, Freewill, Existence and Annihilation; with an oscillation that so generally inclined to the negative and lower side, as to make such Stanzas as the following exceptions to his general Philosophy—

> Oh, if my Soul can fling his Dust aside,
> And naked on the Air of Heaven ride,
>   Is't not a Shame, is't not a Shame for Him
> So long in this Clay Suburb to abide!

> Or is *that* but a Tent, where rests anon
> A Sultán to his Kingdom passing on,
>   And which the swarthy Chamberlain shall strike
> Then when the Sultán rises to be gone?

With regard to the present Translation. The original Rubáiyát (as, missing an Arabic Guttural, these *Tetrastichs* are more musically called), are independent Stanzas, consisting each of four Lines of equal, though varied, Prosody, sometimes *all* rhyming, but oftener (as here attempted) the third line suspending the Cadence by which the last atones with the former Two. Something as in the Greek Alcaic, where the third line seems to lift and suspend the Wave that falls over in the last. As usual with such kind of Oriental Verse, the Rubáiyát follow one another according to Alphabetic Rhyme—a strange Farrago of Grave and Gay. Those here selected are strung into something of an Eclogue, with perhaps a less than equal proportion of the

[*Preface*]

"Drink and make-merry," which (genuine or not) recurs over-frequently in the Original. For Lucretian as Omar's Genius might be, he cross'd that darker Mood with much of Oliver de Basselin Humour. Any way, the Result is sad enough: saddest perhaps when most ostentatiously merry: any way, fitter to move Sorrow than Anger toward the old Tentmaker, who, after vainly endeavouring to unshackle his Steps from Destiny, and to catch some authentic Glimpse of TOMORROW, fell back upon TODAY (which has out-lasted so many Tomorrows!) as the only Ground he got to stand upon, however momentarily slipping from under his Feet.

RUBÁIYÁT
OF
OMAR KHAYYÁM
OF NAISHÁPÚR

I

A WAKE! for Morning in the Bowl of
    Night
Has flung the Stone that puts the Stars to
    Flight:[1]
    And Lo! the Hunter of the East has caught
The Sultán's Turret in a Noose of Light.

II

Dreaming when Dawn's Left Hand was in
  the Sky[2]
I heard a Voice within the Tavern cry,
  "Awake, my Little ones, and fill the Cup
Before Life's Liquor in its Cup be dry."

III

And, as the Cock crew, those who stood
  before
The Tavern shouted—"Open then the Door!
  You know how little while we have to stay,
And, once departed, may return no more."

IV

Now the New Year[3] reviving old Desires,
The thoughtful Soul to Solitude retires,
Where the WHITE HAND OF MOSES on
the Bough
Puts out,[4] and Jesus from the Ground suspires.

V

Irám indeed is gone with all its Rose,[5]
And Jamshýd's Sev'n-ring'd Cup where no
one knows;
But still the Vine her ancient Ruby yields,
And still a Garden by the Water blows.

VI

And David's Lips are lock't; but in divine
High piping Péhlevi, with "Wine! Wine!
    Wine!
Red Wine!"—the Nightingale cries to the
    Rose
That yellow Cheek[7] of her's to'incarnadine.

VII

Come, fill the Cup, and in the Fire of Spring
The Winter Garment of Repentance fling:
    The Bird of Time has but a little way
To fly—and Lo! the Bird is on the Wing.

VIII

And look—a thousand Blossoms with the Day
Woke—and a thousand scatter'd into Clay:
  And this first Summer Month that brings
      the Rose
Shall take Jamshýd and Kaikobád away.

IX

But come with old Khayyám, and leave the
      Lot
Of Kaikobád and Kaikhosrú forgot:
  Let Rustum lay about him as he will,[8]
Or Hátim Tai cry Supper—heed them not.

X

With me along some Strip of Herbage strown
That just divides the desert from the sown,
    Where name of Slave and Sultán scarce is
        known,
And pity Sultán Máhmúd on his Throne.

XI

Here with a Loaf of Bread beneath the
        Bough,
A Flask of Wine, a Book of Verse—and Thou
    Beside me singing in the Wilderness—
And Wilderness is Paradise enow.

Rubáiyát

XII

"How sweet is mortal Sovranty!"—think
    some:
Others—"How blest the Paradise to come!"
  Ah, take the Cash in hand and wave
    the Rest;
Oh, the brave Music of a *distant* Drum!⁹

XIII

Look to the Rose that blows about us—"Lo,
Laughing," she says, "into the World I blow:
  At once the silken Tassel of my Purse
Tear, and its Treasure¹⁰ on the Garden throw."

XIV

The Worldly Hope men set their Hearts upon
Turns Ashes—or it prospers; and anon,
    Like Snow upon the Desert's dusty Face
Lighting a little Hour or two—is gone.

XV

And those who husbanded the Golden Grain,
And those who flung it to the Winds like
        Rain,
    Alike to no such aureate Earth are turn'd
As, buried once, Men want dug up again.

XVI

Think, in this batter'd Caravanserai
Whose Doorways are alternate Night and
Day,
　　How Sultán after Sultán with his Pomp
Abode his Hour or two, and went his way.

XVII

They say the Lion and the Lizard keep
The Courts where Jamshýd gloried and drank
deep:[11]
　　And Bahrám, that great Hunter—the
Wild Ass
Stamps o'er his Head, and he lies fast asleep.

XVIII

I sometimes think that never blows so red
The Rose as where some buried Cæsar bled;
   That every Hyacinth the Garden wears
Dropt in its Lap from some once lovely Head.

XIX

And this delightful Herb whose tender Green
Fledges the River's Lip on which we lean—
   Ah, lean upon it lightly! for who knows
From what once lovely Lip it springs unseen!

XX

Ah, my Belovéd, fill the Cup that clears
TO-DAY of past Regrets and future Fears—
  To-morrow?—Why, To-morrow I may be
Myself with Yesterday's Sev'n Thousand
      Years.[12]

XXI

Lo! some we loved, the loveliest and best
That Time and Fate of all their Vintage prest,
  Have drunk their Cup a Round or two
      before,
And one by one crept silently to Rest.

XXII

And we, that now make merry in the Room
They left, and Summer dresses in new Bloom,
    Ourselves must we beneath the Couch
        of Earth
Descend, ourselves to make a Couch—
        for whom?

XXIII

Ah, make the most of what we yet may spend,
Before we too into the Dust descend;
    Dust into Dust, and under Dust, to lie,
Sans Wine, sans Song, sans Singer, and—
        sans End!

XXIV

Alike for those who for TO-DAY prepare,
And those that after a TO-MORROW stare,
    A Muezzín from the Tower of Darkness
        cries
"Fools! your Reward is neither Here nor
        There!"

XXV

Why, all the Saints and Sages who discuss'd
Of the Two Worlds so learnedly, are thrust
    Like foolish Prophets forth; their Words to
        Scorn
Are scatter'd, and their Mouths are stopt with
        Dust.

XXVI

Oh, come with old Khayyám, and leave the
    Wise
To talk; one thing is certain, that Life flies;
    One thing is certain, and the Rest is Lies;
The Flower that once has blown for ever dies.

XXVII

Myself when young did eagerly frequent
Doctor and Saint, and heard great Argument
    About it and about: but evermore
Came out by the same Door as in I went.

XXVIII

With them the Seed of Wisdom did I sow,
And with my own hand labour'd it to grow:
    And this was all the Harvest that I reap'd—
"I came like Water, and like Wind I go."

XXIX

Into this Universe, and *why* not knowing,
Nor *whence*, like Water willy-nilly flowing:
    And out of it, as Wind along the Waste,
I know not *whither*, willy-nilly blowing.

XXX

What, without asking, hither hurried *whence?*
And, without asking, *whither* hurried hence!
   Another and another Cup to drown
The Memory of this Impertinence!

XXXI

Up from Earth's Centre through the Seventh
       Gate
I rose, and on the Throne of Saturn sate,[13]
   And many Knots unravel'd by the Road;
But not the Knot of Human Death and Fate.

XXXII

There was a Door to which I found no Key:
There was a Veil past which I could not see:
Some little Talk awhile of ME and THEE
There seemed—and then no more of THEE
and ME.[14]

XXXIII

Then to the rolling Heav'n itself I cried,
Asking, "What Lamp had Destiny to guide
Her little Children stumbling in the
Dark?"
And—"A blind Understanding!" Heav'n
replied.

XXXIV

Then to this earthen Bowl did I adjourn
My Lip the secret Well of Life to learn:
    And Lip to Lip it murmur'd—"While you
        live
Drink!—for once dead you never shall
        return."

XXXV

I think the Vessel, that with fugitive
Articulation answer'd, once did live,
    And merry-make; and the cold Lip I kiss'd
How many Kisses might it take—and give!

XXXVI

For in the Market-place, one Dusk of Day,
I watch'd the Potter thumping his wet Clay:
    And with its all obliterated Tongue
It murmur'd—"Gently, Brother, gently, pray!"

XXXVII

Ah, fill the Cup:—what boots it to repeat
How Time is slipping underneath our Feet:
    Unborn TO-MORROW, and dead
        YESTERDAY,
Why fret about them if TO-DAY be sweet!

XXXVIII

One Moment in Annihilation's Waste,
One Moment, of the Well of Life to taste —
  The Stars are setting and the Caravan
Starts for the Dawn of Nothing[15] — Oh, make
      haste!

XXXIX

How long, how long, in infinite Pursuit
Of This and That endeavour and dispute?
  Better be merry with the fruitful Grape
Than sadden after none, or bitter, Fruit.

XL

You know, my Friends, how long since in my
  House
For a new Marriage I did make carouse:
  Divorced old barren Reason from my Bed,
And took the Daughter of the Vine to Spouse.

XLI

For "Is" and "Is-Not" though *with* Rule and
  Line,
And "Up-and-Down" *without,* I could
  define,[16]
  I yet in all I only cared to know,
Was never deep in anything but—Wine.

XLII

And lately, by the Tavern Door agape,
Came stealing through the Dusk an Angel
      Shape
  Bearing a Vessel on his Shoulder; and
He bid me taste of it; and 'twas—the Grape!

XLIII

The Grape that can with Logic absolute
The Two-and-Seventy jarring Sects[17] confute:
  The subtle Alchemist that in a Trice
Life's leaden Metal into Gold transmute.

XLIV

The mighty Mahmúd, the victorious Lord,
That all the misbelieving and black Horde[18]
    Of Fears and Sorrows that infest the Soul
Scatters and slays with his enchanted Sword.

XLV

But leave the Wise to wrangle, and with me
The Quarrel of the Universe let be:
    And, in some corner of the Hubbub
        coucht,
Make Game of that which makes as much of
        Thee.

XLVI

For in and out, above, about, below,
'Tis nothing but a Magic Shadow-show,
   Play'd in a Box whose Candle is the Sun,
Round which we Phantom Figures come
         and go.[19]

XLVII

And if the Wine you drink, the Lip you press,
End in the Nothing all Things end in—Yes—
   Then fancy while Thou art, Thou art but
         what
Thou shalt be—Nothing—Thou shalt not be
   less.

XLVIII

While the Rose blows along the River Brink,
With old Khayyám the Ruby Vintage drink:
  And when the Angel with his darker
      Draught
Draws up to Thee—take that, and do not
      shrink.

XLIX

'Tis all a Chequer-board of Nights and Days
Where Destiny with Men for Pieces plays:
  Hither and thither moves, and mates, and
      slays,
And one by one back in the Closet lays.

L

The Ball no Question makes of Ayes and
      Noes,
But Right or Left as strikes the Player goes;
   And He that toss'd Thee down into the
      Field,
He knows about it all—HE knows—
     HE knows![20]

LI

The Moving Finger writes; and, having writ,
Moves on: nor all thy Piety nor Wit
  Shall lure it back to cancel half a Line,
Nor all thy Tears wash out a Word of it.

LII

And that inverted Bowl we call The Sky,
Whereunder crawling coop't we live and die,
    Lift not thy hands to *It* for help—for It
Rolls impotently on as Thou or I.

LIII

With Earth's first Clay They did the Last
            Man's knead,
And then of the Last Harvest sow'd the Seed:
    Yea, the first Morning of Creation wrote
What the Last Dawn of Reckoning shall read.

LIV

I tell Thee this—When, starting from the
    Goal,
Over the shoulders of the flaming Foal
    Of Heav'n Parwín and Mushtara they
        flung,[21]
In my predestin'd Plot of Dust and Soul

LV

The Vine had struck a Fibre; which about
If clings my Being—let the Súfi flout;
    Of my Base Metal may be filed a Key,
That shall unlock the Door he howls without.

LVI

And this I know: whether the one True Light,
Kindle to Love, or Wrathconsume me quite,
    One Glimpse of It within the Tavern
        caught
Better than in the Temple lost outright.

LVII

Oh Thou, who didst with Pitfall and with Gin
Beset the Road I was to wander in,
    Thou wilt not with Predestination round
Enmesh me, and impute my Fall to Sin?

LVIII

Oh, Thou, who Man of baser Earth didst
    make,
And who with Eden didst devise the Snake;
    For all the Sin wherewith the Face of Man
Is blacken'd, Man's Forgiveness give—and
    take!

*   *   *   *   *   *   *   *

KÚZA-NÁMA

LIX

Listen again. One Evening at the Close
Of Ramazán, ere the better Moon arose,
    In that old Potter's Shop I stood alone
With the clay Population round in Rows.

LX

And, strange to tell, among that Earthen Lot
Some could articulate, while others not:
    And suddenly one more impatient cried—
"Who *is* the Potter, pray, and who the Pot?"

LXI

Then said another—"Surely not in vain
My Substance from the common Earth was
        ta'en,
    That He who subtly wrought me into
        Shape
Should stamp me back to common Earth
        again."

LXII

Another said—"Why, ne'er a peevish Boy,
Would break the Bowl from which he drank
in Joy;
　Shall He that *made* the Vessel in pure
　Love
And Fansy, in an after Rage destroy!"

LXIII

None answer'd this; but after Silence spake
A Vessel of a more ungainly Make:
　"They sneer at me for leaning all awry;
What! did the Hand then of the Potter
　shake?"

LXIV

Said one—"Folks of a surly Tapster tell,
And daub his Visage with the Smoke of Hell;
    They talk of some strict Testing of us—
        Pish!
He's a Good Fellow, and 'twill all be well."

LXV

Then said another with a long-drawn Sigh,
"My Clay with long oblivion is gone dry:
    But, fill me with the old familiar Juice,
Methinks I might recover by-and-bye!"

LXVI

So while the Vessels one by one were
    speaking,
One spied the little Crescent all were
    seeking:[22]
  And then they jogg'd each other, "Brother!
    Brother!
Hark to the Porter's Shoulder-knot a-
    creaking!"

*   *   *   *   *   *   *   *

LXVII

Ah, with the Grape my fading Life provide,
And wash my Body whence the Life has died,
  And in a Windingsheet of Vine-leaf wrapt,
So bury me by some sweet Garden-side.

LXVIII

That ev'n my buried Ashes such a Snare
Of Perfume shall fling up into the Air,
  As not a True Believer passing by
But shall be overtaken unaware.

LXIX

Indeed the Idols I have loved so long
Have done my Credit in Men's Eye much
        wrong:
    Have drown'd my Honour in a shallow
        Cup,
And sold my Reputation for a Song.

LXX

Indeed, indeed, Repentance oft before
I swore—but was I sober when I swore?
  And then and then came Spring, and Rose-
    in-hand
My thread-bare Penitence apieces tore.

LXXI

And much as Wine has play'd the Infidel,
And robb'd me of my Robe of Honour—well,
  I often wonder what the Vintners buy
One half so precious as the Goods they sell.

LXXII

Alas, that Spring should vanish with the Rose!
That Youth's sweet-scented Manuscript
　　　should close!
　The Nightingale that in the Branches sang,
Ah, whence, and whither flown again, who
　　　knows!

LXXIII

Ah Love! could thou and I with Fate
　　　conspire
To grasp this sorry Scheme of Things entire,
　Would not we shatter it to bits—and then
Re-mould it nearer to the Heart's Desire!

LXXIV

Ah, Moon of my Delight who know'st no
    wane,
The Moon of Heav'n is rising once again:
    How oft hereafter rising shall she look
Through this same Garden after me—in vain!

LXXV

And when Thyself with shining Foot shall
    pass
Among the Guests Star-scatter'd on the Grass,
    And in thy joyous Errand reach the Spot
Where I made one—turn down an empty
    Glass!

TAMÁM SHUD

NOTES

[1] Flinging a Stone into the Cup was the Signal for "To Horse!" in the Desert.

[2] The *"False Dawn;" Subhi Kházib*, a transient Light on the Horizon about an hour before the *Subhi sâdhik*, or True Dawn; a well known Phenomenon in the East. The Persians call the Morning Gray, or Dusk, *"Wolf-and-Sheep-While."* "Almost at odds with, which is which."

[3] New Year. Beginning with the Vernal Equinox, it must be remembered; and (howsoever the old Solar Year is practically superseded by the clumsy *Lunar* Year that dates from the Mohammedan Hijra) still commemorated by a Festival that is said to have been appointed by the very Jamshyd whom Omar so often talks of, and whose yearly Calendar he helped to rectify.

"The sudden approach and rapid advance of the Spring," (says a late Traveller in Persia) "are very striking. Before the Snow is well off the Ground, the Trees burst into Blossom, and the Flowers start from the Soil. At *Now Rooz* (*their* New Year's Day) the Snow was lying in patches on the Hills and in the shaded Vallies, while the Fruit-trees in the Garden were budding beautifully, and green Plants and Flowers springing upon the Plains on every side—

Notes

'And on old Hyem's Chin and icy Crown
An odorous Chaplet of sweet Summer buds
Is, as in mockery, set—'—

Among the Plants newly appear'd I recognized some old Acquaintances I had not seen for many a Year: among these, two varieties of the Thistle; a coarse species of the Daisy, like the Horse-gowan; red and white Clover; the Dock; the blue Corn-flower; and that vulgar Herb the Dandelion rearing its yellow crest on the Banks of the Watercourses." The Nightingale was not yet heard, for the Rose was not yet blown: but an almost identical Blackbird and Woodpecker helped to make up something of a North-country Spring.

[4] Exodus iv. 6; where Moses draws forth his Hand—not, according to the Persians, *"leprous as Snow,"*— but *white* as our May-Blossom in Spring perhaps! According to them also the Healing Power of Jesus resided in his Breath.

[5] Irám, planted by King Schedad, and now sunk somewhere in the Sands of Arabia. Jamshyd's Seven-ring'd Cup was typical of the Seven Heavens, 7 Planets, 7 Seas, &c. and was a *Divining Cup.*

[6] *Péhlevi*, the old Heroic *Sanskrit* of Persia. Háfiz also speaks of the Nightingale's *Péhlevi*, which did not change with the People's.

[7] I am not sure if this refers to the Red Rose looking sickly, or the Yellow Rose that ought to be Red; Red, White, and Yellow Roses all common in Persia.

Notes

[8] Rustum, the "Hercules" of Persia, whose exploits are among the most celebrated in the Shah-náma. Hátim Tai, a well-known Type of Oriental Generosity.

[9] A Drum—beaten outside a Palace.

[10] That is, the Rose's Golden Centre.

[11] Persepolis: call'd also *Takht'i Jamshyd*—THE THRONE OF JAMSHYD, "*King-Splendid*," of the mythical *Peeshdádian* Dynasty, and supposed (with Shah-náma Authority) to have been founded and built by him, though others refer it to the Work of the Genie King, Ján Ibn Jann, who also built the Pyramids before the time of Adam. It is also called *Chehl-minar—Forty-column*; which is Persian, probably, for *Column-countless*; the Hall they adorned or supported with their Lotus Base and taurine Capital indicating double that Number, though now counted down to less than half by Earthquake and other Inroad. By whomsoever built, unquestionably the Monument of a long extinguished Dynasty and Mythology; its Halls, Chambers and Galleries, inscribed with Arrow-head Characters, and sculptured with colossal, wing'd, half human Figures like those of Nimroud; Processions of Priests and Warriors—(doubtful if any where a Woman)—and Kings sitting on Thrones or in Chariots, Staff or Lotus-flower in hand, and the *Ferooher*—Symbol of Existence—with his wing'd Globe, common also to Assyria and Ægypt—over their heads. All this, together with Aqueduct and Cistern, and other Appurtenance of a Royal Palace, upon a Terrace-platform, ascended by a double

Notes

Flight of Stairs that may be gallop'd up, and cut out of and into the Rock-side of the *Koh'i Ráhmet, Mountain of Mercy*, where the old Fire-worshiping Sovereigns are buried, and overlooking the Plain of Merdasht.

Persians, like some other People, it seems, love to write their own Names, with sometimes a Verse or two, on their Country's Monuments. Mr Binning (from whose sensible Travels the foregoing Account is mainly condens't) found several such in Persepolis; in one Place a fine Line of Háfiz: in another "an original, no doubt," he says, "by no great Poet," however "right in his Sentiment." The Words somehow looked to us, and the "halting metre" sounded, familiar; and on looking back at last among the 500 Rubáiyát of the Calcutta Omar MS.—*there* it is: old Omar quoted by *one* of his Countrymen, and here turned into hasty Rhyme, at any rate—

> "This Palace that its Top to Heaven threw,
> And Kings their Forehead on its Threshold drew—
>   I saw a Ring-dove sitting there alone,
> And 'Coo, Coo, Coo,' she cried, and 'Coo, Coo, Coo.'"

So as it seems the Persian speaks the English Ring-dove's *Péhlevi*, which is also articulate Persian for "Where?"

BAHRÁM GÚR—*Bahrám of the Wild Ass*, from his Fame in hunting it—a Sassanian Sovereign, had also his Seven Castles (like the King of Bohemia!) each of a different Colour; each with a Royal Mistress within side; each of whom recounts to Bahrám a Romance, according to one of the

57

most famous Poems of Persia, written by Amír Khusraw: these Sevens also figuring (according to Eastern Mysticism) the Seven Heavens, and perhaps the Book itself that Eighth, into which the mystical Seven transcend, and within which they revolve. The Ruins of Three of these Towers are yet shown by the Peasantry; as also the Swamp in which Bahrám sunk, like the Master of Ravenswood, while pursuing his *Gúr*.

¹² A Thousand Years to each Planet.

¹³ Saturn, Lord of the Seventh Heaven.

¹⁴ ME AND THEE; that is, some Dividual Existence or Personality apart from the Whole.

¹⁵ The Caravan travelling by Night (after their New Year's Day of the Vernal Equinox) by command of Mohammed, I believe.

¹⁶ A Laugh at his Mathematics perhaps.

¹⁷ The 72 Sects into which Islamism so soon split.

¹⁸ This alludes to Mahmúd's Conquest of India and its swarthy Idolaters.

¹⁹ *Fanúsi khiyál*, a Magic-lanthorn still used in India; the cylindrical Interior being painted with various Figures, and so lightly poised and ventilated as to revolve round the Candle lighted within.

²⁰ A very mysterious Line in the original;

U dánad u dánad u dánad u ——

Notes

breaking off something like our Wood-pigeon's Note, which she is said to take up just where she left off.

²¹ Parwín and Mushtara—The Pleiads and Jupiter.

²² At the Close of the Fasting Month, Ramazán (which makes the Musulman unhealthy and unamiable), the first Glimpse of the New Moon (who rules their Division of the Year) is looked for with the utmost Anxiety, and hailed with all Acclamation. Then it is that the Porter's Knot may be heard toward the *Cellar*, perhaps. Old Omar has elsewhere a pretty Quatrain about this same Moon—

> "Be of Good Cheer—the sullen Month will die,
> And a young Moon requite us by and bye:
> Look how the Old one meagre, bent, and wan
> With Age and Fast, is fainting from the Sky!"

— FINIS.

TABLES OF CORRESPONDING STANZAS

VARIOUS methods have been adopted in order to help readers find the equivalent stanzas to those in one or other of the editions published in FitzGerald's lifetime. The best would be an electronic text, which could be instantly reconfigured to show the different versions in relation to each other; such a text has been created by the American poet Richard Brodie (http://www.therubaiyat.com), but at the time of writing it contains some errors and misprints which make it less useful than it should be. Decker (p. 229) points out the limitations of the text-based systems adopted by other editors, but his own solution, though I am sure it works, is worthy of Omar the Algebraist and I have found it impossible to follow.

I have attempted a compromise by producing two tables, one showing the sequence of stanzas between *1859* and *1868*, and the second showing the sequence between *1868* and *1872–79* (there is only one discrepancy between *1872* and *1879*: see stanza XLI of *1868* in Table 2). In this way readers can more easily follow the two major phases of revision of the poem, though there will be occasions when they have to navigate between the two tables; but that seemed to me to be simpler than to produce a visually confusing and unwieldy patchwork requiring extensive annotation. A blank entry indicates that the stanza number is the same in the corresponding edition.

TABLE I		TABLE 2	
1859	1868	1868	1872/1879
I		I	
II		II	
III		III	
IV		IV	
V		V	
VI		VI	
VII		VII	
—	VIII [new]	VIII	
VIII	IX	IX	
IX	X	X	
X	XI	XI	
XI	XII	XII	
XII	XIII	XIII	
—	XIV [new]	XIV	[omitted]

TABLE 1

1859	1868
XIII	XV
XIV	XVII
XV	XVI
XVI	XVIII
XVII	XIX
—	XX [transposed from endnote 11]
XVIII	XXIV
XIX	XXV
XX	XXI
XXI	XXII
XXII	XXIII
XXIII	XXVI
XXIV	XXVII
—	XXVIII [new]
XXV	XXIX
XXVI	LVI
XXVII	XXX
XXVIII	XXXI
XXIX	XXXII
XXX	XXXIII
XXXI	XXXIV
XXXII	XXXV
—	XXXVI [new]
XXXIII	XXXVII
XXXIV	XXXVIII
XXXV	XXXIX
XXXVI	XL
—	XLI [new]
—	XLII [new]
—	XLIII [new]
—	XLIV [new]
XXXVII	[omitted]
XXXVIII	XLIX
—	L [new]
—	LI [new]
—	LIII [new]
—	LIV [new]

TABLE 2

1868	1872/1879
XV	XIV
XVI	XV
XVII	XVI
XVIII	XVII
XIX	XVIII
XX	[omitted]
XXI	
XXII	
XXIII	
XXIV	XIX
XXV	XX
XXVI	XXIV
XXVII	XXV
XXVIII	[omitted]
XXIX	XXVI
XXX	XXVII
XXXI	XXVIII
XXXII	XXIX
XXXIII	XXX
XXXIV	XXXI
XXXV	XXXII
XXXVI	XXXIII
XXXVII	XXXIV
XXXVIII	XXXV
XXXIX	XXXVI
XL	XXXVII
XLI	XXXVIII [virtually new in 1872; 1879 restores 1868 text]
XLII	XXXIX
XLIII	XL
XLIV	[omitted]
	[XLI = 1868 LV]
XLV	XLII
XLVI	XLIII
	[XLIV = 1868 LXIX]
	[XLV = 1868 LXX]
XLVII	XLVI
XLVIII	XLVII

TABLE 1		TABLE 2	
1859	1868	1868	1872/1879
—	LV [new]	XLIX	XLVIII
XXXIX	LVI	L	XLIX
XL	LVII	LI	L
XLI	LVIII	LII	LI
—	LIX [new]	LIII	LII
XLII	LX	LIV	LIII
XLIII	LXI	LV	XLI
XLIV	LXII	LVI	LIV
—	LXIII [new]	LVII	LV
—	LXIV [new]	LVIII	LVI
—	LXV [new]	LIX	LVII
	[LXVI = 1859 st. XXVI]	LX	LVIII
—	LXVII [new]	LXI	LIX
—	LXVIII [new]	LXII	LX
—	LXIX [transposed from Preface, p. 14]	LXIII	LXI
		LXIV	LXII
—	LXX [transposed from Preface, p. 14]	LXV	[omitted]
		LXVI	LXIII
—	LXXI [new]	LXVII	LXIV
XLV	[omitted]	LXVIII	LXV
XLVI	LXIII	LXIX	XLIV
XLVII	XLV	LXX	XLV
XLVIII	XLVI	LXXI	LXVI
—	XLVII [new]	LXXII	LXVII
—	XLVIII [new]	LXXIII	LXVIII
XLIX	LXXIV	LXXIV	LXIX
L	LXXV	LXXV	LXX
LI	LXXVI	LXXVI	LXXI
—	LXXVII	LXXVII	[omitted]
LII	LXXVIII	LXXVIII	LXXII
LIII	LXXIX	LXXIX	LXXIII
—	LXXX	LXXX	LXXIV
LIV	LXXXI	LXXXI	LXXV
LV	LXXXII	LXXXII	LXXVI
LVI	LXXXIII	LXXXIII	LXXVII
—	LXXXIV [new]	LXXXIV	LXXVIII
—	LXXXV [new]	LXXXV	LXXIX
—	LXXXVI [new]	LXXXVI	[omitted]
LVII	LXXXVII	LXXXVII	LXXX

TABLE 1		TABLE 2	
1859	1868	1868	1872/1879
LVIII	LXXXVIII	LXXXVIII	LXXXI
LIX	LXXXIX	LXXXIX	LXXXII
—	XC [new]	XC	[omitted]
LX	[omitted]	—	LXXXIII [new]
LXI	XCI	XCI	LXXXIV
LXII	XCII	XCII	LXXXV
LXIII	XCIII	XCIII	LXXXVI
—	XCIV [new]	XCIV	[omitted]
LXIV	XCV		LXXXVII [new]
LXV	XCVI	XCV	LXXXVIII
LXVI	XCVII	XCVI	LXXXIX
LXVII	XCVIII	XCVII	XC
—	XCIX [new]	XCVIII	XCI
LXVIII	C	XCIX	[omitted]
LXIX	CI	C	XCII
LXX	CII	CI	XCIII
LXXI	CIII	CII	XCIV
LXXII	CIV	CIII	XCV
—	CV [new]	CIV	XCVI
—	CVI [new]	CV	XCVII
—	CVII [new]	CVI	XCVIII
LXXIII	CVIII	CVII	[omitted]
LXXIV	CIX	CVIII	XCIX
LXXV	CX	CIX	C
		CX	CI

VARIANTS

The reading of the copy-text, *1859*, is followed by a square bracket and the variant reading:

v. 1   its Rose] his Rose (*1868–79*)

The dates *1868–79* indicate that the variant is found in all editions between those dates, i.e. *1868*, *1872*, and *1879*.

Where a variant affects the whole line or a group of lines, the square bracket follows the stanza and line number(s):

XXXI.4] But not the Master-knot of Human fate (*1868–79*)

Stanza numbers in the notes are those of *1859*, and new or transposed stanzas in *1868–79* are not given with their stanza numbers; for the corresponding stanza numbers in *1868–79*, see the tables on p. 60. Endnote numbers are those of *1859*; to avoid confusion, altered endnote numerals have not been included in passages cited from editions after *1859*.

Three proof copies of *1872* exist (*1872 proof¹*, *1872 proof²*, *1872 proof³*), giving the text in different states; their sequence is demonstrated by Decker (pp. lii–lv). I have only included variants from these copies when they differ significantly from the published version (as in the case of what FitzGerald called 'the infernal Stanza I'). A few additional readings derive from two MS quatrains now in the Rosenbach Library, Philadelphia, and from revisions made by FitzGerald in a copy of *1879* now in the library of Trinity College, Cambridge.

The fourth edition (*1879*) has no endnote numerals in the text of the poem; the notes at the end are keyed to stanza numbers. FitzGerald was the originator of this change, and approved of it when he saw it in proof (*Letters*, iv. 191, 219). I have not recorded the individual occurrences of this revision, except where the status of a note changes between the third (*1872*) and fourth editions.

The title page of *1859* referred to the *Rubáiyát* as 'Translated into English Verse'. *1868–79* have the more equivocal term 'Rendered'.

[Preface]

3   *one of them . . . Toghrul Beg*] one of whom tells the Story of all Three. This was Nizám ul Mulk, Vizyr to Alp Arslan the Son, and Malik Shah the Grandson, of Toghrul Beg (*1868–79*)

3   *Nizám al Mulk*] Nizám ul Mulk (*1868–79*)

6   *the old school-boy friend.*] *1868–79* add a footnote:

> Some of Omar's Rubáiyát warn us of the danger of Greatness, the instability of Fortune, and while advocating Charity to all Men,

recommending us to be too intimate with none. Attár makes Nizám-ul-Mulk use the very words of his friend Omar [Rub. xxxi.], 'When Nizám-ul-Mulk was in the Agony (of Death) he said, "Oh God! I am passing away in the hand of the Wind." '

The reference in square brackets is to st. xxviii in *1859*. FitzGerald came across this anecdote in Garcin de Tassy's French translation of Attar's *Mantic ut-tair* [Parliament of Birds], published in 1863 but which he only read in December 1867 when Tassy sent him a copy; he wrote to Cowell: 'Here is our Omar in his Friend's mouth, is it not?' (28 December 1867, *Letters*, iii. 74).

7 *These severer Studies . . . and his Wine.*] omitted *1868–79*.

8 *(Though all these . . . hereditary calling).*] converted to a footnote in *1868–79*, revising 'Sirname' to 'Surname'.

8 *related in the anonymous preface*] it is told in the anonymous preface (*1868–79*)

8 (footnote)] 'Philosophe Musulman qui a vêcu en Odeur de Sainteté dans la Fin du premier et le Commencement du second Siècle,' no part of which, except the 'Philosophe,' can apply to *our* Khayyám. (*1868–79*)

Decker (pp. lxiv–lxv) emends the texts of all four editions (*1859–79*) to the correct reading of d'Herbelot's text, on the grounds that FitzGerald 'writes the correct quotation in a letter to Cowell' of 23 February 1857 (*Letters*, ii. 254). This is not quite right—FitzGerald made two small slips, writing 'vécu' for 'vêcu' and 'en l'odeur' for 'en odeur'—but in any case it is not certain that when he came to transcribe the passage for *1859* he did not decide to shorten it; his shaky grasp of French grammar would explain his failure to realize that 'dans la Fin' is a solecism (the correct reading would be 'à la fin'). The fact that he left the quotation unchanged strongly implies that he saw nothing wrong with it, in contrast to his noticing the incorrect spelling of 'Bibliothèque'. In addition to this emendation, Decker supplies the phrase 'de l'hegire' after 'Siècle', on the grounds that FitzGerald's version is 'potentially confusing'. Indeed it is; but the context suggests that FitzGerald may have intended the confusion, or at least that he was indifferent to it.

8 *no idle words.*] *1868–79* have a new footnote here, starting with the concluding sentence of the previous note:

The Rashness of the Words, according to D'Herbelot, consisted in being so opposed to those in the Korán: 'No Man knows where he shall die.'—This Story of Omar recalls a very different one [*1872–79*: reminds me of another one] so naturally—and, when one remembers how wide of his humble mark the noble sailor aimed—so pathetically told by Captain Cook—not by Doctor Hawkesworth—in his Second Voyage. When leaving Ulietea, 'Oreo's last request was for me to return. When he saw he could not obtain that promise, he asked for the name of my *Marai*—Burying-place. As strange a question as this was, I hesitated not a moment to tell him "Stepney," the parish in

which I live when in London. I was made to repeat it several times
over till they could pronounce it; and then "Stepney Marai no Tootee"
[*1879*: Toote] was echoed through an hundred mouths at once. I after-
wards found the same question had been put to Mr Forster by a man
on shore; but he gave a different, and indeed more proper answer, by
saying, "No man who used the sea could say where he should be
buried."'

The reference is to James Cook's *Voyage toward the South Pole and round the
World* (2 vols., 1777), i. 374; FitzGerald's transcription has two verbal errors
('pronounce it; and then', which should be 'pronounce it; then', and 'Tootee'
for 'Toote'), and the punctuation is freely altered (e.g. Mr Forster's words are
not direct speech in the original: 'he gave a different, and indeed more proper
answer, by saying no man, who used the sea, [etc.]'. FitzGerald had come
across the passage several years earlier, and sent it to Cowell on 12 November
1860 (*Letters*, ii. 377); this transcription has the same errors and alterations as
those in the published volume, but also others of its own.

9 *from the Calcutta Review.*] *1868–79* add:
> The writer of it, on reading in India this story of Omar's Grave, was
> reminded, he says, of Cicero's Account of finding Archimedes' Tomb
> at Syracuse, buried in grass and weeds. I think Thorwaldsen desired
> to have roses grow over him; a wish religiously fulfilled for him to the
> present day, I believe. However, to return to Omar.

Cowell made this remark about Cicero (*Tusculanae disputationes*, v. 64–6) in
the same letter, sent from Calcutta shortly after his arrival there in November
1856, in which he transcribed for FitzGerald the anecdote about Omar's
prophecy concerning his burial-place (see Explanatory Notes, pp. 139–40);
FitzGerald could, therefore, have included it in the *1859* preface had he wished.
Thorwaldsen is the Danish sculptor Albert Thorvaldsen (1770–1844).

9 *formal Compliment . . . hide under.*] formal recognition of Islamism under
which Omar would not hide. (*1868–79*)

10 *quite as keen . . . compounded of all*] as keen of Bodily Sense as of
Intellectual; and delighting in a cloudy compound [*1872–79*: compos-
ition] of both (*1868–79*)

10 *could be recited . . . or the Tavern.*] might serve indifferently for either.
(*1868–79*)

10 *Things as they were*] Things as he saw them (*1868–79*)

10 *vain mortifications*] vain disquietude (*1868–79*)

10 *It has been seen . . . a Theological direction.*] It has been seen, however,
that his Worldly Ambition was not exorbitant; and he very likely takes
a humorous or perverse pleasure in exalting the gratification of Sense
above that of the Intellect, in which he must have taken great delight,
although it failed to answer the Questions in which he, in common with
all men, was most vitally interested. (*1868–79*)

The remainder of this paragraph ('However this may be . . . expect of Paradise.') and the whole of the following paragraph ('The Mathematic Faculty . . . were Worshippers.') were omitted in *1868–79*.

11 *charily transmitted*] scantily transmitted (*1868–79*)

12 *all that Arms and Science have brought us*] all the acquisitions of Arms and Science (*1868–79*)

12 *There is none*] There is no copy (*1868–79*)

12 *the Bibliothèque Impériale*] the Bibliothèque Nationale (*1879*).

The revision belatedly registers the change from Napoleon III's Second Empire, which fell in 1870, to the Third Republic.

12 *double that Number.*] *1868–72* move the footnote beginning "Since this paper was written" to this point, because of the changes to the text of the following sentences.

12 *the Calcutta with one of Execration . . . to execrate himself.*] the Calcutta with one of Expostulation, supposed (says a Notice prefixed to the MS.) to have risen from a Dream, in which Omar's mother asked about his future fate. It may be rendered thus:—

> 'Oh Thou who burn'st in Heart for those who burn
> In Hell, whose fires thyself shall feed in turn;
>   How long be crying, "Mercy on them, God!"
> Why, who art Thou to teach, and He to learn?'

The Bodleian Quatrain pleads Pantheism by way of Justification.

> 'If I myself upon a looser Creed
> Have loosely strung the Jewel of Good deed,
> Let this one thing for my Atonement plead:
> That One for Two I never did mis-read.' (*1868–79*)

The story of Omar's mother's dream is in d'Herbelot's entry for 'Khiam' (pp. 993–4; see Explanatory Notes, p. 140). FitzGerald had noticed a less accurate version of the 'Bodleian' (i.e. Ouseley MS) quatrain, and mentioned it to Cowell in a letter of 7 November 1867 (*Letters*, iii. 61). But he himself mistook the meaning of the last line, which does not refer to pantheism but to monotheism (Omar claims, or is made to claim, that he has always believed that God is one, not that everything is one).

12 *The Reviewer . . . concludes*] The Reviewer, to whom I owe the Particulars of Omar's Life, concludes his Review (*1868–79*)

13 *Both indeed men . . . Hearts*] Both indeed men of subtle, strong, and cultivated Intellect, fine Imagination, and Hearts (*1868–79*)

13 *who yet fell short*] who fell short (*1879*)

13 *subverted . . . had dawned*] subverted by such better *Hope* as others, with no better Revelation to guide them, (*1868–79*)

13   *consoled himself... no Constructor*] satisfied himself with the theory of so vast a machine [1879: of a vast machine] fortuitously constructed (*1868–79*)

13   *implied no Lawgiver*] implied no Legislator (*1868–79*)

13   *of which he was part Actor*] which he was part Actor in (*1868–79*)

13   *coloured... the outer Sun.*] discoloured with the lurid reflex of the Curtain suspended between the Spectator and the Sun. (*1868–79*)

13   *more careless, of... more than*] more careless of any so complicated System as resulted in nothing but (*1868–79*)

13   *a bitter jest*] a bitter or humorous jest (*1868–79*)

13–14   *and, yielding his Senses... rises to be gone?*] and, pretending sensual pleasure as the serious purpose of Life, only *diverted* himself with speculative problems of Deity, Destiny, Matter and Spirit, Good and Evil, and other such questions, easier to start than to run down, and the pursuit of which becomes a weary sport at last! (*1868–79*)

The two stanzas became LXIX and (heavily revised) LXX in *1868*, transposed to XLIV–XLV in *1872–9*; see below.

14   *(as here attempted)*] (as here imitated) (*1868–79*)

14   *Something*] Sometimes (*1879*)

FitzGerald corrected this to 'Something', the reading of *1859–72*, in a copy of *1879* now in the library of Trinity College, Cambridge. When he first saw the published volume, he wrote to Quaritch requesting an erratum slip with a different reading: 'For "*Sometimes* as in the Greek Alcaic" read "*Somewhat*, etc."' (5 August 1879, *Letters*, iv. 244). Quaritch may have replied to the effect that it was not worth the trouble, or that an erratum slip would be aesthetically displeasing; at any rate FitzGerald reinforced his plea on 10 August: 'It is but a *word* wrong, I know: but a word that alters all the meaning and the fact. The Blank third Line in the Stanza does *not* "sometimes" resemble that in the Alcaic, but does ALWAYS "somewhat" resemble it: which makes all the difference, surely. It may be a trifle: but must it not be more aesthetically wrong than such a very tiny Slip (as small as may be) which may be inserted at the beginning or end to correct it?' In a postscript he made another suggestion: 'I would just as soon—nay, *rather*—have just the one Word corrected by a Pen in the margin' (ibid. 245–6). He wrote to Aldis Wright on 13 August that Quaritch had agreed to make the correction (ibid. 247), but he never did, and FitzGerald never found out.

14   *the third line suspending... the former Two.*] the third line a blank. (*1868–79*)

14   *a strange Farrago*] a strange succession (*1868–79*)

15   *For Lucretian... Humour.*] omitted *1868–79*

15   *Any way*] Either way (*1868–79*)

15 *any way, Fitter*] more apt (*1868–79*)

15 *from under his Feet.*] *1859* and *1879* end here. *1868* has a rule followed by a lengthy addition, retained in a revised form in *1872*:

> While the present Edition of Omar was preparing, Monsieur Nicolas, French Consul at Rescht, published a very careful and very good Edition of the Text, from a lithograph copy at Teheran, comprising 464 Rubáiyát, with translation and notes of his own.
>
> Mons. Nicolas, whose Edition has reminded me of several things, and instructed me in others, does not consider Omar to be the material Epicurean that I have literally taken him for, but a Mystic, shadowing the Deity under the figure of Wine, Wine-bearer, &c., as Háfiz is supposed to do; in short, a Súfi Poet like Háfiz and the rest.
>
> I cannot see reason to alter my opinion, formed as it was a dozen years ago when Omar was first shown me by one to whom I am indebted for all I know of Oriental, and very much of other, literature. He admired Omar's Genius so much, that he would gladly have adopted any such Interpretation of his meaning as Mons. Nicolas' if he could.[1] That he could not appears by his Paper in the Calcutta Review already so largely quoted; in which he argues from the Poems themselves, as well as from what records remain of the Poet's Life.
>
> And if more were needed to disprove Mons. Nicolas' Theory, there is the Biographical Notice which he himself has drawn up in direct contradiction to the Interpretation of the Poems given in his Notes. [1872 omits the whole of the French quotations that follow, and substitutes: '(See pp. 13–14 of his Preface.)'] Here is one of the Anecdotes he produces. 'Mais revenons à Khéyam, qui, resté étranger à toutes ces alternatives de guerres, d'intrigues, et de révoltes, dont cette époque fut si remplie, vivait tranquille dans son village natal, se livrant avec passion à l'étude de la philosophie des Soufis. Entouré de nombreux amis il cherchait avec eux dans le vin cette contemplation extatique que d'autres croient trouver dans des cris et des hurlemens,' &c. 'Les chroniqueurs persans racontent que Khéyam aimait surtout à s'entretenir et à boire avec ses amis, le soir au clair de la lune sur la terrasse de sa maison, entouré de chanteurs et musiciens, avec un échanson qui, la coupe à la main, la présentait à tour de role aux joyeux convives réunis.—Pendant une de ces soirées dont nous venons de parler, survient à l'improviste un coup de vent qui éteint les chandelles et renverse à terre la cruche de vin, placée imprudemment sur le bord de la terrasse. La cruche fut brisée et le vin répandu. Aussitot Khéyam, irrité, improvisa ce quatrain impie à l'addresse du Tout-Puissant: "Tu as brisé ma

---

[1] [FitzGerald's footnote] Perhaps would have edited the Poems himself some years ago. He may now as little approve of my Version on one side, as of Mons. Nicolas' on the other.

cruche de vin, mon Dieu! tu as ainsi fermé sur moi la porte de la joie,
mon Dieu! c'est moi qui bois, et c'est toi qui commets les désordres de
l'ivresse! oh! (puisse ma bouche se remplir de la terre!) serais-tu ivre,
mon Dieu?"

Le poète, après avoir prononcé ce blasphème, jetant les yeux sur
une glace, se serait aperçu que son visage était noir comme du char-
bon. C'était une punition du ciel. Alors il fit cet autre quatrain non
moins audacieux que le premier. "Quel est l'homme ici-bas qui n'a
point commis de péché, dis? Celui qui n'en aurait point commis, com-
ment aurait-il vécu, dis? Si, parce que je fais du mal, tu me punis par
le mal, quelle est donc la différence qui existe entre toi at moi, dis?" [2]

---

[2] [Editor's translation] 'But let us return to Khayyám, who, dwelling apart
from the succession of wars, intrigues, and revolts with which this period was
filled, lived quietly in his native village, passionately devoting himself to the
study of Sufi philosophy. In the company of his many friends he sought,
through wine, that ecstatic contemplation which others think to find through
cries and yells,' etc. 'The Persian chroniclers relate that Khayyám loved above
all to converse and drink with his friends, on moonlit evenings on the terrace
of his house, surrounded by singers and musicians, with a cup-bearer who, cup
in hand, offered it in turn to the happy assembled guests.—During one of
these evenings of which we have just spoken, a gust of wind suddenly arose,
extinguishing the candles and overturning the wine-jar, which had been
unwisely placed on the edge of the terrace. Instantly Khayyám, annoyed,
improvised the following impious quatrain addressed to the Almighty: "You
have broken my wine-jar, my God! in so doing you have closed the gate of
delight upon me, my God! it is I who drink, and you who act like a drunkard!
oh (may my mouth be filled with earth!) can it be that you are drunk, my
God?" The poet, after uttering this blasphemy, is said to have noticed that his
face was black as soot. It was heaven's punishment. He then composed this
other quatrain, not less daring than the first. "Who is the man here below who
has never committed a sin, tell me? He who had never committed one, how
could he have lived, tell me? If, because I do evil, you punish me with evil,
what difference is there between you and me, tell me?"' After 'premier' in the
final paragraph, FitzGerald omitted a passage which allowed him to ignore an
aspect of Omar's alleged Sufism with which he would have sympathized,
namely its opposition to the doctrine of hell. Nicolas adds, after 'premier':
'et qui exprime d'une manière absolue la répulsion du poëte pour la doctrine
des peines futures, décrites dans le Koran, et prêchées si chaleureusement par
les moullahs. Les soufis considèrent cette doctrine, non-seulement comme le
renversement de la leur, mais encore comme indigne de la miséricorde et de la
clémence de la Divinité [and which expresses in absolute fashion the poet's
revulsion towards the doctrine of future punishments, described in the Koran,
and so ardently preached by the mullahs. The Sufis consider this doctrine not

I really hardly knew poor Omar was so far gone till his Apologist informed me. Here we see then that, whatever were the Wine that Háfiz drank and sang, the veritable Juice of the Grape it was which Omar used not only when carousing with his friends, but (says Mons. Nicolas) in order to excite himself to that pitch of Devotion which others reached by cries and 'hurlemens.' And yet, whenever Wine, Wine-Bearer, &c., occur in the Text—which is often enough—Mons. Nicolas carefully annotates 'Dieu' [God] 'La Divinité,' [The Deity] &c.: so carefully indeed that one is tempted to think he was indoctrinated by the Súfi with whom he read the Poems. (Note to Rub. ii. p. 8.)[3] A Persian would naturally wish to vindicate a distinguished Countryman; and a Súfi to enrol him in his own sect, which already comprises all the chief Poets of Persia.

What historical Authority has Mons. Nicolas to show that Omar gave himself up 'avec passion à l'étude de la philosophie des Soufis'? (Preface, p. xiii.) The Doctrines of Pantheism, Materialism, Necessity, &c., were not peculiar to the Súfi; nor to Lucretius before them; nor to Epicurus before him; probably the very original Irreligion of thinking men from the first; and very likely to be the spontaneous growth of a Philosopher living in an Age of social and political barbarism, under sanction of one of the Two and Seventy Religions supposed to divide the world. Von Hammer (according to Sprenger's Oriental Catalogue) speaks of Omar as 'a Free-thinker, and *a great opponent of Sufism*;' perhaps because, while holding much of their Doctrine, he would not pretend to any inconsistent severity of morals. Sir W. Ouseley has written a Note to something of the same effect on the fly-leaf of the Bodleian MS. And in two Rubáiyát of Mons. Nicolas' own edition Súf and Súfi are both disparagingly named.

No doubt many of these Quatrains seem unaccountable unless mystically interpreted; but many more as unaccountable unless literally. Were the Wine spiritual, for instance, how wash the Body with it when dead? Why make cups of the dead clay to be filled with— 'La Divinité'—by some succeeding Mystic? Mons. Nicolas himself is puzzled by some 'bizarres' and 'trop Orientales' [excessively Oriental] allusions and images—'d'une sensualité quelquefois revoltante'

only as an overturning of their own, but also as unworthy of the mercifulness and clemency of the Deity].' Nicolas repeats this point several times in his notes to the poems.

[3] [Editor's footnote] The roman 'ii' is an error for '11'. FitzGerald wrongly implies that Nicolas systematically 'read the poems' with a Sufi interpreter; all Nicolas says in his note is that a Sufi whom he encountered in Tehran made a comment to him about this particular quatrain. Nor does he speak of any Sufi guidance in his preface.

[whose sensuality is sometimes revolting] indeed—which 'les con-
venances' [the proprieties] do not permit him to translate; but still
which the reader cannot but refer to 'La Divinité.'[4] No doubt also
many of the Quatrains in the Teheran, as in the Calcutta, Copies, are
spurious; such *Rubáiyát* being the common form of Epigram in Persia.
But this, at best, tells as much one way as another; nay, the Súfi, who
may be considered the Scholar and Man of Letters in Persia, would be
far more likely than the careless Epicure to interpolate what favours
his own view of the Poet. I observe that very few of the more mystical
Quatrains are in the Bodleian MS., which must be one of the oldest,
as dated at Shiraz, A.H. 865, A.D. 1460. And this, I think, especially
distinguishes Omar (I cannot help calling him by his—no, not
Christian—familiar name) from all other Persian Poets: That,
whereas with them the Poet is lost in his Song, the Man in Allegory
and Abstraction; we seem to have the Man—the *Bonhomme*—Omar
himself, with all his Humours and Passions, as frankly before us as if
we were really at Table with him, after the Wine had gone round.

I must say that I, for one, never wholly believed in the Mysticism of
Háfiz. It does not appear there was any danger in holding and singing
Súfi Pantheism, so long as the Poet made his Salaam to Mohammed at
the beginning and end of his Song. Under such conditions Jeláluddín,
Jámi, Attár, and others sang; using Wine and Beauty indeed as Images
to illustrate, not as a Mask to hide, the Divinity they were celebrating.
Perhaps some Allegory less liable to mistake or abuse had been better

---

[4] [FitzGerald's footnote] A Note to Quatrain 234 admits that, however clear
the mystical meaning of such Images must be to Europeans, they are not
quoted without 'rougissant' [blushing] even by laymen in Persia—'Quant aux
termes de tendresse qui commencent ce quatrain, comme tant d'autres dans ce
recueil, nos lecteurs, habitués maintenant à l'étrangeté des expressions si sou-
vent employés par Khéyam pour rendre ses pensées sur l'amour divin, et à la
singularité des images trop orientales, d'une sensualité quelquefois revoltante,
n'auront pas de peine à se persuader qu'il s'agit de la Divinité, bien que cette
conviction soit vivement discutée par les moullahs musulmans, et meme par
beaucoup de laïques, qui rougissant véritablement d'une pareille licence de
leur compatriote à l'égard des choses spirituelles [As for the endearments
which begin this quatrain, as with so many others in this collection, our read-
ers, accustomed by now to the strangeness of the expressions which Khayyám
so often uses to render his thoughts of divine love, and to the oddness of images
which are excessively oriental, and whose sensuality is sometimes revolting,
will have no trouble persuading themselves that they refer to the Deity, even
though this belief is vigorously contested by the Muslim mullahs, and even
by many among the laity, who verily blush at the freedom with which their
compatriot treats spiritual matters].' [Editor's translation]

among so inflammable a People: much more so when, as some think with Háfiz and Omar, the abstract is not only likened to, but identified with, the sensual Image; hazardous, if not to the Devotee himself, yet to his weaker Brethren; and worse for the Profane in proportion as the Devotion of the Initiated grew warmer. And all for what? To be tantalized with Images of sensual enjoyment which must be renounced if one would approximate a God, who, according to the Doctrine, *is* Sensual Matter as well as Spirit, and into whose Universe one expects unconsciously to merge after Death, without hope of any posthumous Beatitude in another world to compensate for all the self-denial of this. Lucretius' blind Divinity certainly merited, and probably got, as much self-sacrifice as this of the Súfi; and the burden of Omar's Song—if not 'Let us eat'—is assuredly—'Let us drink, for Tomorrow we die!' And if Háfiz meant quite otherwise by a similar language, he surely miscalculated when he devoted his Life and Genius to so equivocal a Psalmody as, from his Day to this, has been said and sung by any rather than spiritual Worshippers.

However, it may remain an Open Question, both with regard to Háfiz and Omar: the reader may understand them either way, literally or mystically, as he chooses. Whenever Wine, Wine-bearer, Cypress, &c., are named, he has only to suppose 'La Divinité;' and when he has done so with Omar, I really think he may proceed to the same Interpretation of Anacreon—and even Anacreon Moore. [1872: However, as there is some traditional presumption, and certainly the opinion of some learned men, in favour of Omar's being a Súfi—and even something of a Saint—those who please may so interpret his Wine and Cup-bearer. On the other hand, as there is far more historical certainty of his being a Philosopher, of scientific Insight and Ability far beyond that of the Age and Country he lived in; of such moderate worldly Ambition as becomes a Philosopher, and such moderate wants as rarely satisfy a Debauchee; other readers may be content to believe with me that, while the Wine Omar celebrates is simply the Juice of the Grape, he bragg'd more than he drank of it, in very defiance perhaps of that Spiritual Wine which left its Votaries sunk in Hypocrisy or Disgust.]

Cowell had objected to the direct quotations from Nicolas; in a letter of 25 March 1872, FitzGerald wrote: 'If it be reprinted, I will cut out from the Preface all I quoted from Mr. Nicolas about Omar's Defiance to the Deity (which you did not like) and perhaps end with a few words leaving the Question of real, or mystical, Wine a more open Question' (*Letters*, iii. 336). The last comment bears on the revision to the final paragraph of the added material. FitzGerald deleted the whole of this addition in the proofs of *1879* (letter to Quaritch of March 1879, *Letters*, iv. 191).

'Anacreon Moore' refers to the Irish poet Thomas Moore (1779–1852), who acquired the nickname after his translation of Anacreon's odes appeared in 1800; there are several drinking-songs in Moore's own light verse, e.g. 'Drink of this cup' (*Irish Melodies*), which begins 'Drink of this cup;—you'll find there's a spell in | Its every drop 'gainst the ills of mortality'. The slight note of disparagement in FitzGerald's mention of Moore (as self-evidently frivolous) may owe something to the cheerful inauthenticity of his popular 'Oriental' narrative poem *Lalla Rookh* (1817), and to the fact that he published, in 1831, a fulsome biography of the Irish rebel leader Lord Edward Fitzgerald (1763–98); *our* FitzGerald had a low opinion of the book ('dull very') and of his namesake, so clearly identified with the *vita activa*: 'I think he is a poor creature as to mind—he had the valour of a brute' (letter to Thackeray of 10 October 1831, *Letters*, i. 107).

[*The Poem*]

1]   Wake! For the Sun behind yon Eastern height
        Has chased the Sessions of the Stars from Night;
           And, to the field of Heav'n ascending, strikes
        The Sultán's Turret with a Shaft of Light. (*1868*)

        Wake! For the Sun before him into Night
        A Signal flung that put the Stars to flight;
           And, to the field of Heav'n ascending, strikes
        The Sultán's Turret with a Shaft of Light. (*1872 proof*¹)

        Wake! For the Sun before him into Night
        A Signal launch'd that put the Stars to flight;
           And, now the field of Heav'n ascending, strikes
        The Sultán's Turret with a Shaft of Light. (*1872 proof*²)

        Wake! For the Sun who scatter'd into flight
        The Stars before him from the Field of Night,
           Drives Night along with them from Heav'n, and strikes
        The Sultán's Turret with a Shaft of Light. (*1872–79*)

In March 1872, when FitzGerald and Quaritch were debating whether to reprint the second edition or return to the first, Quaritch asked FitzGerald whether one version was more accurate as a translation, and FitzGerald replied: 'As to the relative fidelity of the two Versions, there isn't a Pin to choose—not in the opening Stanzas you send' (*Letters*, iii. 339). In a letter of 18 June, FitzGerald wrote to Cowell: 'I shall be glad of any Light upon the infernal Stanza I—which I have corrected (as it stands) so far as the two verbs "flung" and "strikes" do not clash to Quaritch's—and perhaps other's—Ears' (ibid. 356). He is presumably referring to the reading introduced in *1872 proof*², which replaces 'flung' by 'launch'd', though this was still not the final version.

II]   Before the phantom of False morning died,
          Methought a Voice within the Tavern cried,
              'When all the Temple is prepared within,
          Why lags [1879: nods] the drowsy Worshipper outside?' (*1868–79*)

V.I   its Rose] his Rose (*1868–79*)

V.3]   But still a Ruby gushes from [1879: kindles in] the Vine, (*1868–79*)

V.4   still a Garden] many a Garden (*1868–79*)

VI.4   yellow] sallow (*1868–79*)

VII.2   The Winter Garment] Your Winter-garment (*1868–79*)

VII.4   To fly—and Lo!] To flutter—and (*1868–79*)

After st. VII: Whether at Naishápúr or Babylon,
                  Whether the Cup with sweet or bitter run,
                      The Wine of Life keeps oozing drop by drop,
                      The Leaves of Life keep falling one by one. (*1868–79*)

There is a Persian source for the first two lines of this stanza in both the
Ouseley and Calcutta MSS, but neither mentions Naishapur; Heron-Allen
(1899, p. 16) suggests that FitzGerald was, to use his phrase in the *1868*
Preface, 'reminded' of it by Nicolas, whose version of the stanza does mention
Naishapur. The Persian original of this stanza was one of those FitzGerald
translated into Latin, though neither has an equivalent of the last two lines.

VIII.1–2] Morning [*1872–79*: Each morn] a thousand Roses brings, you say;
           Yes, but where leaves the Rose of yesterday? (*1868–79*)

IX.1–2]   Well, let it take them! What have we to do
           With Kaikobád the Great, or Kaikhosrú? (*1868–79*)

IX.3–4]   Let Rustum cry 'To Battle!' as he likes,
           Or Hátim Tai 'To Supper!'—heed not you. (*1868*)

               Let Zál and Rustum thunder [1879: bluster] as they will,
           Or Hátim call to Supper—heed not you. (*1872–79*)

Zál is Rustum's father.

X.I   some Strip] the Strip (*1868–79*)

X.3–4]   Where name of Slave and Sultán is forgot—
           And peace to Máhmúd on his golden Throne! (*1868–79*)

XI.1–2]   A Book of Verses underneath the Bough,
           A Jug of Wine, a loaf of Bread—and Thou (*1872–79*).

1868 has 'a little Bread' for 'a Loaf of Bread' in l. 1.

XI.4]   Oh, Wilderness were Paradise enow! (*1868–79*)

XII]   Some for the Glories of This World; and some
           Sigh for the Prophet's Paradise to come;
               Ah, take the Cash, and let the Promise go,
           Nor heed the music [*1872–79*: rumble] of a distant Drum!

After st. XII: Were it not Folly, Spider-like to spin
                 The Thread of present Life away to win—
                     What? for ourselves, who know not if we shall
                 Breathe out the very Breath we now breathe in? (*1868*)

XIII.1   the Rose that blows] the blowing Rose (*1868–79*)

XIV–XV   These stanzas are transposed in *1868–79*.

XIV.4   is gone] was gone (*1868–79*)

XV.1   And those] For those (*1868*)

XVI.2   Doorways] Portals (*1868–79*)

XVI.4   his Hour or two] his destin'd Hour (*1868–79*)

XVII.4   and he lies fast asleep] but cannot break his Sleep (*1868–79*)

After XVII: The Palace that to Heav'n his pillars threw,
                 And Kings the forehead on his threshold drew—
                     I saw the solitary Ringdove there,
                 And 'Coo, coo, coo,' she cried; and 'Coo, coo, coo.' (*1868*)

This stanza appears in endnote 11 in *1859* (see p. 57), and was restored to the
endnotes in *1872–79* (see below, p. 89).

XVIII–XXII   The order of these stanzas in *1868* is XXI, XXII, XXIII, XVIII, XIX;
                 1872–79 revert to the *1859* order.

XVIII.4   its Lap] her Lap (*1868–79*)

XIX.1   delightful Herb] reviving Herb (*1872–79*)
                 tender Green] living Green (*1868–79*)

XX.2   past Regrets] past Regret (*1868–79*)

XXI.1   Lo!] For (*1868–79*)
                 and best] and the best (*1868–79*)

XXI.2]   That from his Vintage rolling Time has [*1879*: hath] prest,
                     (*1868–79*)

After XXIV: Another Voice, when I am sleeping, cries,
                 'The Flower should open with the Morning skies.'
                     And a retreating Whisper, as I wake—
                 'The Flower that once has blown for ever dies.' (*1868*)

The last line is the same as that of st. XXVI, which in *1868* was transposed to a
later point in the poem (see below).

XXV.2   so learnedly,] so wisely—they (*1879*)

XXVI]   Transposed in *1868*, with a revised first line: see note following
                 st. XLIV.

XXVII.4   as in] where in (*1872–79*)

XXVIII.2   my own] mine own (*1879*)
                 labour'd it] wrought to make it (*1868–79*)

xxx.3–4]   Ah, contrite Heav'n endowed us with the Vine
To drug the memory of that insolence! (*1868*);

Oh, many a Cup of this forbidden Wine
Must drown the memory of that insolence! (*1872–79*)

xxxi.3   many knots] Many a knot (*1872–79*)

xxxi.4]   But not the Master-knot of Human fate (*1868–79*)

xxxii.1   a Door] the Door (*1868–79*)

xxxii.2   a Veil past which] the Veil through which (*1868–79*)
I could not] I might not (*1879*)

xxxii.4   There seemed] There was (*1868–79*)

After xxxii: Earth could not answer; nor the Seas that mourn
In flowing Purple, of their Lord forlorn;
Nor Heaven, with those eternal Signs reveal'd
[*1872–79*: Nor rolling Heaven, with all his Signs reveal'd]
And hidden by the sleeve of Night and Morn. (*1868–79*)

The image of the mourning sea comes from Attar's *Mantic ut-Tair* [Parliament of Birds]; Cowell remembered discussing the passage with FitzGerald 'in his early Persian days at Oxford in 1855', adding that 'the idea seized his imagination from the first' (Heron-Allen 1899, p. 55); he later cited the stanza to a friend as an example both of FitzGerald's 'wonderful instinct or *flair* for anything that was really poetical' and of his willingness to 'introduce many touches' from Persian sources other than Omar (*Life of Cowell*, 433).

xxxiii]   Then of the THEE IN ME who works behind
The Veil of Universe I cried to find
A Lamp to guide me through the darkness; and
Something then said—'An Understanding blind.' (*1868*)

Then of the THEE IN ME who works behind
The Veil, I lifted up my hands to find
A Lamp amid the Darkness; and I heard,
As from Without—'THE ME WITHIN THEE BLIND!' (*1872–79*)

Heron-Allen (1899, p. 57) expounds the revised stanza as 'an exposition of the Sufi doctrine of the emanation of the mortal Creature from God the Creator, and his re-absorption into God', and traces it to 'two intricate passages' in Attar's *Mantic ut-Tair* [Parliament of Birds]; but this cannot apply to the *1859* text. FitzGerald wrote to Quaritch when *1879* was in proof that '[s]ome people' preferred the *1868* version of this stanza: 'It has the merit of a fuller Rhyme; whether any other advantage I know not; and will leave to you and your able Critic Overseer to choose whether to restore or not. I am quite indifferent about it' (3 June 1879, *Letters*, iv. 219).

xxxiv.1–2]   Then to the Lip of this poor earthen Urn
I lean'd, the secret Well of Life [*1872–79*: the Secret of my Life] to learn: (*1868–79*)

XXXV.3]   And drink; and that impassive [*1872–79*: and Ah! the passive]
                     Lip I kiss'd, (*1868–79*)

XXXVI.1–2]   For I remember stopping by the way
                     To watch a Potter thumping his wet Clay: (*1868–79*)

XXXVII]   Not *1868–79*.

After XXXVII: The revisions and transpositions that follow are among
the most extensive and complicated of those made by FitzGerald in
successive editions. In *1868* he added eight stanzas (the second of which
he had already partially translated into Latin in 1857: see Arberry,
pp. 62, 123–4):

> For has not such a Story from of Old
> Down Man's successive generations roll'd
>   Of such a clod of saturated Earth
> Cast by the Maker into Human mould?
>
> And not a drop that from our Cups we throw
> On the parcht herbage but may steal below
>   To quench the fire of Anguish in some Eye
> There hidden—far beneath, and long ago.
>
> As then the Tulip for her wonted sup
> Of Heavenly Vintage lifts her chalice up,
>   Do you, twin offspring of the soil, till Heav'n
> To Earth invert you like an empty Cup.
>
> Do you, within your little hour of Grace,
> The waving Cypress in your Arms enlace,
>   Before the Mother back into her arms
> Fold, and dissolve you in a last embrace.
>
> And if the Cup you drink, the Lip you press,
> End in what All begins and ends in—Yes;
>   Imagine then you *are* what heretofore
> You *were*—hereafter you shall not be less.
>
> So when at last the Angel of the drink
> Of Darkness finds you by the river-brink,
>   And, proffering his Cup, invites your Soul
> Forth to your Lips to quaff it—do not shrink.
>
> And fear not lest Existence closing *your*
> Account, should lose, or know the type no more;
>   The Eternal Sáki from that Bowl has pour'd
> Millions of Bubbles like us, and will pour.
>
> When you and I behind the Veil are past,
> Oh but the long long while the World shall last,
>   Which of our Coming and Departure heeds
> As much as Ocean of a pebble-cast.

1872 has a different first stanza:

> Listen—a moment listen!—Of the same
> [*1872 proof¹*: For, in your ear a moment—of the same]
> Poor Earth from which that Human Whisper came
>   The luckless Mould in which Mankind was cast
> They did compose, and call'd him by the name.

In the second stanza, l. 2, *1872–79* read:

> For Earth to drink of, but may steal below.

The third stanza in *1872–79* reads:

> As then the Tulip for her morning sup
> Of Heavenly Vintage from the soil looks up,
> [*1872 proof¹*: Of Wine from Heav'n her little Tass lifts up,]
>   Do you devoutly do the like, till Heav'n
> To Earth invert you like [*1879*: you—like] an empty Cup.

1872–79 omit the fourth stanza, and substitute the following one, slightly revised and transposed from its later position in *1868* (for which see below, note following st. XXXVIII); this change was made in *1872 proof²*:

> Perplext no more with Human or Divine,
> To-morrow's tangle to the winds resign,
>   And lose your fingers in the tresses of
> The Cypress-slender Minister of Wine.

Following the fourth stanza, *1872–79* have revised versions of the remaining *1868* stanzas, but they also interpolate two other stanzas transposed from their later position in *1868* (for which see below, note following st. XLIV):

> And if the Wine you drink, the Lip you press,
> [*1872 proof¹*: And if the Cup, and if the Lip you press,]
> End in what All begins and ends in—Yes;
>   Think then you are TO-DAY what YESTERDAY
> You were—TO-MORROW you shall not be less.
>
> So when the Angel of the darker Drink
> At last shall find you by the river-brink,
> [*1872 proof¹*: So when at last the Angel of the drink
> Of Darkness finds you by the river-brink,]
>   And, offering his Cup, invite [*1872 proof¹*: invites] your Soul
> Forth to your Lips to quaff—you shall not shrink.
>
> Why, if the Soul can fling the Dust aside,
> And naked on the Air of Heaven ride,
>   Were't not a Shame—were't not a Shame for him
> In this clay carcase crippled to abide?
>
> 'Tis but a Tent where takes his one-day's rest
> A Sultan to the realm of Death addrest;
>   The Sultan rises, and the dark Ferrásh
> Strikes, and prepares it for another guest.

And fear not lest Existence closing your
Account, and mine, should know the like no more;
   The Eternal Sáki from that Bowl has pour'd
Millions of Bubbles like us, and will pour.

When you and I behind the Veil are past,
Oh but the long long while the World shall last,
   Which of our Coming and Departure heeds
As the SEV'N SEAS [*1879*: the Sea's self] should heed a pebble-cast.

'Ferrásh' = 'servant'. In a copy of *1879* now at Trinity College, Cambridge,
FitzGerald altered 'the Angel' (in the stanza beginning 'So when') to 'that
Angel'. The stanza beginning 'And fear not' has no original in the Ouseley
or Calcutta MSS; it was based on no. 137 in Nicolas's edition (Heron-Allen
1899, p. 73).

XXXVIII.4   Starts for] Draws to (*1868*)
1872–79 revise the whole stanza:

A Moment's Halt—a momentary taste
Of BEING, from the Well amid the Waste—
   And Lo!—the phantom Caravan has reach'd
   [*1872 proof*: Before the starting Caravan has reach'd]
The NOTHING it set out from—Oh, make haste!

The *1872* revision was prompted by a remark of Tennyson's, who wrote to
FitzGerald in late March 1872, praising the poem but adding: 'You stole a bit
in it from the Gardner's [*sic*] Daughter, I think: perhaps not, but it would be
quaint if the old poet had the same expression' (*Letters*, iii. 337). FitzGerald
replied in jocular-defensive tone (the letter is addressed to Emily Tennyson;
'paltry Poet' was a long-standing joke; 'Oh, Dem!' is the catchphrase of
the feckless Mr Mantalini, who sponges off his wife in Dickens's Nicholas
Nickleby; and the ironic allusion to Browning stems from FitzGerald's indig-
nation that some contemporary critics ranked him higher than Tennyson):
'*I*—*I*—! crib from the Gardener, which the paltry Poet charges me with!
Oh, Dem! But really, I should like to hear what this *Paltry Innuendo-maker*
alludes to: if it be any gloss of mine on Omar, very little doubt it came from
some of those paltry poems: but if it *should* be old Omar's, not even the spite
of a Poet *inferior to Browning* can accuse the old Persian of Theft. I should like
to find that three *so-called* Poets had jumped at one thought. So do tell me
what rankles in poor Alfred's mind: and I will relieve him at once' (ibid. 338).
Mrs Tennyson explained that the alleged 'theft' was from ll. 16–17: 'The
summer pilot of an empty heart | Unto the shores of nothing', and FitzGerald
responded (on 7 April, this time directly to Tennyson): 'I positively forgot to
what passage in Omar Mrs. AT's Quotation referred till I looked back and
saw about the Caravan starting for the Dawn of Nothing. I remembered then
having been at a loss for a word to express the "*no*-thing"—Nothingness,
Non-existence; Non-entity, etc., failing from clumsiness in one way or other: so

the word "Nothing" which is unsuitable for Omar's purpose as it is suitable to yours came to be adopted. I have not Eyes to look over the Persian to see how far Omar's Metaphor goes: so you may set it down as an Echo of yourself if you will. I remember often wanting a word like the French *"Néant"* to express what is so much the burden of the old Song' (ibid. 342). Meanwhile Tennyson himself had had second thoughts; on 11 April he wrote that he had misremembered FitzGerald's text: 'I see—rather to my confusion—that your words or Omar's are not "bound to the shores of nothing" but "Starts for the dawn of nothing" wherefore I repent that I made the least-little allusion to the passage. Nothing can well be finer than that passage in your translation—or indeed than almost the whole of it' (ibid. 345). Nevertheless FitzGerald revised the stanza and made a point of telling Tennyson that he had done so: '[I] altered about the "Dawn of Nothing," etc., as AT pointed out its likeness to his better Property' (to Emily Tennyson, Dec 1872, ibid. 389). Decker (pp. liii–liv) acutely remarks that 'starting' in *1872 proof*⁷ salvages 'Starts' from *1859*, but that FitzGerald in the end drew back from the 'mere recollection of the phrasing Tennyson had read'.

After XXXVIII: Would you that spangle of Existence spend
      About THE SECRET—quick about it, Friend!
        A Hair, they say, [*1872–79*: A Hair perhaps] divides the
          False and True—
      And upon what, prithee, does Life depend?

      A Hair, they say, [*1872–79*: A Hair perhaps] divides the
        False and True;
      Yes; and a single Alif were the clue,
        Could you but find it, to the Treasure-house,
      And peradventure to THE MASTER too;

      Whose secret Presence, through Creation's veins
      Running, Quicksilver-like eludes your pains:
        Taking all shapes from Máh to Máhi; and
      They change and perish all—but He remains;

      A moment guess'd—then back behind the Fold
      Immerst of Darkness round the Drama roll'd
        Which, for the Pastime of Eternity,
      He does Himself contrive, enact, behold.

      But if in vain, down on the stubborn floor
      Of Earth, and up to Heav'n's unopening Door,
        You gaze To-day, while You are You—how then
      To-morrow, You when shall be You no more?
        [*1872 proof*⁷: when You shall be You no more?]

      Oh, plagued no more with Human or Divine,
      To-morrow's tangle to itself resign,
        And lose your fingers in the tresses of
      The Cypress-slender Minister of Wine.

(*1868–79*, except that *1872–79* transpose the last stanza to an earlier position: see above; in a copy of *1879* now at Trinity College, Cambridge, FitzGerald revised 'does Life' in line 4 of the first stanza to 'may Life')

a single Alif: the first letter of the alphabet, a symbol of the oneness of God.
from Máh to Máhi: for FitzGerald's gloss in his added endnote, see below.

XXXIX.1]   Waste not your Hour, nor in the vain pursuit (*1868–79*)

XXXIX.2   dispute?] dispute. (*1868–79*)

XXXIX.3   merry] jocund (*1872–79*)

XL.1   how long since] how bravely (*1868–79*)

XL.2]   I made a Second Marriage in my house; (*1872–79*)

XLI.2   *without,* I could define] by Logic I define (*1868–79*)

After XLI: Ah, but my Computations, People say,
                 Have squared the Year to human compass, eh?
                    If so, by striking from the Calendar
                 Unborn To-morrow, and dead Yesterday. (*1868–79*, except
that ll. 2–3 in *1872–79* read: Reduced the Year to better reckoning?—
Nay, | 'Twas only)

XLII.2]   Came stealing] Came shining (*1868–79*)

XLIII.3   subtle Alchemist] sovereign Alchemist (*1868–79*)

XLIII.4   transmute.] transmute: (*1868–79*), connecting this quatrain syntactically to XLIV.

XLIV.1   the victorious Lord] Allah-breathing Lord, (*1868–79*)

XLIV.4]   Scatters before him with his whirlwind Sword. (*1868–79*)

FitzGerald consulted Cowell about 'whirlwind': '*Conquering, victorious, triumphant,* etc. are weak, because implied. But this Whirlwind which has just struck me may be Bombastes Furioso—and "forcible Feeble"' (29 January 1868, *Letters*, iii. 78).

After XLIV: *1868–79* omit st. XLV. *1868* has a series of new, revised, and transposed stanzas. The third was cut in *1872–79*; the seventh and eighth, which originally appeared in FitzGerald's preface in *1859*, were placed at an earlier point in *1872–79* (see above). The Persian original of the ninth was one of those translated by FitzGerald into Latin (Arberry, pp. 59, 112–13).

           Why, be this Juice the growth of God, who dare
           Blaspheme the twisted tendril as a Snare?
              A Blessing, we should use it, should we not?
           And if a Curse—why, then, Who set it there?

           I must abjure the Balm of Life, I must,
           Scared by some After-reckoning ta'en on trust,
              Or lured with Hope of some Diviner Drink,
           When the frail Cup is [*1872–79*: To fill the Cup—when]
              crumbled into Dust!

If but the Vine and Love-abjuring Band
Are in the Prophet's Paradise to stand,
 Alack, I doubt the Prophet's Paradise
Were empty as the hollow of one's Hand.

Oh threats of Hell and Hopes of Paradise!
One thing at least is certain—*This* Life flies:
 One thing is certain and the rest is Lies;
The Flower that once is blown for ever dies.

Strange, is it not? that of the myriads who
Before us pass'd the door of Darkness through
 Not one returns to tell us of the Road,
Which to discover we must travel too.

The Revelations of Devout and Learn'd
Who rose before us, and as Prophets burn'd,
 Are all but Stories, which, awoke from Sleep
They told their fellows, and to Sleep return'd.

Why, if the Soul can fling the Dust aside,
And naked on the Air of Heaven ride,
 Is't not a shame—is't not a shame for him
So long in this Clay suburb to abide!

But that is but a Tent wherein may rest
A Sultan to the realm of Death addrest;
 The Sultan rises, and the dark Ferrásh
Strikes, and prepares it for another guest.

I sent my Soul through the Invisible,
Some letter of that After-life to spell:
 And after many days my Soul return'd
 [*1872–79*: And by and by my Soul return'd to me,]
And said, 'Behold, [*1872–79*: And answer'd 'I] Myself
  am Heav'n and Hell:'

Heav'n but the Vision of fulfill'd Desire,
And Hell the Shadow of a Soul on fire,
 Cast on the Darkness into which Ourselves,
So late emerg'd from, shall so soon expire.

We are no other than a moving row
Of visionary Shapes [*1872–79*: Of Magic Shadow-shapes]
  that come and go
 Round with this Sun-illumin'd Lantern held
In Midnight by the Master of the Show;

MS versions of the two stanzas beginning 'I sent my Soul' and 'Heaven but
the Vision' are in the Rosenbach Library in Philadelphia. The first has the
1872 reading of the first three lines, followed by a draft: 'And said "O Man,
Thyself art Heaven and Hell."' which FitzGerald corrected to 'And answered,

"Thou Thyself art Heaven and Hell."' The second stanza deletes 'fulfilled' in line 1 and replaces it with 'attained'; it also has 'from a Soul' for 'of a Soul' in the second line, and omits 'Ourselves' at the end of line 3 (this last is almost certainly a slip). Accompanying these MS stanzas is a note: 'Cowell suggested "attained," but it is not the verb. Fulfilled is more sonorous. It shall go. "O Man" is scarcely Persian and I doubt if it can be justified. E FG.' The note is undated; if it forms part of a letter, the likelihood is that FitzGerald was writing either to his publisher, Quaritch, or to Quaritch's reader, while preparing the third edition in 1872. Alternatively the note may be a memorandum made to himself in the same period; this would fit better with the fact that the text contains draft readings and unique variants, and that FitzGerald expresses an intention to *restore* the reading 'fulfilled', which is in fact what he did in 1872.

XLVII–XLVIII]   These stanzas were revised and transposed to an earlier point in 1868–79 (see above).

XLIX.1–2]   Impotent [1879: But helpless] Pieces of the Game He plays
              Upon this chequer-board of Nights and Days; (1868–79)

XLIX.3   and mates] and checks (1868–79)

L.2   Right or Left] Here or There (1879).

The reading in 1859–72 is closer to the Persian original (Heron-Allen 1899, p. 105). Both Heron-Allen and Arberry (p. 224) mistakenly state that the revision dates from 1872.

L.3   toss'd Thee] toss'd you (1868–79)

LI.2, 4   thy Piety . . . thy Tears] your Piety . . . your Tears (1868–79)

After LI: For let Philosopher and Doctor preach
              Of what they will, and what they will not—each
                  Is but one Link in an eternal Chain
              That none can slip, nor break, nor over-reach. (1868)

LII.3   thy hands] your hands (1868–79)

LII.4]   As impotently rolls [1879: moves] as you or I. (1868–79)

LIII.1   the Last Man's] the Last Man (1868–79)

LIII.2   And then] And there (1868–79)

LIII.3   Yea,] And (1868–79)

After LIII: Yesterday *This* Day's Madness did prepare;
              To-morrow's Silence, Triumph, or Despair:
                  Drink! for you know not whence you came, nor why:
              Drink! for you know not why you go, nor where. (1868–79)

One of FitzGerald's Latin versions translates the Persian quatrain from which he took the last two lines of this stanza (Arberry, pp. 59, 113–14).

LIV.1]   I tell you this—When, started from the Goal, (1868–79)

LIV.3   Mushtara] Mushtari (1868–79).

Cowell told FitzGerald that the final 'a' was an error, and FitzGerald explained: 'I find it *Mushtara*' in the Dictionary. I suppose that ʾ expresses the *i* you give instead of *a*. As I love the *a* best, could I print it Mushtara', as in Dictionary?' (29 January 1868, *Letters*, iii. 78). But Cowell was inexorable. The change was also made in endnote 21.

LV.2   the Súfi] the Dervish (*1868–79*)

LVI.2   Wrathconsume] Wrath-consume (*1868–79*)

LVI.3   One Glimpse] One Flash (*1868–79*)

After LVI: What! out of senseless Nothing to provoke
              A conscious Something to resent the yoke
                  Of unpermitted Pleasure, under pain
              Of Everlasting Penalties, if broke!

              What! from his helpless Creature be repaid
              Pure Gold for what he lent us dross-allay'd—
                  Sue for a Debt we never did contract,
              And cannot answer—Oh the sorry trade!

              Nay, but, for terror of his wrathful Face,
              I swear I will not call Injustice Grace;
                  Not one Good Fellow of the Tavern but
              Would kick so poor a Coward from the place.
                  (*1868*; *1872–79* cut the third stanza)

LVII.3   Predestination] Predestin'd Evil (*1868–79*)

LVII.4   Enmesh me] Enmesh, and then (*1868–79*)

LVIII.1   Oh, Thou] Oh Thou (*1868–79*)

LVIII.2   who with Eden didst] ev'n with Paradise (*1868–79*)

LVIII.3–4   wherewith . . . blacken'd] the Face of wretched Man | Is
              black with—(*1868–79*)

After LVIII: The heading 'Kúzá-Námá' is omitted in *1868–79*.

FitzGerald wrote to Elizabeth Cowell on 10 December 1867 asking her to pass on a query to her husband: 'Was I wrong in printing Kúza Náma—the Persian (as I understand) and not the Arabic Form? It *looks* so much pleasanter. Somehow I couldn't care to use the Arabic: there is no need to use either. I only did it for fun' (*Letters*, iii. 66). On 29 January 1868 he wrote again, this time directly to Cowell: 'I think of *dele*-ing *Kuza Nama*: first because it looks gawky in the page (and I love my "pretty Page") and secondly because it seems to be the heading of another Poem; as I found from the Printers by their Proof' (*Letters*, iii. 78). The 'pretty Page' alludes to the opening words of Thackeray's poem 'The Age of Wisdom', 'Ho, pretty page', which FitzGerald later set to music (*Letters*, iii. 727).

LIX] As under cover of departing Day
Slunk hunger-stricken Ramazán away,
    Once more within the Potter's house alone
I stood, surrounded by the Shapes of Clay. (*1868–79*)

LX] And once again there gather'd a scarce heard
Whisper among them; as it were, the stirr'd
    Ashes of some all but extinguisht Tongue,
Which mine ear kindled into living Word. (*1868*)

Shapes of all Sorts and Sizes, great and small,
That stood along the floor and by the wall;
    And some loquacious Vessels were; and some
Listen'd perhaps, but never talk'd [*1872 proof*: spoke] at all.
(*1872–79*)

LXI.1 Then said another—] Said one among them—(*1872–79*)

LXII.1 Another said—'Why, ne'er] Then said a Second—'Ne'er
(*1872–79*)

LXII.2 the Bowl] the Cup (*1868*)

LXII.3–4] Shall He that of his own free Fancy made
The Vessel, in an after-rage destroy!' (*1868*);
And He that with his hand the Vessel made
Will surely not in after Wrath destroy.' (*1872–79*)

LXIII.1] After a momentary silence spake (*1872–79*)

LXIII.2 A Vessel] Some Vessel (*1868–79*)

After LXIII: Thus with the Dead as with the Living, *What?*
And *Why?* so ready, but the *Wherefor* not,
    One on a sudden peevishly exclaim'd,
'Which is the Potter, pray, and which the Pot?' (*1868*)

Whereat some one of the loquacious Lot—
I think a Súfi pipkin—waxing hot—
    'All this of Pot and Potter—Tell me then,
Who makes—Who sells—Who buys—Who *is* the Pot?'
[*1879*: Who is the Potter, pray, and who the Pot?'] (*1872–79*)

FitzGerald's uncertainty about line 4 dates back to a query in his letter to Cowell of May–June 1857: 'I must transcribe my *Sketch* for the second of those *Potter* Tetrastichs, as I am not sure of the meaning of the last line[.] I have taken it to be—"What? does he who moulds the Pots *traffic* in them?" . . . But does it only mean—"here are we Pots made—*by* whom, *for* whom, and for what end?" Which I suppose is right after all' (*Letters*, ii. 275). *1872* is closer to the version Cowell included in his *Calcutta Review* article (p. 161): 'Where is the pot-maker, the pot-buyer, the pot-seller?'—though FitzGerald still finds a way of keeping his own existential question. Cowell's translation is literally accurate, and his 'Where' correctly renders the Persian interrogative *kū*, but FitzGerald had always been determined to change this: in his Latin version, he translated the line 'At, precor, quid denique sint Vasa, quid qui fingit illa?' [But, pray, which after all are the pots, and he who makes them?]. The correct term would have been *quo*. Arberry (p. 111) comments 'The error was perpetuated in Stanza LX', but I do not think it was an error; FitzGerald knew perfectly well that *kū* means 'where', since a pun on this word forms the climax of the stanza found by Binning at Persepolis and translated by FitzGerald in endnote 11 (p. 57).

LXIV.1   Tapster] Master (*1868*)

LXIV.1–3]   "Why," said another, "Some there are who tell
              Of one who threatens he will toss to Hell
                   The luckless Pots he marr'd in making—Pish! (*1872–79*)

LXV.1]   "Well," said another, "Whoso will, let try, (*1868*)
              "Well," murmur'd one, "Let whoso make or buy, (*1872–79*)

LXVI.4   Hark to] Now for (*1868–79*)

LXVII.2   my Body] the Body (*1872–79*; this change originated in *1872*
proof²)

LXVII.3–4]   And lay me, shrouded in the living Leaf,
              By some not unfrequented Garden-side. (*1868–79*)

After LXVII: Whither resorting from the vernal Heat
              Shall Old Acquaintance Old Acquaintance greet,
                   Under the Branch that leans above the Wall
                   To shed his Blossom over head and feet. (*1868*)

1868 consisted of 110 stanzas, cut down in *1872* to 101. In the course of revising the text for *1872*, FitzGerald wrote to Cowell: 'I still want to omit the Stanza about "Whither resorting from the vernal heat," partly for the absurd reason that I want 101 Stanzas rather than 102!' (18 June 1872, *Letters*, iii. 356–7).

LXVIII.1   That] Then (*1868–79*)

LXVIII.2   Of Perfume] Of Vintage (*1868–79*)

LXIX.2   in Men's Eye] in this World (*1879*)

LXIX.3   my Honour] my Glory (*1868–79*)

LXXI.3   I often wonder] I wonder often (*1872–79*)

LXXI.4   the Goods] the ware (*1868*); the stuff (*1872–79*)

LXXII.1   Alas,] Yet Ah, (*1868–79*)

After LXXII: Would but the Desert of the Fountain yield
              One glimpse—if dimly, yet indeed reveal'd,
                   Toward which the fainting Traveller might spring,
                   As springs the trampled herbage of the field!

Oh if the World were but to re-create,
That we might catch ere closed the Book of Fate,
   And make The Writer on a fairer leaf
Inscribe our names, or quite obliterate!

Better, oh better, cancel from the Scroll
Of Universe one luckless Human Soul,
   Than drop by drop enlarge the Flood that rolls
Hoarser with Anguish as the Ages roll. (*1868*)

1872–79 have the first two stanzas only, with a minor revision in the first
('To' for 'Toward' in l. 3), and a heavily revised version of the second, which
in *1872 proof¹* is not grammatically coherent, and only reached its final form
in *1872 proof³*:

Would [*1872 proof¹*: And] but some winged Angel ere too late
Arrest [*1872 proof¹*: Wrested] the yet unfolded Roll of Fate,
   And make the stern Recorder otherwise
   [*1872 proof¹*: And make The Writer on a fairer leaf]
Enregister [*1872 proof¹*, *1872 proof²*: Inscribe our names], or quite
    obliterate!

This stanza has no original in the Ouseley or Calcutta MSS; it is based
on no. 457 in Nicolas's edition, to which the *1868* version is more faithful
(Heron-Allen 1899, p. 143).

LXXIII.1   Thou and I] you and I (*1868–79*)
               with Fate] with Him (*1872–79*)

After LXXIII: *1872–79* have a line of asterisks between sts. LXXIII and
               LXXIV.

LXXIV]   But see! The rising Moon of Heav'n again
               Looks for us, Sweet-heart, through the quivering Plane:
                  How oft hereafter rising will she look
               Among those leaves—for one of us in vain! (*1868*)

               Yon rising Moon that looks for us again—
               How oft hereafter will she [*1872 proof¹* and *1872 proof²*:
                  shall it] wax and wane;
                  How oft hereafter rising look for us
               Through this same Garden—and for *one* in vain! (*1872–79*)

The reading 'Sweet-heart' in *1868* is the only place in any version of the poem
where the sex of the addressee is demonstrably female.

LXXV.1   Thyself with shining Foot] Yourself with silver Foot (*1868*);
               Yourself with silver step (*1872 proof¹*, *1872 proof²*); like her, oh
               Sáki, you (*1872–79*; this reading was introduced in *1872 proof³*).

LXXV.3   thy joyous] your joyous (*1868*, *1879*); your blissful (*1872*,
               introduced in *1872 proof³*).

After LXXV: TAMÁM SHUD] TAMÁM (*1868–79*)

[*FitzGerald's endnotes*]

1] Not *1868–79*.

2] The last two sentences are omitted *1868–79*.

3 (says a late Traveller in Persia)] says Mr Binning, (*1868–79*)

3 *Now Rooz*] *Naw Rooz* (*1868–79*)

5 King Schedad] King Shaddád (*1868–79*)

7 if this refers] if the fourth line refers (*1879*)

7 in Persia.] in Persia. I think Southey, in his Common-Place Book, quotes from some Spanish author about a Rose [*1872*: about Rose; *1879*: the Rose] being White till 10 o'clock; 'Rosa perfecta' at 2; and 'perfecta incarnada' at 5. (*1868–79*)

8 of Persia, whose exploits] of Persia, and Zál his Father, whose exploits (*1872–79*)

11 *Peeshdádian*] *Peshdádian* (*1879*)

11 (with Shah-náma Authority)] (according to the Shah-náma) (*1868–79*)

11 built by him, though others] built by him. Others (*1868–79*)

11 Ján Ibn Jann, who also built the Pyramids] Ján Ibn Ján—who also built the Pyramids—

11 It is also called . . . articulate Persian for 'Where?'] not *1868–79*.

In *1868* FitzGerald placed the stanza about the ring-dove in the text of the poem, after XVII, and added an endnote keyed to l. 4 which uses some of the material from this passage; *1872–79* transpose the stanza, and the *1868* note, to the end of this note, and *1879* adds a further paragraph (see below).

11 from his Fame in hunting it] not *1868–79*

11 within side;] within; (*1868–79*)

11 recounts to Bahrám a Romance, according to] tells him a Story, as told in (*1868–79*)

11 these Sevens] all these Sevens (*1868–79*)

11 while pursuing his *Gúr*.] *1872–79* add:

> The Palace that to Heav'n his pillars threw,
> And Kings the forehead on his threshold drew—
>   I saw the solitary Ringdove there,
> And 'Coo, coo, coo,' she cried; and 'Coo, coo, coo.'

This Quatrain Mr Binning found, among several of Háfiz and others, inscribed by some stray hand among the ruins of Persepolis. The Ringdove's ancient *Péhlevi*, *Coo, Coo, Coo*, signifies also in Persian '*Where? Where? Where?*' In Attár's 'Bird-parliament' she is reproved by the Leader of the Birds for sitting still, and for ever harping on that one note of lamentation for her lost Yúsuf.

1879 has a further addition:

> Apropos of Omar's Red Roses in Stanza xix [xviii in *1859*], I am reminded of an old English Superstition, that our Anemone Pulsatilla, or purple 'Pasque Flower,' (which grows plentifully about the Fleam Dyke, near Cambridge), grows only where Danish Blood has been spilt.

After 11: *1868* has a new footnote, keyed to l. 4 of the stanza about the ringdove which was placed in the text of the poem; the text is as above ('This Quatrain . . . her lost Yúsuf.').

14] ME-AND-THEE: some dividual Existence or Personality distinct from the Whole. (*1868–79*)

After 14: *1872–79* have a new note, keyed in *1872* to l. 4 of xxxvii (xl in *1859*):

> One of the Persian Poets—Attár, I think—has a pretty story about this. A thirsty Traveller dips his hand into a Spring of Water to drink from. By and by comes another who draws up and drinks from an earthen Bowl, and then departs, leaving his Bowl behind him. The first Traveller takes it up for another draught; but is surprised to find that the same Water which had tasted sweet from his own hand tastes bitter from the earthen Bowl. But a Voice—from Heaven, I think—tells him the Clay from which the Bowl is made was once *Man;* and, into whatever shape renew'd, can never lose the bitter flavour of Mortality.

After 14: *1868–79* have two new notes. The first is keyed to l. 1 of the second stanza added after xxxvi (see above):

> The custom of throwing a little Wine on the ground before drinking still continues in Persia, and perhaps generally in the East. Mons. Nicolas considers it 'un signe de liberalité, et en même temps un avertissement que le buveur doit vider sa coupe jusqu'à la dernière goutte [a sign of liberality, and at the same time a warning that the drinker must empty his cup to the last drop].' Is it not more likely an ancient Superstition; a Libation to propitiate Earth, or make her an Accomplice in the illicit Revel? Or, perhaps, to divert the Jealous Eye by some sacrifice of superfluity, as with the Ancients of the West? With Omar we see something more is signified; the precious Liquor is not lost, but sinks into the ground to refresh the dust of some poor Wine-worshipper foregone.
>
> Thus Háfiz, copying Omar in so many ways: 'When thou drinkest Wine pour a draught on the ground. Wherefore fear the Sin which brings to another Gain?'

The second is keyed to l. 1 of the transposed stanza xlviii (see above), and was itself revised. In *1868*:

> According to one beautiful Oriental Legend, Azräel accomplishes his mission by holding to the nostril an Apple from the Tree of Life.

In *1872–79* this is followed by another sentence:

> This, and the two following Stanzas would have been withdrawn, as somewhat *de trop*, from the Text but for advice which I least like to disregard.

The phrasing suggests Cowell, or his wife; in a letter to Mrs Cowell of 1 February 1868, FitzGerald wrote: 'My dear Lady, you know that what I used to do with your own Verses was, to cut out; and now you won't let me do so with mine!' (*Letters*, iii. 79). But this letter refers to the second edition; and in a letter of 18 June 1872, FitzGerald wrote to Cowell that Quaritch 'was much opposed to leaving out some things which you wished omitted' (ibid. 363). On balance I think FitzGerald is alluding to the advice given by Elizabeth Cowell in 1868, because any omissions urged by Cowell for *1872* would be likely to relate to stanzas containing objectionable religious views, and that is not the case with the ones at issue here.

15] The Caravans travelling by night, after the Vernal Equinox—their New Year's Day. This was ordered by Mohammed himself, I believe. (*1868*). This note was cut in *1872–79*.

After 15: *1868–79* have a new note, keyed to l. 3 of the third stanza added after XXXVIII (see above):
From Máh to Máhi; from Fish to Moon.
FitzGerald has got the terms reversed; it should be 'from Moon to Fish', 'a common Oriental metaphor for universality' (Heron-Allen 1899, p. 83).

16] A Jest, of course, at his Studies. A curious mathematical Quatrain of Omar's has been pointed out to me; the more curious because almost exactly parallel'd by some Verses of Doctor Donne's, and quoted [*1872–79*: that are quoted] in Izaak Walton's Lives! Here is Omar: 'You and I are the image of a pair of compasses; though we have two heads (sc. our *feet*) we have one body; when we have fixed the centre for our circle, we bring our heads (sc. feet) together at the end.' Dr Donne:

> If we be two, we two are so
>   As stiff twin-compasses are two;
> Thy Soul, the fixt foot, makes no show
>   To move, but does if the other do.
>
> And though thine in the centre sit,
>   Yet when my other far does roam,
> Thine leans and hearkens after it,
>   And grows erect as mine comes home.
>
> Such thou must be to me, who must
>   Like the other foot obliquely run;
> Thy firmness makes my circle just,
>   And me to end where I begun. (*1868–79*)

The poem by Donne is 'A Valediction: forbidding mourning'; the 'pointer-out' was probably Cowell, but may have been FitzGerald's friend W. B. Donne, whose family claimed descent from the poet's. FitzGerald alters the first line of the text in Izaak Walton's *Life* (1640; often reprinted with his other biographies, hence *Lives*): 'If they be two, they are two so'; in line 4 Walton has 'doth', and in line 5 'though it'.

17] The Seventy-two Religions supposed to divide the World: *including* Islamism, as some think: but others not. (*1868–79*)

This revision was prompted by a note in Nicolas's edition which spoke not of seventy-two sects but seventy-two 'Kingdoms of the World'. FitzGerald wrote to Elizabeth Cowell that when Cowell 'taught me the Poems at Rushmere, he rendered it the *seventy-two Sects*; and I think (not at all sure) that I understood from him the seventy-two Sects into which *Islamism* split. So I printed it in a Note but had misgivings directly afterward; and somewhere (I cannot recall where) read that it was Christianity which Mohammedans thought so split up' (10 December 1867, *Letters*, iii. 66). Cowell may have told FitzGerald of Muhammad's prediction that the world would be divided between Islam and seventy-two *other* religions, but FitzGerald's revised phrasing leaves this unclear. Did Cowell also scotch the notion that the phrase applied to Christianity? He would not have been happy with a Muslim satire on the divisions between Christians.

18] Alluding to Sultan Mahmúd's Conquest of India and its dark people. (*1868–79*)

19   the Candle lighted] the lighted Candle (*1868–79*)

After 21: *1872–79* have a new note, keyed to l. 4 of the revised version of the stanza added after LXIII (see above):

> This Relation of Pot and Potter to Man and his Maker figures far and wide in the Literature of the World, from the time of the Hebrew Prophets to the present; when it may finally take the name of 'Pot-theism,' by which Mr. Carlyle ridiculed Sterling's 'Pantheism.' *My* Sheikh, whose knowledge flows in from all quarters, writes to me—
>
> 'Apropos of old Omar's Pots, did I ever tell you the sentence I found in "Bishop Pearson on the Creed"?' 'Thus are we wholly at the disposal of His will, and our present and future condition, framed and ordered by His free, but wise and just, decrees. *"Hath not the potter power over the clay, of the same lump to make one vessel unto honour, and another unto dishonour?"* (Rom. ix. 21). And can that earth-artificer have a freer power over his *brother potsherd* (both being made of the same metal), than God hath over him, who, by the strange fecundity of His omnipotent power, first made the clay out of nothing, and then him out of that?'
>
> And again—from a very different quarter—'I had to refer the other day to Aristophanes, and came by chance on a curious Speaking-pot story in the Vespæ, which I had quite forgotten.

> Φιλοκλέων. Ἄκουε, μὴ φεῦγ᾽· ἐν Συβάρει γυνή ποτε   l. 1435
>   κατέαξ᾽ ἐχῖνον.

Κατηγορος. Ταῦτ' ἐγὼ μαρτύρομαι.

Φι.   Οὐχῖνος οὖν ἔχων τιν' ἐπεμαρτύρατο·
        Εἶθ' ἡ Συβαρῖτις εἶπεν, ἐι ναὶ τὰν κόραν
        τ ἠν μαρτυρίαν ταύτην ἐάσας, ἐν τάχει
        ἐπίδεσμον ἐπρίω, νοῦν ἄν εἴχες πλείονα.

'The Pot calls a bystander to be a witness to his bad treatment. The woman says, "If, by Proserpine, instead of all this 'testifying' (comp. Cuddie and his mother in 'Old Mortality!') you would buy yourself a trivet [*1879*: rivet], it would show more sense in you!" The Scholiast explains *echinus* as' ἄγγος τι ἐκ κεράμον.'

Carlyle's quip occurs in his *Life of John Sterling*, which FitzGerald read when it was first published in 1851 (*Letters*, ii. 40–1). '*My* Sheikh' refers to Cowell; FitzGerald says he intends to use the two quotations in a letter of 12 April 1872 (*Letters*, iii. 347). 'Bishop Pearson' is John Pearson (1613–86), Bishop of Chester; his *Exposition of the Creed*, published in 1659, remained a standard reference work in English divinity (*DNB*). Cowell uses the Latin title 'Vespæ' for Aristophanes' play *The Wasps*, and paraphrases rather than translates the passage. The interpolated reference to characters in Walter Scott's novel *Old Mortality* (1816) would have appealed to FitzGerald; Scott was his favourite novelist. 'Testify' is a word associated with the jargon of the Cameronians, the extreme Protestant sect to which Cuddie Headrigg and his mother Mause belong; for example, when the hero Henry Morton is arrested in their house, Mause rebukes her son: 'if you and thae thowless gluttons, that are sitting staring like cows bursting on clover, wad testify wi' your hands as I have testified wi' my tongue, they should never harle the precious young lad awa' to captivity' (ch. 8).

1879 has a further addition, which FitzGerald enclosed in a letter to Quaritch of 21 January 1879 (*Letters*, iv. 176):

One more illustration for the oddity's sake from the 'Autobiography of a Cornish Rector,' by the late James Hamley Tregenna. 1871.

'There was one old Fellow in our Company—he was so like a Figure in the "Pilgrim's Progress" that Richard always called him the "ALLEGORY," with a long white beard—a rare Appendage in those days—and a Face the colour of which seemed to have been baked in, like the Faces one used to see on Earthenware Jugs. In our Country-dialect Earthenware is called *"Clome"*; so the Boys of the Village used to shout after him—"Go back to the Potter, Old Clome-face, and get baked over again." For the 'Allegory,' though shrewd enough in most things, had the reputation of being *"saift-baked,"* i.e., of weak intellect.

22   with all Acclamation] with Acclamation (*1868–79*)

22   Old Omar] Omar (*1868–79*)

22   this same Moon] the same Moon (*1879*)

APPENDIX I

CRITICAL RESPONSES TO THE *RUBÁIYÁT* IN FITZGERALD'S LIFETIME: FOUR REVIEWS AND A POLEMICAL ARTICLE

THE following pieces are representative of the published criticism of the *Rubáiyát* in FitzGerald's lifetime. They comprise the only substantial notice taken of the first edition (1859); two reviews of the second edition (1868), which appeared in American and British journals in 1868 and 1870; a review-article based on the third edition (1872), which appeared in 1876, and was the first publication in Britain to name FitzGerald as author/translator; and the first scholarly critique of FitzGerald's version of Omar, which appeared in 1879. FitzGerald does not mention the review of *1859* in the *Literary Gazette*, and may not have seen it, and there is no direct evidence that he saw the piece in the *North American Review*; we know that he saw the others.

None of the reviews of the *Rubáiyát* was written by a Persian scholar, and all make liberal use of FitzGerald's Preface in their biographical and critical assessments of Omar. (It is a bit disconcerting to find a scholar such as Charles Eliot Norton passing FitzGerald's phrases off as his own, or at any rate quoting them without acknowledgement, but FitzGerald himself behaved in exactly the same way towards his sources, and in Victorian periodical criticism the practice would have been taken for granted.) Jessie Cadell's article of 1879 is the first published response to the *Rubáiyát* by someone competent in Persian, for although FitzGerald continued his dialogue with Edward Cowell on the subject, Cowell was far too loyal a friend to publish any reservations he had about FitzGerald's version.

I have abbreviated the four reviews, indicating where they copy the Preface, and with one or two exceptions giving stanza numbers instead of the full text of the verse they quote; readers who do not have independent copies of the other texts of the poem will have to consult the Tables of Corresponding Stanzas on p. 60 and then look up the relevant stanzas in the Variants. I have reprinted Cadell's piece in full because it sets the terms of the debate about FitzGerald as a translator, and makes the case for the prosecution with fair-minded stringency. It also has the advantage of giving the reader some literal translations of Omar from the same period as FitzGerald's work.

Minor slips in the articles, e.g. in quotations from the poem or spellings of proper names, have not been corrected.

FitzGerald wrote to Cowell that he was 'well pleased to be so belauded' in the *Fraser's* review of 1870, even though 'I cannot say there is much in it: the piece from Rabelais was interesting, and to the point' (8 July 1870, *Letters,* iii. 231). It is perhaps significant that he does not comment on the much more pertinent allusions to Tennyson's *In Memoriam* and 'The Two Voices'. The author of the 1876 review-article in the *Contemporary Review*, Henry Schütz Wilson, wrote to Quaritch requesting permission to make FitzGerald's name public and asking for some biographical details about him. Quaritch forwarded the request to FitzGerald, and seems to have pressed him at the same time to allow his name on the title page. FitzGerald refused the title page request, on the grounds that there were too many Edward FitzGeralds in the world: one was an 'Ex-policeman' who lived nearby, another a parson in a neighbouring village; 'In fact one of us was generally hanged in Ireland once a Year till the Law was altered'. However, he allowed that since one of these multiple namesakes was 'known to be the Culprit by several among the small Circles of Omarians', Wilson could go ahead and '[name] one of us as the understood Translator'. He signed this letter "One of the E.F.G.'s' (25 January 1870, *Letters,* iii. 651–2). When Wilson's article appeared, FitzGerald wrote to him: 'I have had many felicitations from Friends on account of your very handsome praises in the *Contemporary,* which you will think it sham modesty in me to say were far beyond desert: but I do sincerely think so' (26 April 1876, *Letters,* iii. 676).

The 'Literary Gossip' section of the *Athenaeum* of 10 March 1877 announced, as FitzGerald put it a little nervously, 'some Lady's Edition of Omar which is to discover all my Errors and Perversions. So this will very likely turn the little Wind that blew my little Skiff on' (to Elizabeth Cowell, 11 March 1877, *Letters,* iv. 16–17). The 'Lady' was Jessie Cadell, who did not live to complete her edition; FitzGerald read her article in *Fraser's Magazine* in 1879 and commented that it was 'temperate and just' (to Cowell, June 1879, *Letters,* iv. 225).

1. Anonymous Review, *Literary Gazette,* NS 66 (1 October 1859), 326

OMAR KHAYYÁM is a Persian poet who is little known in Persia, and who is still less known in Europe. Verbosity was certainly not one of his characteristics, and wanting this, he might possibly lack the passport to Oriental fame; but if the astronomer-poet of Persia appears as well in his native garb as he appears in English, it was certainly high time that he should be brought out of his obscurity. We learn that he was born at Naishápúr, in Khorassán, in the latter half of the eleventh century, and died within the first quarter of the twelfth. He was much more celebrated for his astronomical and mathematical studies and acquirements than for his poetical powers; and yet it would appear that his poems are the only remains which have been preserved to perpetuate his memory. His history is intimately connected . . .

[The reviewer gives a short paraphrase of FitzGerald's Preface on the schoolboy pact between Omar, Nizám ul-Mulk, and Hasan Sabbah, concluding with Omar's life of devotion to knowledge.]

Omar's Epicurean freedom of thought and expression rendered him the dread of the Súfis. The oriental mysticism of his age was altogether distasteful to him, and he soon made it apparent that he would make no compromise between faith and unbelief, between spiritualism and materialism, between this world and the next, between the religion of Mahomet and absolute scepticism. With more courage than the majority of orientals, he refused to disguise his creed in gorgeous draperies. He did not allow himself the luxury of floating through the lazy hazes in which the Sufis hid their real mistrust and misbelief; but spoke out boldly, rashly, and—in the light of Christianity—impiously, on the most momentous topics. He made no pretence of allegory; his wine was the veritable juice of the grape; his beauties were no divine harmonies, but consisted of flesh and blood; his gardens were not the haunts of houris, but plots of earthly flowers; he preferred the tavern to the temple; and as his meditations, though sufficing to undermine his belief in the false religion in which he had been nurtured, had failed to find any anchorage of supernal truth, he believed only in the visible and the tangible, and ridiculed those who believed in anything else. His whole creed is expressed in the following stanza:—

> But leave the wise to wrangle, and with me
> The quarrel of the universe let be:
>   And, in some corner of the hubbub coucht,
>   *Make game of that which makes as much of thee.*

No Persian poet of whom we have heard has written so few verses as Omar Khayyám, and none has written so earnestly, or with so much poignancy, and richness and depth of feeling. His poems, though evidently written occasionally, are not the utterances of occasional frames of mind, but are the expressions of life-long habitudes of thought; and nothing can be more dreary than the merriment in which he seeks to drown his despair, and nothing more beautiful than the manner in which he discourses of both. What could be better expressed than the following?

[quotes stanzas XVI–XIX]

The deep questions of all time pressed heavily upon this Persian poet of the middle-ages; and few poets, ancient or modern, have given fuller utterance to the subtlest speculations with which the human intellect can be occupied. The quaint beauty of the following extract must be the excuse for its length:

[quotes stanzas LIX–LVI]

Everywhere the same crushing fatalism presents itself. The poet maintains that man must be unaccountable, because he has not the choice of his actions; his volitions are but the subordinate pulsations of an invisible Destiny; he is tossed as a ball, to and fro, and has no right to make questions of "Ayes or Noes," but must go left or right as he is impelled; that the finger of Fate is writing and moving on, and that whatever is written can never be cancelled by human wisdom or human agony and penitence:—

> And that inverted bowl we call the sky,
> Whereunder crawling coop't we live and die,
>   Lift not thy hands to *it* for help—for it
> Rolls impotently on as thou and I.

A melancholy creed, but one on which, after his own tragical fashion, the poet contrived to make merry. We must thank the modest translator of this powerful and original poet for the valuable contribution—slight, so far as bulk is concerned, though it be—which he has made to our current literature. Never was the Gospel of Despair preached more fervently than it is in the pages of Khayyám, and few of our modern fatalists could express their convictions with so much terse vigour, or deck their repulsive theories with so many quaint beauties, as this Eastern poet and sage.

2. Anonymous Review of *Rubáiyát* (2nd edition) and of Nicolas's
Les Quatrains de Khèyam, *North American Review*, 109
(October 1869), 565–84

[The author was the American scholar and critic Charles Eliot Norton
(1827–1908), who was later instrumental in revealing FitzGerald's iden-
tity as author/translator of the *Rubáiyát*; in 1875 he began an epistolary
friendship with FitzGerald, though he never told him of his authorship
of this piece.]

The prevailing traits of the genius of Omar Khayyám are so coinci-
dent with certain characteristics of the spiritual temper of our own
generation, that it is hardly surprising that his poetry, of which hith-
erto the Western world knew nothing, is beginning to excite the
interest it deserves, and has lately been made accessible to us in
translation. The fame of Omar, certainly one of the most remarkable
poets of Persia, has been narrowly confined within the limits of his
own language, and even his name has scarcely been heard outside his
own land. This is hardly to be wondered at; for there is much in the
quality of his verse to render it unacceptable to the generality of
orthodox readers of poetry, and to those who read only *with* and not
through their eyes. The transcendental character of much of his
poetry takes it out of the range of common appreciation, and that it
may be understood at all it requires to be read with something of the
same spirit with which it was written.

Omar Khayyám was born near Naishápúr in Khorassan in the
second quarter of our eleventh century, and died, it is said, in the
year 1123; thus preceding Hafiz by more than three centuries, and
Saadi by about a century. It is a striking illustration of this early
bloom of Persian culture, that Omar precedes Dante by two hundred
years.

[Quotes biographical account from FitzGerald's Preface, some of it practic-
ally verbatim, including the story of the schoolboy pact and its aftermath,
and Omar's prophecy of his burial-place; the order is changed so that the
comment on the meaning of the name 'Khayyám' follows the latter story,
and Norton adds a detail here from his own knowledge:]

In obedience to the custom that prevails in Persia, that every
poet should take a distinguishing name in addition to his own,
Omar chose that of Khayyám, or Tent-maker, as indicating, it is said,

the occupation which he himself carried on and which had been that of his father. The Persians declare that it was the modesty of the poet that prevented him from assuming a more brilliant name, such as that of *Firdusi*, "the Celestial," or *Hafiz*, "the Preserver."

His poetry is wholly composed of independent stanzas, called *Rubáiyát*, "consisting each of four lines of equal, though varied, prosody; sometimes all rhyming, but oftener the third line a blank. As usual with such Oriental verse, the Rubáiyát follow one another according to alphabetic rhyme,—a strange succession of grave and gay." And not merely a strange succession of grave and gay, but of such dark interior meaning that the two translators, M. Nicolas, and the anonymous English versifier, though apparently not at odds as to the literal meaning, are completely at variance as to the true interpretation and significance of Omar's verse. They agree, indeed (for this at least is plain), that Omar was a sceptic, a free-thinker, no true believer, but a very thorn in the side of the orthodox disciples of the prophet. But while M. Nicolas regards him as essentially a mystic, concealing secret meanings in his verse,—a *Súfi*,—in a word, devoted to the contemplation of Divinity, and to the attainment of perfection, shadowing the Deity in his poetry under figures and tropes of Wine, Wine-bearer, and the like, the English translator, on the other hand, believes him to have been a materialistic Epicurean, audacious in thought and expression,

[Quotes three passages on Omar's materialism from the original concluding paragraph of the Preface (i.e. before the addition made in *1868* in response to Nicolas)]

The study of Omar's verse helps but little to reconcile this wide difference of judgment. Many of his quatrains, as the English translator admits, seem unaccountable unless mystically interpreted; but many more as unaccountable unless literally. May it not be that there are two sides to Omar's shield,—one of mystic gold, the other of plain silver? It belongs to the true poet to represent more completely than other men the double nature of man,—the spiritual and the sensual alike; in him the vision and the faculty divine are indissolubly bound to the delight of the eye in the beauty of the actual world, and to the joy of the heart in the present life. The higher the spiritual imagination reaches, the broader must be the foundation on which it rests, of love and knowledge of material existence. Omar may

have sung, in a literal sense, the praises of the wine which gladdens
the hearts of men, without any feeling of incongruity when he sings
that wine which is the spiritual reviver and comforter of the soul.
The common literal object easily becomes a type of divine excellence,
and other Persian poets have used wine and beauty as images to illus-
trate the divinity they were celebrating. The English translator,
indeed, who denies to Omar's verse the spiritual significance which
many of his Persian readers attribute to it, admits that the chief
Persian poets, including Háfiz, borrowed largely of Omar's material,
"but turning it to a mystical use more convenient to themselves and
the people they addressed,—a people quite as quick of doubt as of
belief; as keen of bodily sense as of intellectual, and delighting in a
cloudy compound of both, in which they could float luxuriously
between heaven and earth, and this world and the next, on the wings
of a poetical expression, that might serve indifferently for either."
It is true that, however much of spiritual significance may be allowed
to Omar's verse, many of his quatrains refuse to be thus interpreted,
and compel us to accept them as simple expressions of earthly
passion and of sensual delights. But whatever allowance be required
for the sensual side of Omar's character, his quatrains give proof of
the delicacy no less than of the strength of his poetic nature, of
the subtility no less than of the elevation of his thought. The deepest
questions that perplex mankind occupy him. Seeking with a shrewd,
inquisitive, and independent intelligence, he fails to find a trust-
worthy answer to the problems of existence and eternity; and his
penetrating imagination serves him no better than his understanding
in the attempt to reach assurance concerning the nature of God and
man. But he does not rest in simple negative conclusions, in mere
denial of the unfounded assertions, and reaction from the vain super-
stitions, of the popular religious creed. He doubts, indeed, at times,
as he watches the perverse course of human affairs, whether there
be a God; he presents clearly the dilemmas involved in the concep-
tion of a divine power creating and sustaining the universe; for him
there is neither heaven nor hell outside of his own soul. If there be a
God, he has made man weak, liable to error, and full of passions,
and has left him in doubt as to his destiny; but if there be a God, he
must know the nature of the beings he has made, and is surely not
worse than they, and will not punish them for being such as he
has made them. If we interpret some of Omar's quatrains mystically,

we find him sometimes seeking satisfaction in pantheistic abstractions, in efforts towards communion with, and absorption in, the Divine, and sometimes betaking himself to atheistic speculations, and admitting no other guiding principle in the universe than a blind, impartial fate. But, perplexed or baffled as he may be, he maintains a manly independence, and, finding nothing outside or beyond this world to rest upon, fixes himself solidly here, and resolves, while all things are fleeting and changing around him to enjoy at least the present hour, and to make the best of the life which is his to-day, but may not be his to-morrow. However shifting and uncertain are his thoughts respecting the invisible and the unknown, his practical philosophy does not vary, and, like the Hebrew preacher, he constantly repeats: "There is nothing better for a man than that he should eat and drink, and that he should make his soul enjoy good in his labor. This also I saw that it was from the hand of God."

Strokes of a vigorous imagination, strongly grasping the reality, constantly occur in his verse. His boldness of expression often runs into audacity. Things held sacred he treats with a free hand, and what he ventures to think he ventures also to speak. The bitter contrast between the wretchedness of men in this life and their undefined expectations of a better lot in another life moves him at times to contemptuous irony of human hopes and efforts, at times to indignant scorn of the supposed divine order of the universe. From the illusions of earth,—the palace of misery,—he turns to the real, if transient, gladness of wine, and celebrates the joys of self-forgetfulness in the embrace of the twisted tendrils of the grape. He professes no wisdom but that of honest integrity of thought, which authorizes him to speak plain truth whether it be acceptable or not. He has no disposition to make terms with the true believers. He is unsparing in his rebukes of pretenders to religion, and in his satire of its ministers. But his fancy chiefly occupies itself with the transitoriness and uncertainty of human affairs, with the ignorance of man concerning his own destiny, with the quick passage of life, and with the means of enjoyment which the hour affords.

In a literal translation much of the charm of the original must be lost, and much of its spirit evaporates. But even in the dry version of M. Nicolas the transcendental character of Omar's poetry is apparent, and its essential qualities do not altogether disappear.* The English anonymous translator, of the character of whose version I have yet to speak, has confined his work within such narrow limits that, before proceeding to it, it may be well to give some passages from the French rendering, which illustrate the nature of the genius and of the speculations of the poet:—

[Quotes fifty-one passages, mostly whole quatrains, from Nicolas's edition, translating the French text into English; of these, approximately fourteen (it is difficult to calculate exactly because of FitzGerald's habit of combining material from different quatrains) have some equivalent in the *Rubáiyát*.]

Such passages as these, suffering from the accumulated injuries of a double translation, and reproducing neither the poetic form nor the style of the original verse, while they but imperfectly render its substance, can hardly fail in spite of all these drawbacks to leave a strong impression on the mind of the reader—especially if he be a little versed in the usual manner of the Persian poets—of the originality of Omar's genius, and of the vigor of his character as shown in the independence of his attitude toward the popular belief and predominant opinions of his time. The individual quality of the poet's imagination, the clear, defined, precision of his expression, the spiritual insight of his speculation, and the realistic truth of his rendering of feeling, unite to give him a high place among the poets of his country; while his direct dealing with subjects of universal import, and his grasp of thoughts and moods common to the latest generation, set him among the few poets who have more than a mere historic or literary interest for men of different race, of different language, and of another age than his. Leaving altogether out of view the striking contrast which his poetry offers to the contemporary poetic productions of the Western world, and the picture it affords of the material civilization no less than of the spiritual culture of Persia at the period when it was composed, it possesses an intrinsic claim to record, as the imaginative utterance of one who in his time was busied with the questions which from the days of Adam to the latest day have occupied the best and wisest of the sons of men, and to which each has striven—and shall we say each as vainly as Omar

---

* M. Nicholas gives the original text as well as the translation of Omar's work,—four hundred and sixty-four quatrains in all. His notes are copious and useful.

himself?—to discover the answer which shall satisfy the doubting, sceptical, sad heart of man. That such a view, at least, of the significance and worth of the poetry of Omar has been held by his English translator, is plain from the manner of the work which he has given us. He is to be called 'translator' only in default of a better word, one which should express the poetic transfusion of a poetic spirit from one language to another, and the re-presentation of the ideas and images of the original in a form not altogether diverse from their own, but perfectly adapted to the new conditions of time, place, custom, and habit of mind in which they reappear. In the whole range of our literature there is hardly to be found a more admirable example of the most skilful poetic rendering of remote foreign poetry than this work of an anonymous author affords. It has all the merit of a remarkable original production, and its excellence is the highest testimony that could be given, to the essential impressiveness and worth of the Persian poet. It is the work of a poet inspired by the work of a poet; not a copy, but a reproduction, not a translation, but the redelivery of a poetic inspiration.

Much in the English work has been simply suggested by the original. Hints supplied by Omar are enlarged; thoughts touched upon by him are completely grasped; images faintly shadowed by him, fully developed. The sequence of the Persian quatrains, depending on the rhyme and not upon the contents of the verse, admits of no progressive development of feeling, and no logical continuity of thought. The poet is compelled by his form into sententiousness, into gnomic sayings, into discontinuous flashes of emotion, and finds himself obliged to recur often to the same idea, in order to present it under a new image or in a different aspect. The English Omar has not troubled himself to follow this peculiarity of his model. He has strung his quatrains together in an order which, if it fail to unite them all in a continuous and regularly developed whole, into a poem formed of the union of the separate stanzas, does at least so bind together many of them that the various portions seem like fragments of an Oriental eclogue. Moreover, a minor key of sadness, of refined melancholy, seems to recur in the English composition more frequently than in the Persian. The sentiment of the original Omar is often re-enforced by the English, is expressed in stronger, tenderer, and more delicate strokes. Every now and then a note of the nineteenth century seems to mingle its tone with those of the twelfth;

as if the ancient Oriental melody were reproduced on a modern European instrument. But it is very striking to see, and much more to feel, how close the thought and the sentiment of the Persian poet often are to the thought and sentiment of our own day. So that in its English dress it reads like the latest and freshest expression of the perplexity and of the doubt of the generation to which we ourselves belong. There is probably nothing in the mass of English translations or reproductions of the poetry of the East to be compared with this little volume in point of value as *English* poetry. In the strength of rhythmical structure, in force of expression, in musical modulation, and in mastery of language, the external character of the verse corresponds with the still rare interior qualities of imagination and of spiritual discernment which it displays.

It needs no further introduction. The English Omar gives us one hundred and ten quatrains in all, from which the following citations are selected:—

[Quotes (without giving the stanza numbers) I, VII–XV, XVII–XXIII, XXVI, XXIV–XXV [out of sequence], XXX–XL, XLVIII, XLVII [transposed], XLV–XLVI [out of sequence], LIV–LVI, LXI [isolated from context], LXVII–LXVIII, LXXI–LXXX, LXXXIII–XCVII, CIV–CV, XCVIII–C [out of sequence], CVI–CX; the article concludes without further comment.]

3. Anonymous Review, *Fraser's Magazine* (June 1870), 777–84

[The author was Thomas W. Hinchliff (1825–82), founder and first president of the Alpine Club; he identified himself in a letter to Quaritch of 1876 (Wrentmore, pp. 42–3).]

It is little more than two years since Mr. Chenery, the accomplished Professor of Arabic at Oxford, gave us his translation of the Makámát, or 'Assemblies of El Harírí,' and thereby furnished to English readers a valuable picture of Persian life about the end of the eleventh and beginning of the twelfth century. Born at Bussorah in A.D. 1054 and dying in 1122, El Harírí, 'the silk-merchant,' was in the prime of life at the time of the first Crusades, and the origin of his book was derived from the accident of meeting with one of the few survivors from the city of Serúj, which was attacked and destroyed by Baldwin, brother of Godfrey of Bouillon, during the period of his establishment at Edessa. The readers of the seventh volume of Gibbon will appreciate the historical interest of such a link between the East and the West at a time when they were engaged in deadly conflict, and the Sultans of the Seljukian dynasty were preparing to drive the Roman power out of Asia. During almost precisely the same period as that in which El Harírí lived near the mouths of the Euphrates, Omar Khayyám, the Astronomer-Poet of Persia, was flourishing at Naishápúr in Khorassan, and sunning himself in the courtly favour of the Sultans Alp Arslán and Malik Shah, the two immediate successors of Toghrul Beg and Tartar, who wrested Persia from the son of Mahmúd the Great. Under the rule of these victorious Seljukian Sultans the language and literature of Persia revived, and Omar Khayyám, in his doubt capacity of poet and mathematician, was doubtless a man of great mark in his time. As an astronomer he was one of the eight learned men who were employed by Malik Shah to reform the Calendar, and who established the Gelalæan or Jaláli era: all errors either past or future were corrected, says Gibbon, by a computation of time which surpasses the Julian and approaches the accuracy of the Gregorian style. As a poet, he has bequeathed to the world his Rubáiyát, a gem of the finest water, which is now introduced to Englishmen by the poetical translation of an anonymous author.

The translator, who can hardly be too much congratulated on the excellence and elegance of his performance, prefaces it by a very interesting account of what is known concerning this Epicurean Persian philosopher, who, in Khorassan, two centuries before the time of Dante, could with such force of language and power of imagery express the ideas of a sceptical mind.

[Relates the story of the schoolboy pact and its aftermath from FitzGerald's Preface, partly by paraphrase and partly by direct quotation, and tells the story of his prophecy of his burial-place.]

Having thus been introduced to Omar Khayyám in his Persian home, we must in the next place proceed to consider the particulars of his work. It appears that, like many other prophets, the Tentmaker was not over popular in his own country, and has therefore been scantily transmitted abroad.

[Further paraphrase and quotation from the Preface on the manuscripts, on the parallel between Omar and Lucretius, on the form of the *ruba'is*, and on FitzGerald's selection.]

He has certainly achieved a remarkable success, and it would be difficult to find a more complete example of terse and vigorous English, free from all words of weakness or superfluity. The rhythm of his stanzas is admirable, and that with which the poem begins may be taken as a fair specimen of the pointed force with which he expresses himself:

[Quotes stanza I]

The only notice that we have seen of this English version is in the *North American Review*, where it is said that 'the translator is only to be called "translator" in default of a better word, one which should express the poetic transfusion of a poetic spirit from one language to another, and the representation of ideas and images of the original in a form not altogether diverse from their own, but perfectly adapted to the new conditions of time, place, custom, and habit of mind in which they reappear. . . . It is the work of a poet inspired by the work of a poet; not a copy, but a reproduction; not a translation, but the redelivery of a poetic inspiration.' There can be no shadow of doubt as to the merits of this poem, in the vigour of its language and the beauty of its imagery, whatever may be thought of the opinions which it expresses. And this leads us at once to the real controversy about Omar Khayyám.

While the English translator was engaged on his work, M. Nicolas, French consul at Rescht, was also occupying himself with the work of the Tentmaker, and published a very careful and very good edition of the text from a lithograph copy at Teheran, comprising 464 Rubáiyát, with a translation and notes of his own. While he and the Englishman are fully agreed as to the literal meaning of the original, they are quite at variance as to the inner meaning of it. The former, as we have seen, is content to look upon Omar as a merely sensual and material Epicurean, who, finding that his knowledge comes to nothing, and that all his science will not enable him 'to solve the riddle of this earth,' denies all that he cannot fathom, and proclaims aloud, 'Let us drink, for to-morrow we die.' M. Nicolas, on the other hand, takes him for a mystic, shadowing the Divinity under the names of Wine, Wine-bearer, &c., as Háfiz is supposed to do—in short, a Súfi poet like Háfiz and the rest. There is something analogous to this in the prologue of Rabelais, where, wishing to show that there was a vast amount of great value and secret meaning hidden under the jesting exterior of his book, he quotes the description of Socrates by Alcibiades, who compared the great philosopher to one of the quaint and ludicrous little boxes which were used to contain the most inestimable of essences and drugs. Rabelais devotes a considerable part of his book to the consultation of the subterranean oracle of the Holy Bottle, where the motto was 'In vino veritas,' and where the priestess whispered in the ear of Panurge to repeat:

> Bottle! whose mysterious deep
> Does ten thousand secrets keep,
> With attentive ear I wait;
> Ease my mind and speak my fate,
> Soul of joy, like Bacchus we
> More than India gain by thee:
> Truths unborn thy juice reveals
> Which futurity conceals.
> Antidote to fraud and lies,
> Wine that mounts us to the skies,
> May thy father Noah's brood
> Like him drown but in thy flood.

And after giving them the exquisite draught she finally dismissed them, saying, 'Now, my friends, you may depart, and may that intellectual sphere whose centre is everywhere, and circumference nowhere, whom we call God, keep you in his Almighty protection. When you come into your world, do not fail to affirm and witness that the greatest treasures are hidden under ground.'

Rabelais might have been well quoted by M. Nicolas in favour of his mystical interpretation of Omar Khayyám, who in one of his quatrains speaks of recommending wine as a means of raising, not of lowering himself, and in others as a means of acquiring truth.

In spite of Omar's frequent praises of the vine in an apparently material sense, it is highly improbable that he, the learned philosopher and astronomer, honoured by the highest confidence and favour of the great Malik Shah, should have been in reality a vulgar toper. It may be that he has two faces, the one literal and the other mystical: some of his tetrastichs seem only intelligible in the first sense, and others only in the second. The English translator is not convinced by M. Nicolas, but admits that it may be an open question how we are to understand such writers as Háfiz and Omar: we have only to substitute Dieu, Divinité, for Wine and Wine-bearer; and when we have done that with Omar we may, he says, 'proceed to the same interpretation of Anacreon, and even of Anacreon Moore.' Such mystical interpretations, however, ought to present no overwhelming difficulty to those who are content to see the Song of Solomon described and intituled in the Authorised Version as the Loves of Christ and the Church. Omar Khayyám speaks often enough of wine in a very unequivocal sense, at others he rather treats it as the wine that inspires truth and is given to us to gladden and strengthen man's heart. He says:

[Quotes stanzas LX–LXII]

Omar Khayyám has been charged with downright infidelity, and there is no doubt of the frequent audacity of his words; but we ought to remember that he was writing, more than 700 years ago, under the shadow of Persian Mohammedism, and saw through the errors of the popular faith, though he had no further revelation to substitute for it. It would be unfair to accuse of Atheism a man who, finding himself surrounded by falsehood and honestly labouring in the fields of scientific truth, was unable to arrive at the real solution of the mysteries of creation. As we find in *In Memoriam*—

> So runs my dream, but what am I?
> An infant crying in the night;
> An infant crying for the light,
> And with no language but a cry—

so we find Omar Khayyám singing:

[Quotes stanzas XXXIV–XXXVII, LI–LIII, LXXIII–LXXV]

Perhaps two of his most powerful verses are these:

[Quotes stanzas LXXI–LXXII]

The scepticism of Omar is but the 'old old story' clad in a more than usually poetical dress: it reminds us of the saying of a Frenchman, Royer-Collard, that philosophy is the art of tracing back human ignorance to its fountain-head: it has flowed down to us from the days of *Vanitas vanitatum*, in a continued succession till the day when our own Laureate set the great battle of the human soul before us in his poem of *The Two Voices*. The doubts and difficulties of thinking and intelligent man are there set forth in much the same way as in the verses of the old Tentmaker. Tennyson there says, through the medium of the evil voice which tempts man to despair and suicide, in consequence of his inability to arrive at the absolute knowledge of truth:

> To which he answered scoffingly;
> Good soul! suppose I grant it thee,
> Who'll weep for *thy* deficiency?
>
> Or will one beam be less intense,
> When *thy* peculiar difference
> Is cancelled in the world of sense?

Omar Khayyám by way of anticipation, seven centuries ago, said what our translator puts as follows:

[Quotes stanzas XLVII–XLVIII]

It is the scepticism of a man who, after working through all the fields of science open to him, finds himself disposed to weep despairingly over the unsatisfactory result of human knowledge. Tennyson, in the masterly poem alluded to, was as unable as Omar to untie the knot in a logical manner; but, with the better light of modern thought to guide him, he cut it by an assertion of faith in the beauty and life and happiness of the world around him.

To the old Persian sage such a lofty stage of thought was perhaps impossible: he knew the difficulty equally well, but he was not prepared with such a happy solution of it. We must be content to admire his verses for their intrinsic beauty. The vigour of his thought and expression, and their harmony with much that is now going on around us, inspire us with a strange feeling of sympathy for him who in the darkest ages of Europe filled himself with all knowledge accessible to him before he went to his last sleep under the roses of Naishápúr.

The work before us is very short; and in spite of its beauty we must not indulge ourselves in quoting much more from it, great as would be the pleasure of doing so. We can but hope that many who have not yet heard of the Astronomer-Poet of Persia may take him and enjoy the many beautiful images with which he has in so

short a space presented them. But it seems impossible to conclude
without giving the last few of these charming verses:

[Quotes five concluding stanzas of poem in *1868*]

4. Review by H. Schütz Wilson, *Contemporary Review*, 27 (March 1876), 559–70

[Henry Schütz Wilson (1824–1902), author and critic, was, like Thomas
Hinchliff, a member of the Alpine Club, and it seems likely that the two
men shared their admiration for the *Rubáiyát*. Was Quaritch's faulty
memory or exaggeration responsible for the errors Wilson commits as to
the original edition ('unadvertised, and unnoticed, at the price of half-
a-crown' . . . 'one American bought two hundred copies')? At any rate this
is an early example of what Wilson himself calls the 'romance of bibliog-
raphy' associated with the work.]

> *"Lucretius, nobler than his mood,*
> *Who dropped his plummet down the broad*
> *Deep Universe, and said, 'No God.'*
>
> *Finding no bottom: he denied*
> *Divinely the divine; and died*
> *Chief poet on the Tiber-side*
>
> *By grace of God."*   E. B. Browning

Between the years 1050 and 1125 (the exact dates are not accurately
known) there lived in Persia one Omar Khayyám, Khayyám being
his *Takhallus,* or poetical name, and signifying tentmaker, who was
further known in his own day, and is known in our day, as the
astronomer-poet of Persia.

[Paraphrases biography of Omar from FitzGerald's Preface, including the
schoolboy pact and its aftermath.]

Contented with his modest competence and with his career of
science, disturbed by no yearnings of ambition, by no desire for
riches, Omar lived and died enjoying a great reputation amongst
contemporaries as the greatest sage in science of his land and time.

Had he, however, been merely a man of science, he would not much
have concerned us now. His science, superseded by later and better
knowledge, would have died with him, or might, at most, have been

faintly known to a few black-letter *savans* groping dimly in curious old Persian lore; but Omar has another reputation, somewhat slightly esteemed, indeed, by contemporaries, but very living at this far-off hour. He was also a poet. He may, indeed, in some respects be ranked amongst the first and greatest of poets. After so many centuries of oblivion, his work has recently been exhumed; and he, though dead, yet liveth, and will live. There were strong reasons, as we shall presently see, why his verses should have remained somewhat of a secret during his lifetime; but that secret is now an open secret for us. In order to estimate vividly the remoteness of the times in which he lived, considered with reference to Europe, it may be useful to remember that Omar's life extended over the Norman Conquest and the Crusades; that the curfew bell was tolling in England while Omar may have listened to the muezzin's call to prayer; that his time comprises the English kings from William I. to Henry II.; and that he was a contemporary of Thomas à Beckett and of Fair Rosamond. For the English reader, with whom we have now chiefly to do, these few landmarks of time will realize sufficiently the period in which Omar lived that inner life of thought and feeling which he poured into passionate poetry, full alike as of splendour, which, though little recognized in his own time, is yet eloquent and vital for ours. For it is his own deep, secret, inner life, his spiritual existence, his doubts, struggles, sorrows, deepest thoughts, that he sings of magnificently well. His poems are truly vital with the genuine records of a human soul which, though it existed in the far-off long ago, thought thoughts and felt feelings that we, and almost all men since, as before his time, have also had to entertain, to wrestle with, to conquer, or to be conquered by.

For our knowledge in England of Omar and his works we have to thank a thin volume, published by Bernard Quaritch. This work consists of a translation of 101 of the Rubáiyát, or verses, of the Persian poet; of a preface, and of notes to the poetry. This small work has undergone vicissitudes which make of the story of the book a romance of bibliography. Originally produced some fifteen years ago, unadvertised, and unnoticed, at the price of half-a-crown, the book did not sell at all; and Mr. Quaritch gradually reduced the price to a shilling, to threepence, and even to a penny, at which latter price some purchasers were found. By chance the work fell into the hands of competent judges, and the volume began silently and slowly to make its way among those who could critically estimate and enjoy it. It had a certain success in a small section of American society, and one American bought two hundred copies to give away to friends. Both in England and in America Omar won for himself friends and admirers, and his poems are now going through a third edition, which sells well at the price of seven shillings and sixpence. So much for the early fortunes of a translation, which now the world will not willingly let die. There will be, I think, more editions yet; but it may be here recorded that the work has not hitherto yielded any direct pecuniary return to the translator.

The translation appeared under the veil of an anonymous, but amongst the audience, fit though few, that such work found, the name of the translator became privately known; and I am now permitted to state publicly that the translator of Omar is Mr. Edward Fitzgerald.

The translation itself may justly be termed masterly; the preface and notes are decidedly the work of a thoughtful scholar. Mr. Fitzgerald has, as already stated, translated 101 verses, but he has by no means rendered the whole of Omar's poetical work. Of the MS. one copy is in the Bodleian, and contains 158 Rubáiyát; one is at Calcutta, and comprises 516 verses; Von Hammer has another copy containing about 200; while the Lucknow MS. is said to contain 400. This information we owe to Mr. Fitzgerald himself. He seems to have left untranslated all the amatory and sensual parts of the work, and to have devoted his attention chiefly to Omar's philosophy, and to those views of the relations of man to the Infinite which so deeply occupied that great wild heart. It is the soul's essence of Omar that Mr. Fitzgerald has delivered to us. He has most successfully reproduced for us, when reproducing Omar's song, that "something, as in the Greek Alciac, when the penultimate line seems to lift and suspend the wave that falls over in the last," and we may consider, with satisfaction and gratitude, that the verbal music, as well as the deepest meaning of Omar, is before us to delight us. The translation, indeed, reads like an original work, and that work the work of a poet. Eastern scholars vouch for the fidelity; every competent reader can certify the beauty of the thing translated, as of the translation itself.

Goethe maintains that all highest poetry can be translated; nay, that it is a note of the highest work that it has a vital force that will bear to be re-told in other tongues. Mr. Fitzgerald's admirable work is an illustration of the great poet-critic's theory. In the easy flow and nervous strength of his glorious verses, which seem owing to their very excellence, to be modern work—and his own work—we require to set our thought backward in order to realize the fact that we are face to face with the thoughts and imagery of a Persian poet of the eleventh century. All high abstract thought transcends the local and temporary. Omar has only so much of the East as lends colour to his imagery and magic to his music. The perennial essence of his song might belong to almost any country, and is scarcely limited by any particular century.

Thus much premised, in the way of needful explanation and information, we will pass on to an attempt to analyze these glowing and still vital verses, and to show, by sufficient extract, proof of their claim to the high character which they bear already in the estimation of the judicious few.

Omar is a sceptic, but he is no commonplace sceptic. His is no shallow and petulant negation. His doubts do not spring from thin and sour logic. He "denied divinely the divine." To be more accurate, he rather doubted than denied. He was full of that unconscious faith which complains to the Deity of its inability to comprehend the divine. His sense of the transient, his regretful protest against inscrutability, are deeply pathetic, are never irreverent. His was a sincere and earnest soul, profound in its dark depths, gay with sad humour upon its light surface. To him negation affords no repose; he does not rest content in it, but has to set the struggles of his soul to music, to express sorrow in song. He flies, defiantly, from the unrest of ceaseless questioning to Epicurean enjoyment; he seeks to drown doubt in the wine-cup, to stupefy mental yearning in the arms of beauty. He tries to employ his senses as allies to assist him in stilling the voice of the ever vainly searching soul. Love and wine are called in as narcotics to sooth restless attempts to solve the mystery of life and death, to read the riddle of the earth, to help him to bear the burden of this unintelligible world. His grief is that no thought, no effort of his, can pierce behind the veil. He does not deny the existence of the Divine Idea behind appearances; but he despairs because he cannot attain to any insight into thickly hidden things. Despair is commensurate with desire. He is not victor, but he never ceases to struggle and to long. He eats, drinks, and sleeps, because to-morrow he dies, and because he cannot recognize life through death. His doubts are the doubts which have perplexed so many noble thinking souls.

His is no poor, thin, incredulous soul; he is noble, deep, imaginative, and he pours out despair, depression, doubt, in the sadness and the splendour of his song. He is not complacent in doubt; he has nothing of the vanity of a little *esprit fort*. He burns to know, and, not attaining knowledge, his grief flows into deep and passionate musical utterance. His song suggests depths greater than he, with his rare lyrical gift, can get expressed; his plaint is sincere, his yearning is genuine. Towards the mass of men he affects a grave orthodoxy, but behind his loose Eastern sleeve he laughs in mockery—or sighs in melancholy. The Koran is to him a doubtful revelation, which does not explain the facts of life, and which leaves the great *why* of human life and death unanswered. He revolts against the dark mystery in which mysteries are shrouded; he resents the jealous care with which the great secret is kept so well. Like all men who possess deep and real humour he is also melancholy, thoughtful, profound; with a mind which cannot turn aside from revolving incessant question and feeling constant longing toward the Infinite. Forced gaiety does not silence restless cogitation, and Omar has to live lonelily his inner life of aspiration and disappointment. His temperament, like that of many poets, may have been pleasure-loving and sensuous, may have had varying moods and widely differing moments; but he turned defiantly to sensuality, he drank the forbidden wine, and revelled in the charm of woman, mainly as a palliative against the soul's unrest, chiefly in the hope of lulling that gnawing and eager doubt which led to no conviction.

Separated from Omar himself by so many centuries, and further divided from him by the great difference between the East and the West, by the differing habits of life and methods of thought and feeling which divide the Oriental and the Mahommedan from us in our European civilization, it is difficult to divine how far he may have been driven towards unbelief, or the want of belief, by the priesthood of his day and land. He could not have held priestcraft in any reverence or respect. He might temporize scornfully in order to live easily with the clergy, but it is most improbable that he should have had any belief in the order of the priesthood. In all times the great enemy of religion is the "religious world." To the true priesthood many indeed are called, but very few are chosen. Omar probably found no help from his priests towards answering the ardent importunity of the more urgent and hopeless of the "Two Voices" within his breast. He would turn contemptuously from priestly juggling and formal observance. His nature was too deep and real to be satisfied with the shows of things, or with mere hearsays. He longed to pierce to the very heart of the great mystery, and to look eye to eye upon a living deity; and he gazed hopelessly upon the inscrutable in deep and passionate dejection. His objective images of the transitory in human things belong to the finest utterances of poetry; this quest of light behind the veil has all the passion of emotion blended with and sinking into the repose of utter sadness. His was no light, trivial, querulous nature; he had a deep, earnest soul, which longed for light, and desired to believe. Hence the vital human interest of his song of sorrow and of doubt.

Many a small, dry, withered soul is rather pleased at, and vain of, its infidelity; but Omar is an instance of the almost unspeakable pathos of a man who gladly would, and yet who cannot fully believe, and comprehend, and trust. Unbelief, or failure to attain the comfort of conviction, affords no joy to him. He has to resort to active means, were it only dissipation or debauchery, to still or divert the unquiet cravings of a soul which longed for light, and desired ever a confidence which it yet could never obtain. Those inexplicable facts of life which appear to contradict the belief of man in the beneficence and tenderness of a living and ideal divinity sorely puzzled his will. He could not realize a divine government of the world by force, or law, or will. His is not the "mystic unfathomable song" of Dante, which is unfathomable because it deals with the mystery of affirmation. Omar's song is fathomable, because it is restricted to the blankness of negation, of nonentity, and fails to apprehend Divine significance in the relations between the Creator and the creature; but yet we may call it a real song nevertheless, since it is the product of a heart which is "rapt into true passion of melody," so that the "very tones of him become musical by the greatness, depth, and music of his thoughts." He recognizes the splendour, the wonder, and, almost, the terror that lie hid in the being of every man; but he cannot reconcile the mystic being of man with the holiness of sympathetic relation with God. He does not wish not to do so, but he fails, is unable so to think. Still, he is a genuine, true singer; if he cannot pierce through appearance to the inner truth, he can yet set his sad failure to most magnificent melody.

My attempt to analyze the essence of Omar's strife and song must now be tested by some quotations from his "Rubáiyát." I shall select some of those verses which convey his deepest meaning in most perfect music.

[Quotes extensively from *1868* text, with brief accompanying comments: stanzas VII–IX, XVII–XVIII, XXI–XXV, XXVII–XXXIII, XLVII, XLIX–LII, LIV, LXIII–LXXIV]

In another passage, Omar's instinct presages, and denies scornfully, the dark Calvinistic doctrine:—

LXXVIII.

"What! out of senseless nothing to provoke
A conscious something to resent the yoke
    Of unpermitted pleasure, under pain
Of everlasting penalties, if broke!

LXXIX.

"What! from his helpless creature be repaid
Pure gold for what he lent us dross-allay'd—
    Sue for a debt we never did contract,
And cannot answer—oh! the sorry trade!

LXXX.

"O Thou, who didst with pitfall and with gin
Beset the road I was to wander in,
    Thou wilt not with predestin'd evil round
Enmesh, and then impute my fall to sin!"

Again, Omar thinks out St. Paul's image of the potter—"Hath not the potter power over the clay, of the same lump to make one vessel unto honour, and another unto dishonour?"—and impugns the justice of the doctrine, as applied to human beings, in several fine quatrains.

One more characteristic verse will conclude my extracts:—

"O Thou, who man of baser earth didst make,
And ev'n with Paradise devise the snake;
    For all the sin wherewith the face of man
Is blacken'd—man's forgiveness give—and take!"

This verse shows, through doubt, a lurking trust in the divinity of Deity, and his usual strong repugnance to the popular priestborn forms of religious belief. Omar hated particularly the current sect of the Súfis, who seem to have been a somewhat hypocritical body, and to have veiled contemptuous unbelief under the most rigid formalism.

I have been guided, in my choice of extracts, by the principle which has actuated Mr. Fitzgerald in translating—that is, I have sought to present the passages which exemplify most clearly the heights and depths of Omar's philosophy. With a poet's love of beauty, Omar willed that his tomb should be "in a spot where the north wind may scatter roses over it;" and his pupil, Khwájah Nizámi, relates that he visited the poet's grave, and found it just outside a garden at Naishápúr, and saw that trees stretched their boughs over the garden wall, and dropped flowers upon the tomb, "so as the stone was hidden under them" And there the high-soaring, pleasure-loving, doubting poet slept fitly and well, and had, perhaps, beneath the roses, answer to his long, sorrowful doubts.

Doubt, like faith, is not always quite clear to its possessor. A man cannot always define the limits of his questioning, as he is frequently unable to define clearly the mysterious bounds of his belief. Omar, whose external form of revelation was the Koran, with Allah and his one prophet, became one of the sad, sincere inquirers whose cry is, "I would believe if I could." The intense longing of all genuine souls for light, for insight into the awful mystery of the Unseen, is sometimes answered so. There are doubts common to all thinking men—to all men who can think highly and deeply. Some of these men stop sadly at doubt, while others press on victoriously to light, and joy, and faith; and answer ultimately, after toil and storm, the awful mystery with a triumphant and "everlasting yea." The thoughts which seem so long to be "beyond the reaches of our souls," lead heroic souls to that pure white light of reason, and that glow of exalted feeling, which give a man conviction of his Maker. But Omar, with an intellect subtle and strong, with an imagination full of fire and fervency, with a poet's transcendental gift, remains, unhappy, on the shadow side of clear faith; but has yet expressed, with rare clearness and beauty, all the doubt which lofty natures feel. He who lived and sang so long ago, is only now flowering into fame. His thoughts about a problem which does not change with time seem very vital, and even very modern. It is the blank of negation set to sweet and subtle music; it is endless question sung in saddest but most splendid strains.

Omar could not lift the veil, but he has sung his inability in verses which must deeply touch the human heart. Even Lucretius, with whom Omar is most naturally compared, seems to me to be inferior in depth, in force, in beauty and glory of rhythm. The extracts which I have given will, I believe, send all my readers to Mr. Fitzgerald's charming book. They will be rewarded by finding, through his admirable translation, that they have learned to know a new and real poet in OMAR THE TENTMAKER.

5. Article by J.E.C., 'The True Omar Khayam', *Fraser's Magazine*, NS 19 (May 1879), 650–9

[Jessie Cadell (1844–84), Orientalist and novelist, was married to an Indian Army officer and lived for many years in Peshawur.]

That we have heard a good deal of late about Omar Khayam is not due, we fear, to any increase in the number of Persian scholars, but to the fact that the existing translation harmonises with a special phase of modern thought. It has been much read, and notices of it have appeared in different places, of which the earliest was one in *Fraser's Magazine* for June 1870. As very beautiful English verse, no one can doubt that Mr. Fitzgerald's *Khayam* fully deserves its fame. As a translation, we are less satisfied with it. While acknowledging that the translator has been on the whole successful in catching the sound of the Persian lines, wonderfully so in setting thoughts and phrases from the Persian in his English verses, we contend that this is hardly enough to satisfy us in the translation of a set of epigrams. It is a poem on Omar, rather than a translation of his work, and its very faults have, to English readers, taken nothing from its charm and added much to its popularity. Its inexactness has allowed for the infusion of a modern element, which we believe to exist in the Persian only in the sense in which the deepest questions of human life are of all time. Its occasional obscurity, too, has rather helped than hindered the impression of the whole. People expect obscurity in a Persian writer of the twelfth century—even like it—as it leaves dark corners which the mind can light up any way it pleases, and regard what it finds there as one of the peculiar beauties of Eastern thought. These points have less attraction for those who, knowing Khayam in the original, have learnt to value him for himself.

It is true that there are obscurities in the Persian, but they are in great part technical difficulties, natural enough in a work handed down for nearly eight centuries in manuscript, and which has been interpolated, imitated, and borrowed from to a truly marvellous extent. It is not always easy to know exactly what Khayam has said: but that known, there is not much difficulty in seeing what he means.

The position of Khayam among Persian poets is peculiar. Von Hammer speaks of him as 'one of the most notable of Persian poets, unique in the irreligious tone of his verses.' He died about a hundred years after Firdusi, and with him, according to the authority above quoted, closes the period of 'primitive purity in Persian verse.' He may be said to stand midway between the age of Firdusi, and that of the great Sufi poets. He still writes the pure simple Persian of the former, but he gives us no narrative poetry, and occupies himself with the problems of life and death, sin and fate, past, present, and future, which, dealt with unsatisfactorily to Persian minds by Mohammedan theology, gave rise to the mysticism of Attar, Jelal-ud-din Rumi and Sáadi. He is the sole representative of the age of free thought, which is said to be everywhere the forerunner of mysticism. Though he is certainly not orthodox, he seems to us more of a doubter than a disbeliever. He questions, mocks, and rebels, but produces nothing positive of his own. However, we are not in a position to say even this with certainty. He wrote very little, and that little has been so mixed up with later additions as to be difficult to recognise. What we feel most sure of, reads like the product of leisure hours: his moods vary, he is not always consistent; he will say the same thing in two or three shapes, or will contradict himself in quatrains which we cannot help believing to be genuine if there ever existed a Khayam. And though not much is known of his life, there is quite enough to establish his identity. He was an astronomer and mathematician, and his school-boy connection with Nizam ul Mulk, and Hasan ibn Sabbah, gave him a place in history. The *Calcutta Review* of March 1858 tells us all that is known of his life, which is repeated in Mr. Fitzgerald's preface: but his fame, which extends wherever Persian is read, rests on his poetry.

This consists only of rubáis, i.e. four-line stanzas or quatrains, from the Arabic numeral '*arba*,' four. There are great numbers of these current under his name, of which there seems no doubt that the larger portion are spurious. We have collected 1,040 of them from the material within our reach. The MS. copies are rare, both in Europe and the East, though some of the older MSS. are so short that they could be transcribed in a few hours by an apt penman. Still they are not as rare as Mr. Fitzgerald seems to consider. We have seen eleven MS. copies, of which seven are in England and four in Paris. Then there is M. Nicholas's edition of his text, published in Paris, 1868. Of these collections the smallest contains 158 rubáis, the largest 516. Some of the rubáis are mere paraphrases of one another, and some, not many, are repetitions; but after all possible weeding has been done, there will remain at least a thousand which we have collected from these MSS., and a few minor sources, claiming to be the work of Khayam. The opinion of those best qualified to judge would place the number of undoubtedly genuine quatrains at about 250 to 300. The copyists seem to have been calmly indifferent as to true or false readings. Helped very much by the fame of this particular poet, this has been for ages the common form of epigram in the East; and rubáis, scored by an imitator on the margin of one copy, have been included in the text of the next; or the copyist, if something of a poet, has thought well enough of work of his own as to give it the chance of immortality under the famous name. By some processes of this kind extraneous matter has been lent wholesale to Khayam, till the original is in danger of being lost in the mass of additions. On the other hand, we find rubáis previously known to us as Khayam's in the works of well-known poets, such as Hafiz (in Brockhaus's careful edition), Anwari, Sulman Savah Sáadi, and, above all, a mysterious person named Afzul Kashi, who in style and mode of thought has very much in common with Khayam.

Besides manuscript evidence, the tests most to be trusted are simplicity of language, perfection in rhythm and sound, and epigrammatic completeness. Khayam was a clear-headed person, and master of his own language in its best days, and we may discard rubáis at once when there is looseness of grip in the thought. We do not believe he wrote the following:

> Until the loved one gives me the soul-entrancing wine,
> The heavens will shower no kisses upon my head and feet.
> They tell me to repent, when repentance's hour shall come:
> If God Himself command it not, be sure I'll not repent.

Here the first two lines refer to divine ecstasy, and the last two are derived from a saying of Khayam, which we find in other places, that the command to repent and renounce wine, evil, or whatever it may be, must come from the God who made him and his fallible nature.

Each rubái is complete in itself, and has no connection with what goes before or follows after. The first three lines introduce the subject, and the fourth is thus described by Mirza Sáib: 'The last line of a rubái drives the nail through the heart.' They are arranged by the terminal letters of the rhyming word or phrase: all those ending in *a* are classed together, and followed by those in *b*. It occasionally happens that succeeding verses take up the same subject, but this is rare, and one is never a continuation of the other. We quote two from M. Nicholas:

227.

They have gone, and of the gone no one comes back
From behind the secret veil, to bring you word
That matter will be opened to your need, not prayer:
For what is prayer without faith and earnest longing?

228.

Go, thou, cast dust on the heaven above us,
Drink ye wine, and beauty seek to-day!
What use in adoration? What need for prayer?
For of all the gone no one comes back.

Here we have in the latter verse something very like a contradiction of the former, certainly written in a different mood, possibly by another hand. It is the last which has the genuine Khayam flavour.

Mr. Fitzgerald's No. 69 (of the 1872 edition):

Strange, is it not? that of the myriads who
Before us pass'd the door of Darkness through,
No one returns to tell us of the road
Which to discover we must travel too—

is rather the expression of an idea found in many rubáis than the translation of any one, and it lacks the point. It would be easy enough to put 'the door of darkness' into Persian, but we have not found it there. Khayam does not stop to wonder, but he does make some practical suggestions. He says in many shapes, 'While you live enjoy

all that is.' The following, which is as close as any to Mr. Fitzgerald,
may be taken as a specimen of the rest:

> Of all the trav'llers on that weary road,
> Where's one returned to bring us news of it?
> Take heed that here, in feigned goodness, you
> Pass nothing pleasant by—you'll not come back.

More interesting than parallels of this kind may be an examination
of what we have found in Khayam, with occasional references to
Mr. Fitzgerald. Our translations are as near as possible literal, and
come from what we believe to be the best reading of the given rubái.
We have not followed any one MS.

The leading ideas are pleasure, death, and fate, and his predom-
inant states of mind are the sensuous, the gruesome, and the rebel-
lious. He mocks, questions, laments, enjoys; is a person of varying
moods, strong feelings, and remarkable boldness; but he has some
sort of belief at the bottom of it all. He has no doubt about his enjoy-
ment of the pleasant things round him, while they last. He can chafe
against the sorrows of life and its inevitable end, the folly of the
hyprocrites, and the cruelty of fate; but he never doubts the existence
of an oppressor, nor questions the reality of sorrow any more than
that of death. He can feel strongly the charms of nature:

> The day is sweet, its air not cold nor hot,
> From the garden's cheek the clouds have washed the dew;
> The bulbul softly to the yellow rose
> Makes his lament, and says that we must drink.

Again:

> The new day's breath is sweet on the face of the rose:
> A lovely face among the orchards too is sweet;
> But all your talk of yesterday is only sad.
> Be glad, leave yesterday, to-day's so sweet.

This is on spring time:

> To-day, when gladness overpowers the earth,
> Each living heart towards the desert turns;
> On every branch shine Moses' hands to-day,
> In every loud breath breathes Jesus' soul.

Of these allusions, the hand of Moses signifies the white blossoms of spring, and the soul or breath of Jesus is His power of giving life to the dead—the shape taken in Persian by all metaphorical allusions to our Lord.

We find in the Persian other two variations of this; but we think it the best, and Mr. Fitzgerald has used it in the fourth of his stanzas:

> Now the New Year, reviving old desires,
> The thoughtful soul to solitude retires
> When the white hand of Moses on the bough
> Puts out, and Jesus from the ground suspires.

Here is another kind of pleasure:

> Drink wine, for it is everlasting life;
> It is the very harvest of our youth
> In time of roses, wine, and giddy friends.
> Be happy, drink, for that is life indeed.

Of the love verses of the collection the following are specimens:

> When my heart caught thy fragrance on the breeze,
> It left me straight and followed after thee.
> Its sad master it no more remembers.
> Once loving thee, thy nature it partakes.

> Each drop of blood which trickles from mine eye
> Will cause a tulip to spring freshly up,
> And the heart-sick lover, seeing that,
> Will get hope of thy good faith.

> For love of thee I'll bear all kinds of blame,
> Be woe on me if I should break this faith.
> If all life long thy tyranny holds good,
> Short will the time from now to judgment be.

> Love which is feigned has no lustre;
> Like a half-dead fire it burns not:
> Nights, days, months, years, to the lover
> Bring him no rest or peace, no food or sleep.

Both of these last might be claimed by those who hold the mystic interpretation of Omar's wine and love as proof of their theory. He certainly wrote little about love. His sense of the beauty of nature is marred perpetually by the thought of the death and decay in store for all.

> See the morning breeze has torn the garment of the rose,
> With its loveliness the nightingale is wildly glad.
> Sit in the rose's shade, but know, that many roses,
> Fair as this is, have fallen on earth and mixed with it.

Another in much the same mood:

> The cloud's veil rests on the rose's face still,
> Deep in my heart is longing for that wine.
> Sleep ye not, this is no time for sleep.
> Give wine, beloved, for there's sunshine still.

Wine is the favourite theme; we get wearied with the constant recurrence of the praise of wine, and with exhortations to drink and be drunken, through hundreds of musical lines; till at last, without agreeing with those who look on it all as simply a figure for Divine love, 'the wine of the love of God,' we come to regard it as representing more than mere sensual pleasure. We must remember that drinking had in the East at that time no vulgar associations. Wine parties were common in the houses of the great men, and in the courts of the princes. We have heard much of those of Harun-al-Rashid and the Barmakides, and we learn that such parties owed great part of their charm to music and song, witty talk, and sparkling verse. 'Vers de société' were then, and have always been, a rage in Oriental good society. These wine parties were in fact the nurseries of all the intellectual life of the time, which was unconnected with religion, and did much to counteract the dullness of orthodox Mohammedan life. So little growth to be got in what was lawful, it was small wonder that stirring minds turned from it; and as including so much else that they valued, we find these idolising the pleasure which seemed so fertile as a metaphor for the rest. This seems to us to account for a great deal of Khayam's wine. Still there are some good quatrains which seem undeniably mystic, and modern explanations given in the East point that way. But we do not believe that Khayam habitually used his own language in the strained and artificial sense of the great Sufi writers. We believe that, in as far as he was mystic, he was so at first hand, and was certainly much else into the bargain. We find the more mystic verses are generally those of least authority, and most of the genuine verses on wine are explicable on the hypothesis that it means social enjoyment. The reiterated 'Drink, you will sleep in the dust,' seems to show that the wine was something practical. 'Drink, the past day comes not back again;' 'time will not return on its steps;' 'other moons will rise;' 'no one stays or returns,' all this would be without point if the wine were some draught of love, or longing for the divine which might be enjoyed equally in any stage of being. The same may be said for the following: 'I am the slave of that coming moment when the Saki says, "Take another cup," and I shall not be able.' This moment is the hour of death, putting an end to human pleasure in whatever shape our poet cared most for it.

Khayam's view of death is coloured by a strong dash of materialism; whatever he may think, he talks of nothing but the death of the body—a kind of materialism common enough in Eastern thought, and which even its mystics never escape. In pious biography no spiritual grace is ever conferred without its visible sign—a fragment of dirty paper on which is inscribed the name of God, a piece of roast fowl from a master's mouth, a praying mat, a well-worn blanket—such are the media by which the highest spiritual graces reach the soul of man. No wonder that there should be confusion between seen and unseen; that Eastern mysticism is open to all sorts of interpretation, and that a shrewd, many-sided doubter like Khayam has been classed as a mystic while contemplating death mainly from the gruesome side of bodily corruption and decay.

He refers again and again to burial, the washing of the body, the making of the bier, the loosening of joints, the separation of the members, the mixing with earth, and the return to the elements—being used in the course of time by the builder and the potter to build walls, porticos, and palaces, to make jars, jugs, and pots: the future he contemplates with most complacency is that of returning to his old haunts and old friends in the form of a wine jug, when he is sure the wine will revive some sort of life in him. The grievance to him of death is not the dim future for his soul, but rather the leaving of pleasant things in his mouth and by his side. When he thinks of the future, death is no trouble to him:

> I am not the man to fear to pass away,
> That half to me better than this half seems;
> God as a loan my life has given me;
> I'll give it back when payment time shall come.

And another, which Mr Fitzgerald's readers will recognise:

> In the sphere's circle, far in unseen depths,
> Is a cup which to all is given in turn;
> Sigh ye not then, when it to thy turn comes,
> Its wine drink gladly, for 'tis time to drink.

Of these, the first is certainly genuine, the second doubtful. But there is very little of this strain in proportion to the talk about the decay of the body and its afterwards serving natural purposes:

> Wherever there is a garden of tulips or roses,
> Know that they grow from the red hot blood of kings;
> And every violet tuft which is springing
> From earth, was once a mole on some fair cheek.

Or this:

> As I mused in the workshop of the potter
> I saw the master standing by his wheel;
> Boldly we made covers and handles for his jars
> From the head of the king or the foot of the beggar.

The following is found in every MS. we have seen:

> To the potter's shop yesterday I went,
> Noisy or mute, two thousand pots I saw,
> There came a sudden shout from one of them—
> 'Where is the potter, the seller, the buyer of pots?'

We would draw the reader's attention to stanzas 82, 83 and 87 of Mr. Fitzgerald's translation, for which this one rubái, beat out thin and otherwise freely dealt with, has served as foundation. We have so far seen no other rubái we could connect with Mr. Fitzgerald's from 82 to 88 inclusive.

As another specimen of the way the translation has been made we quote two beautiful stanzas on this part of the subject—death and the future—though they have less to do with it in the Persian than in the English:

> 66.
> I sent my soul through the invisible,
> Some letter of that after life to spell,

And by-and-bye my soul returned to me,
And answered—I myself am heaven and hell.

67.

Heaven's but the bosom of fulfilled desire,
And hell the shadow of a soul on fire,
Lost in the darkness into which ourselves,
So late emerg'd from, shall so soon expire.

No. 66 is found in all the oldest MSS. we have seen in this shape:

On the first day, my heart above the spheres
Was seeking pen and tablet, hell and heaven,
Till the right-thinking master said at last,
'Pen, tablet, heaven and hell are with thee.'

No. 67 is also undoubtedly genuine, and, in its Persian form, found in every copy we have seen, with one exception:

The universe is a girdle for our worn bodies,
The Oxus but a trace of our blood-stained tears;
Hell is a spark from our senseless sorrow,
And heaven a breath from a moment of ease.

These translations are absolutely literal. We feel dissatisfied with Mr. Fitzgerald's verses, fine as they are, for in them we get some ideas the Persian lines do not contain, and lose many that they do.

The shadow on the darkness from which we have come and to which we shall return, we seem to have met with somewhere, but not in Khayam. We lose the 'right-thinking master,' who is a striking feature in the Persian in the one rubái, and in the other we lose the stupendous claim the Persian poet is making, as well as the peculiar beauty of what he has to say of heaven and hell.

After this we shall not expect much deference from Khayam to the religious system in which he had been educated, nor much recognition of eternal consequences to follow the keeping or breaking Mohammedan laws; what we wonder at is the heed he seems to take to them after all, and the presence of a rueful semi-penitent strain in some very authentic verses. It would seem that with all his boldness he never succeeded in convincing himself that he was in the right, and that his attitude of mind towards God, the law, and moral obligation, was that of rebellion, not negation. Hence what we have said about

Fate. One of his main ideas is Fate's cruelty, and his most frequent state of mind the rebellious. This is his originality; others have moaned and lamented, he attacks, and boldly. Fate is immutable; he says:

> Long, long ago, what is to be was fixed,
> The pen rests ever now from good and bad;
> That must be, which He fixed immutably,
> And senseless is our grief and striving here.

In a cruder form, 'whether you drink or not, if you are bound for hell you will not enter heaven.' Fate appears commonly under the title of the 'wheel of heaven,' and the doings of the wheel are very unsatisfactory:

> This tyrannous wheel which is set on high
> Has never loosed hard knots for any man,
> And when it sees a heart which bears a scar,
> It adds another scar to that sore place.

Again:

> Never has a day been prosperous to me;
> Never has a breath blown sweetly towards me;
> And never was my breath drawn in with joy,
> But the same day my hand was filled with grief.

But we doubt the authenticity of these; beside manuscript argument the tone is too much of a lament. Khayam prefers to accuse the wheel of being 'ungrateful, unfaithful, and unkindly.' In the following he deprecates its ill will in a whimsical style, of which we have other specimens:

> O wheel, I am not content with thy turnings;
> Free me, I am not fit to be thy slave.
> The fool and the unwise you favour most;
> Why not me too? I am not over-wise.

Fate favours fools, it is indifferent to the sighs of its victims, it rubs salt on wounds, it adds sore to sore, it delights in ruthlessly cutting short the moment when, by help of wine or love, a man has drawn in his breath in ease 'that breath returns not.' It is fertile in devices to cause and prolong suffering in life, and ever holds death as a final blow over every head—the one certainty amid the changing possibilities of both worlds.

About the origin of things, the only fact of which Khayam is quite sure is that they were not made to please him.

> About existence, O friend, why fret thee?
> And weary soul and heart with senseless thought?
> Enjoy it all, pass gaily through the world:
> They took no counsel with thee at the first.

Far better it would have been not to have come at all. 'If those who have not come only knew what we endure from life, they would stay away.' Again, 'We come with anguish, we live in astonishment, we go with pain, and we know not the use of this coming, being, and going.' Stronger even than the above is the following:

> If coming had been of myself, I'd not have come,
> Or, if going was of myself, I would not go;
> But, best of all if in this world of earth
> Were no coming, no being, no going.

He is sad enough, and we know of no outward cause for his sadness. When he speaks of his favourite wine, he says, 'Slander it not, it is not bitter: the bitterness is that of my life.' Though many of the moaning rubáis are interpolations (Khayam's style was rather bold than plaintive), it is he who cries out: 'Oh, oh, for that heart in which there is no burning!' and, 'As mine eyes are never without tears, I must either die or sorrow will overwhelm me.'

After this we must either suspect him of being sad for sheer idleness, or believe that he was oppressed by the awfulness and weariness of life and its mystery of evil to the extent of real suffering. His longings towards good were real and sincere; but meeting with death and sin, and making no more of them than other men, he was, perhaps, the readier to despair that he had put his estimate of the good in life very low. The pleasant thing he sings of could not help him much in lessening the pains of doubt, or in softening his discontent at the hypocrisy and wrong about him. He says:

> Of the eternal secret none has loosed the knot,
> Nor trod one single step outside himself.
> I look from the pupil to the master,
> And each one born of woman helpless see.

> From deepest heart of earth to Saturn's height
> I solved all problems of the universe;

> I leapt out free from bonds of fraud and lies,
> Yes, every knot was loosed but that of Death.

> Of the eternal past and future, why
> Discourse? they pass our powers of wit and will;
> There's nought like wine in pleasant hours, be sure:
> Of every tangle it doth loose the knots.

This last has the mocking tone in which he scouted at the learned of his day who chose to discourse of the past and future, of which they knew so very little. They might not unfairly retort that his wine and cupbearer had not saved him from the sorrows of life. However, he mocks on: it is his pleasure. He mocks at believers and unbelievers, priests and mystics; and when he comes to moral responsibility, he mocks at the God in whom he believes, as it were, in spite of himself. In the following quatrain he mocks at the Moslem Paradise:

> They tell us in heaven that houris will be,
> And also honey, sugar, and pure wine;
> Fill then the wine cup and place it in my hand,
> For better is one coin than boundless credit.

Here he uses the promise of the Koran as an excuse:

> We hear of houris in heaven and fountains
> That will run with honey and pure wine:
> If here we worship these, what is the harm,
> Since at the end of time we meet the same?

It is no inanimate wheel of heaven which is ultimately responsible for his sorrow, for he says, 'Do not accuse the wheel of causing joy and sorrow, good and evil, for verily it is more helpless than you are,' and he holds the Creator responsible for evil as for the rest.

> Some God has fashioned thus my body's clay;
> He must have known the acts I should perform:
> No sin of mine but comes from laws of his:
> What reason then for burning fires at last?

He asks what is evil? what is sin? The law taught him that some things were permitted, some forbidden; and he asks why? What is it that makes this action right and that wrong, when there is not much to choose between them, and when towards both he has the same strong natural desire, which after all seems so much more like a Divine command than the capricious utterances of the Mollahs. Still sin exists; he can but rebel; he can conquer nothing, not even peace of mind. He says:

> Abstain then from impossible commands.
> How can the soul triumph o'er the body?
> Wine is my sin, but so is abstinence forbidden.
> To sum all up, he says, 'Hold the cup awry, and spill it not.'

> What are we that he should speak evil of us,
> And make a hundred of each one of our faults?
> We are but his mirrors, and what he sees in us
> And calls good or evil that sees he in himself.

After this we can at least understand how it came to pass that Khayam was very miserable. We must now quote Mr. Fitzgerald:

78.

> What! out of senseless nothing to provoke
> A conscious something to resent the yoke
> Of unpermitted pleasure under pain
> Of everlasting penalties if broke.

79.

> What! from his helpless creatures be repaid
> Pure gold for what he lent us dross-allay'd,
> Sue for a debt we never did contract,
> And cannot answer. Oh, the sorry trade!

80.

> Oh Thou who didst with pitfall and with gin
> Beset the road I was to wander in,
> Thou wilt not with predestined evil round
> Enmesh, and then impute my fall to sin!

81.

> Oh Thou, who man of baser earth didst make,
> And e'en with Paradise devise the snake,
> For all the sin wherewith the face of man
> Is blacken'd, man's forgiveness give, and take!

Rebellious as Khayam certainly was, we do not think he went as far as this. Mr. Fitzgerald's stanzas 78, 79 are a free rendering of various things scattered through the Persian, which hardly have quite the same meaning in their own places, those we have recently quoted being the nearest we know to them. Khayam has at least the grace to be miserable, not jaunty, when he says: 'We are helpless: thou hast made us what we are—we sin—and suffer profoundly, but do not see any way out of it.' For the 80th we find the following:

> In my path in many places thou layest snares,
> Saying, I will take thee if thou put foot in one.
> No least atom of the world is empty of thy law;
> I but obey that law, and thou callest me a sinner.

We think the 81st is a misconception of the meaning of a Persian line. We speak under correction, for the readings of the various MSS. differ so greatly that this may be a translation of something we do not know; but we doubt it, as we seem to have the material of which the most important line was compounded.

We remember several quatrains on repentance. One is as follows:

> As this world is false, I'll be nothing else,
> And only remember pleasure and bright wine;
> To me they say, May God give thee repentance!
> He does it not; but did He, I would not obey.

Here we have the Mohammedan notion of repentance as the gift of God, and such repentance is strong on the practical side of the renunciation of evil. Khayam speaks of repentance as something outside him, but often adds that he would rebel against it if it were given him. Another on the same subject:

> May there be wine in my hand for ever,
> And ever love of beauty in my head.
> To me they say, May God give thee repentance!
> Say He gives it, I'll not do it, far be it from me.

The following is, we think, where Mr. Fitzgerald has got his line about forgiveness. We have no notion where the snake, Paradise, and blackened face may come from, they are not unlikely allusions, but we do not know them:

> Oh Thou, knower of the secret thoughts of every man,
> Thou in the time of weakness the helper of every man,

> O God, give me repentance and accept the excuse I bring,
> O giver of repentance and receiver of the excuses of every
>   man!

This last line Mr. Fitzgerald seems to have read—

> O repent ye and excuse thy self to every man—

a sense which we believe the Persian will not naturally convey; but we again remark that Mr. Fitzgerald may have had another quatrain or another reading of this. Khayam was bold enough at times, but we do not think he reached the point of offering forgiveness to God for man's sins. What we have just quoted is not bold at all, being evidently a prayer for a better mind. Its authenticity is doubtful, however. The following is a more trustworthy expression of Khayam's better mood:

> Ever at war with passion am I. What can I do?
> Ever in pain for my actions I am. What can I do?
> True thou may'st pardon all the sin, but for the shame
> That thou hast seen what I have done, what can I do?

Another:

> Though I've ne'er threaded thy obedience's pearl,
> And though through sin I have not sought thy face,
> Still of thy mercy hopeless am I not,
> For I have never called the great One two.

Here he hopes for mercy, spite of sin, because he has never attacked the unity of God.

Of course, in such a collection, much stress cannot be laid upon one or two quatrains, but there is much else to justify us in holding that our poet was not without some faith in God and duty. In many respects Khayam contradicts preconceived notions of Oriental character. Though fond of pleasure, he was not attracted by a sensual Paradise. He was not indifferent to death—he was not passive under the hand of Fate, or at all remarkable for resignation. He is a discovery, a light on the old Eastern world in its reality, which proves, as do most realities, different from what suppositions and theories would make them. Finally, though we have at times disagreed with Mr. Fitzgerald in reading Khayam, we are not much the less grateful for his poem and the introduction.

APPENDIX II

ALFRED TENNYSON, 'TO E. FITZGERALD'

[TENNYSON originally wrote this poem in early June 1883, intending it as an introduction to 'Tiresias'; the opening lines recall his last meeting with FitzGerald, in September 1876, when he and his son Hallam came to Woodbridge (see Terhune, pp. 320–2). FitzGerald, who died on 14 June, never saw the poem. After receiving the news, Tennyson added a concluding section, and when he published 'Tiresias' in 1885 the two sections formed a frame around that poem. The text here is that of the first edition. For the textual history of the poem, and notes on its personal and literary allusions, see *The Poems of Tennyson*, ed. Christopher Ricks, 2nd edn., 3 vols. (Harlow: Longman, 1987), iii. 105–10.]

> Old Fitz, who from your suburb grange,
>   Where once I tarried for a while,
> Glance at the wheeling Orb of change,
>   And greet it with a kindly smile;
> Whom yet I see as there you sit
>   Beneath your sheltering garden-tree,
> And while your doves about you flit,
>   And plant on shoulder, hand and knee,
> Or on your head their rosy feet,
>   As if they knew your diet spares
> Whatever moved in that full sheet
>   Let down to Peter at his prayers;
> Who live on milk and meal and grass;
>   And once for ten long weeks I tried
> Your table of Pythagoras,
>   And seem'd at first 'a thing enskied'
> (As Shakespeare has it) airy-light
>   To float above the ways of men,
> Then fell from that half-spiritual height
>   Chill'd, till I tasted flesh again
> One night when earth was winter-black,
>   And all the heavens flash'd in frost;
> And on me, half-asleep, came back
>   That wholesome heat the blood had lost,

And set me climbing icy capes
   And glaciers, over which there roll'd
To meet me long-arm'd vines with grapes
   Of Eshcol hugeness; for the cold
Without, and warmth within me, wrought
   To mould the dream; but none can say
That Lenten fare makes Lenten thought,
   Who reads your golden Eastern lay,
Than which I know no version done
   In English more divinely well;
A planet equal to the sun
   Which cast it, that large infidel
Your Omar; and your Omar drew
   Full-handed plaudits from our best
In modern letters, and from two,
   Old friends outvaluing all the rest,
Two voices heard on earth no more;
   But we old friends are still alive,
And I am nearing seventy-four,
   While you have touch'd at seventy-five,
And so I send a birthday line
   Of greeting; and my son, who dipt
In some forgotten book of mine
   With sallow scraps of manuscript,
And dating many a year ago,
   Has hit on this, which you will take
My Fitz, and welcome, as I know
   Less for its own than for the sake
Of one recalling gracious times,
   When, in our younger London days,
You found some merit in my rhymes,
   And I more pleasure in your praise.

['Tiresias' followed here: its concluding lines evoke 'those who mix all odour to the Gods | On one far height in one far-shining fire.']

   'One height and one far-shining fire'
      And while I fancied that my friend
   For this brief idyll would require
      A less diffuse and opulent end,

And would defend his judgment well,
　　If I should deem it over nice—
The tolling of his funeral bell
　　Broke on my Pagan Paradise,
And mixt the dream of classic times,
　　And all the phantoms of the dream,
With present grief, and made the rhymes,
　　That miss'd his living welcome, seem
Like would-be guests an hour too late,
　　Who down the highway moving on
With easy laughter find the gate
　　Is bolted, and the master gone.
Gone into darkness, that full light
　　Of friendship! past, in sleep, away
By night, into the deeper night!
　　The deeper night? A clearer day
Than our poor twilight dawn on earth—
　　If night, what barren toil to be!
What life, so maim'd by night, were worth
　　Our living out? Not mine to me
Remembering all the golden hours
　　Now silent, and so many dead,
And him the last; and laying flowers,
　　This wreath, above his honour'd head,
And praying that, when I from hence
　　Shall fade with him into the unknown,
My close of earth's experience
　　May prove as peaceful as his own.

EXPLANATORY NOTES

References to the 'Introduction' are to the introduction to this edition. FitzGerald's own introduction is referred to as the 'Preface'.

Explanatory notes relating to FitzGerald's endnotes do not occupy a separate section, but are given as part of the notes to the stanzas to which they are keyed: so, for example, the notes on endnote 11 will be found with the notes to stanza XVII.

For FitzGerald's English spelling and orthography, see the Note on the Text, pp. lviii–lix, and for his spelling and accentuation of Persian words and proper names, see the Note on Pronunciation, pp. lx–lxi. Spelling in FitzGerald's sources (e.g. d'Herbelot's Bibliothèque Orientale) has not been modernized.

[Preface]

3 *Title*: the title is the same as that of Edward Cowell's article in the *Calcutta Review*, which FitzGerald cites further on.

Hasan al Sabbáh . . . Synonym for Murder: referring to the (supposed) etymology of the word 'assassin' in English; FitzGerald is less certain of this derivation further on in the Preface.

Nizám al Mulk . . . the Crusades: this historical account is condensed from the article in the *Calcutta Review* which FitzGerald has not yet formally cited: see below. 'Alp the Lion' is Alp Arslan (1029–72), nephew, not son, of Toghrul Beg (*c*.990–1063; the relationship is correctly stated in d'Herbelot, p. 102); the 'feeble Successor of Mahmúd the Great' was Massoud; for Mahmud himself see notes to sts. X.4 and XLIV.

Vizyr: not recorded as a variant spelling in *OED*; it remained constant in all four editions, and appears in FitzGerald's letters (e.g. to Tennyson, 31 Oct. 1876, *Letters*, iii. 716). The more usual 'Vizier' is preserved in the extract FitzGerald goes on to quote from the *Calcutta Review*.

as quoted in the Calcutta Review: the anonymous article in vol. 30, no. 59 [Mar. 1858], 149–62 was by FitzGerald's friend and mentor in Persian, Edward Cowell (see Introduction, pp. xix–xx). The article begins by evoking 'the story of the crusades' and '*the old man of the mountains*,— that mysterious potentate, round whose inaccessible retreat hangs such a cloud of fable' (p. 149). Cowell's approach to Omar is made via this figure: 'how wide seems the interval between this man of blood in his mountain home, and a poet of Persia! It is indeed a strange piece of forgotten history, which thus joins two such different characters'. Cowell then fills in the historical background concerning the rise of the Seljuk dynasty, which 'caused the crusades'. He goes on: 'But the crusades were still future at the time our narrative opens. Alp Arslán, or Alp the Lion, was on the throne of his father Toghrul Beg . . . when three youths were studying together under the great doctor of Islam, Mowaffak of Naishápur' (p. 150). FitzGerald begins not with 'the old man of the mountains' but with a plain statement of the facts of Omar's life and death, which is oddly enough nowhere to be found in Cowell; he radically compresses Cowell's account of the historical context, which he does not in any case attribute to the *Calcutta Review* article, and he changes the emphasis from an opposition between two figures (the 'man of blood' and 'a poet of Persia') to a more complicated relationship between the 'three youths'. Once he begins to quote directly from the *Calcutta Review*, FitzGerald 'edits' the extract in his usual fashion, leaving out some material, rewriting and paraphrasing at will; and much of the information he gives outside the quoted passages also comes from Cowell. The story of the schoolboy pact cannot be historically accurate (Nizam ul-Mulk was thirty years older than the other two, and there is no evidence that Hasan studied in Naishapur); it may have arisen from the desire to connect three famous Persians who were 'in one way or another upholders of the Persian way of life and values' (Avery and Heath-Stubbs, p. 118).

3 *Mirkhond's History of the Assassins*: 'Mirkhond' is the Persian historian Muhammad ibn Khawand Shah ibn Mahmúd (1433–98); his account of the Assassins is contained within his monumental *Rauzât-us-safâ* [Garden of Purity].

4 *Hakim*: honorific title in Arabic, meaning 'the Wise'.

heretical in his creed and doctrine: it may seem odd that such a man should send his son to a great orthodox teacher; FitzGerald has omitted a passage which explains that Ali did this to divert suspicion from his heretical tendencies.

5 *Transoxiana*: the region to the east of the river Oxus (modern Abu Darya), roughly corresponding to Afghanistan.

disgraced and fell. FitzGerald omits the sentence which follows: 'His subsequent adventures are one of the romances of oriental history.'

the Persian sect of the Ismailians: the phrasing is ambiguous; the sense is 'the Persian branch of the Ismailian sect', not that the Ismailians were originally a Persian sect. The name derives from Isma'il, eldest son of Ja'far as-Sadiq, the sixth Shi'i Imam; their main base was in Egypt. In Persia their influence was opposed to the ruling Seljuk dynasty, which had adopted the Sunni form of Islam.

6 *it is yet disputed . . . founder of the dynasty*: the first of these theories is now generally accepted.

a yearly pension of 1,200 mithkáls of gold: a 'mithkal' or 'miskal' is a measure of weight of about 4.5 grams. In his letter of 23 December 1857 (*Letters*, ii. 306–7), FitzGerald asked Cowell about Omar's pension: one authority gave the sum as 2,022 mithkals, another mentioned a gift of land in Naishapur, and FitzGerald was taken with this latter idea: see note below.

7 *Merv*: or Meru, in modern Turkmenistan, an oasis-city on the ancient trade route known as the Silk Road; from the eleventh century a centre of Seljuk rule and famous for its commercial and cultural wealth; it was sacked by the Mongols in 1221.

says Gibbon: the remark comes in ch. 57 ('The Turks') of *The History of the Decline and Fall of the Roman Empire* (vol. v, 1788). Gibbon does not mention Omar, attributing the reform of the calendar to 'a general assembly of the astronomers of the East'.

entitled Ziji-Malikshahí," and the French: the double quotation marks here signal a suspension in the quotation from the *Calcutta Review*; everything from 'and the French' to 'and his Wine' at the end of the next paragraph is presented as though by FitzGerald himself, though in fact it is mostly a paraphrase of Cowell.

the French . . . Algebra: the translation was by F. Woepke, *L'Algèbre d'Omar Al-Khayyámi* (Paris, 1851); FitzGerald sent a copy to Cowell in May 1858 (*Letters*, ii. 315 and 316 n. 1).

These severer Studies . . . little else to record: the phrase 'severer Studies', taken with the phrase on p. 11 about Omar's 'Mathematic Faculty . . . which regulated his Fansy', echoes Cowell's remark in the *Calcutta Review* that Omar offers 'an example of the perfect compatibility of the severest studies in the exact sciences with that play of fancy and delicacy of feeling which we associate with the poet' (pp. 153–4). The substance of the remark about Omar's uneventful life is also Cowell's: 'Of the particular incidents of his life we know little enough, but probably there was little to know. A life, like his, spent in quiet toil, "And hiving knowledge with each studious year," leaves little for the chronicler to record' (pp. 152–3; Cowell is quoting Byron on Gibbon, *Childe Harold's Pilgrimage*, iii, st. 107).

Perhaps he liked . . . his Wine: cp. the letter to Cowell cited above, in which FitzGerald relishes the idea that Omar might have been rewarded in land as well as money: 'Now if there be this *Land* also, it is not only a pleasant addition to his Story, but explains somewhat the constant لب کشت in his Quatrains:—the side of the "Arable" where he wished to lie with his book, and a Bit of Mutton, and a moderate Bottle of Wine.' See sts. x–xi of the poem.

Diwán: collection, volume; Cowell uses the term in his *Calcutta Review* article, in his translation of the Persian original of st. xi.

8 *Sirname*: this spelling was becoming rare in the nineteenth century but is common in the literature of the seventeenth and eighteenth centuries, FitzGerald's favourite reading.

the following whimsical lines: Cowell's translation of No. 22 in the Ouseley MS (Heron-Allen 1898, p. 4).

one more anecdote . . . prefixed to his poems: Cowell transcribed this anecdote from the preface to the Calcutta MS, and sent it to FitzGerald in his first letter from Calcutta, written shortly after his arrival there in November 1856 (Arberry, pp. 49–50).

8 *Hyde's Veterum Persarum Religio*: Thomas Hyde, *Historia religionis veterum Persarum* (1700); the Latin text is reprinted in Decker (pp. lxvii–lxviii). Like d'Herbelot (see next notes) Hyde follows the story of Omar's burial-place with that of his mother's dream, and gives a Latin version of the quatrain which FitzGerald later included in the Preface in *1868* (see Variants, p. 66).

D'Herbelot alludes to it in his Bibliothèque: Barthélemy d'Herbelot, *Bibliothèque orientale ou Dictionaire universel contenant généralement tout ce qui regarde la connaissance des peuples de l'Orient* (Paris: Compagnie des Libraires, 1697). 'This erudite, discursive, and vastly entertaining work is said to have been written first in Arabic and translated into French for printing' (Sir Paul Harvey and J. E. Heseltine (eds.), *Oxford Companion to French Literature* (Oxford: Clarendon Press, rev. edn. 1969)).

[FitzGerald's footnote] D'Herbelot's entry (pp. 993–4) begins: 'KHIAM. Nom d'un Philosophe Musulman qui a vécu en odeur de Sainteté dans sa Religion, vers la fin du premier, & le commencement du second Siècle de l'hegire [Name of a Muslim Philosopher who lived, with a reputation for holiness in his religion, towards the end of the first, and beginning of the second, century of the Hegira]'. D'Herbelot then relates the story of Omar's prophecy of his burial-place, adding one important detail to the account cited in the *Calcutta Review*, about Omar's claim to foreknowledge being in opposition to the Koran. He follows this with the story of Omar's mother's dream (see above). FitzGerald telescopes 'dans sa religion, vers la fin' to 'dans la Fin'; see Variants, p. 66. By omitting 'de l'hegire' at the end, FitzGerald misleadingly suggests that d'Herbelot's dating is wildly inaccurate (the Hegira, the date of Muhammad's journey from Mecca to Medina which marks the beginning of the Muslim calendar, took place in AD 622; d'Herbelot is out by a couple of centuries, not eight). FitzGerald then jokes that 'odeur de sainteté', which means literally 'odour of sanctity', might correspond to Omar's wish that his remains should be scented with wine, and he refers the reader to his own text—but gives the wrong stanza numbers. The first edition only goes up to 75; FitzGerald means nos. 67 and 68 (LXVII and LXVIII, p. 66). The joke was dropped in subsequent editions.

FitzGerald had registered puzzlement at d'Herbelot's description of Omar in a letter to Cowell of February 1857: 'look for "Khiam" in your d'Herbelot, and see your story in *his* Version—"qui a vécu en l'odeur de Sainteté dans sa Religion?" I *suppose* this is our Omar since the Flower story goes with him; but here is a different version of Omar's Orthodoxy' (*Letters*, ii. 254). He returned to the subject in a letter of 23 December: 'I think D'Herbelot's notion of Omar being a *Saint* rises from that Story which Nizámí tells (and D'Herbelot quotes) about Omar's Tomb covered with Flowers' (*Letters*, ii. 307).

9 *without fear of Trespass*: FitzGerald has, so far, cited only matters of information, not interpretation. What follows is more polemical, and FitzGerald knew that his view of Omar would not appeal to Cowell.

Epicurean Audacity of Thought and Speech: see Introduction, p. xxv.

the Súfis: so-spelt here; in st. LV 'Sufi'. In his article 'Háfiz, the great lyric poet of Persia', published in *Fraser's Magazine* in September 1854, Cowell defines Sufi doctrine as FitzGerald understood it, and as it applies to the supposed mystical interpretation of his poems:

> sufeyism is a form of that Pantheism which has been native to the dreamy East from the earliest times of Gentile history. But the purer creed of Mohammedanism, as compared with idolatry, has exercised a most beneficial influence on its development . . . The world, say the Sufis, and the things of the world are not what they seem; our life here is a fall and a ruin; for the soul has once been absorbed in God, and only in re-absorption can one hope to find rest. All its higher aspirations here, as it vaguely expresses them in heroism, poetry, or music, are unconscious yearnings after its better home; and in the odes of Sufeyism these unconscious feelings and dumb longings are supposed to find their utterance. Human speech is weak and imperfect, and can only express these deeper emotions by images drawn from the sensuous and temporal. Hence arises the two classes of Sufi metaphors, those drawn from wine and those from love. Thus in some odes wine is the love of God, and ebriety represents religious ardour and abstraction from earthly thoughts; in others, which apparently express the joys and sorrows of an earthly passion, the beloved object in reality means the Deity; and all the woes of separation and hopes for reunion with which they are filled, shadow forth the soul's spiritual exile, and its longings for the hour of re-absorption into the Divine Nature.

FitzGerald had reservations about the application of this allegorical system to Háfiz (see below), and he was confident that it did not apply to Omar. Here he had support from Cowell himself, at least at this date; in his *Calcutta Review* article Cowell stated that 'Omar was no mystic,—we find no trace of Sufeyism in his book. His roses bloom in an earthly summer, his wine is of mortal vintage; unlike all other Persian poets, every thing with him is real and concrete' (p. 157). FitzGerald borrowed and expanded the last sentence: see below.

In the second edition FitzGerald considerably expanded his discussion of Omar's attitude to the mystical philosophy of Sufism, through an attack on the French scholar J. B. Nicolas: see Variants (pp. 69–73). For a concise and helpful account of Sufism and the historical Omar Khayyám, see Avery and Heath-Stubbs, pp. 13–18.

Their Poets: i.e. the poets of Sufism.

9 *Háfiz*: celebrated fourteenth-century Persian poet; FitzGerald read him in
the early period of his Persian studies, well before he encountered Omar.
In a letter of 8 June 1854, written while he was staying with Tennyson at
Farringford, he told Cowell that he and Tennyson had been 'trying at
some Háfiz' together in an anthology of Persian verse, and that Tennyson
would 'only look at Háfiz—in whom he takes interest' (*Letters*, ii. 131).
Háfiz's poems about wine and sensual pleasure are as frank as Omar's, and
at times his outlook is identical: 'The season of spring has arrived:
endeavour now to be merry and gay while thou art able; for the roses will
bloom again and again, after thou art laid under the sod.' Binning (whose
translation this is) also expresses scepticism about Háfiz's mysticism; he
remarks of another of the poems he translates: 'Spiritual meaning it may
have for aught I know; but I am too obtuse to discover any' (Binning,
i. 256, 259). It suited FitzGerald to characterize Háfiz here as either a
convinced Sufi, or a hypocritical juggler; in the second edition he repeats
the charge that Háfiz copied Omar, but he also declared that he had 'never
wholly believed in the Mysticism of Háfiz' (see Variants, pp. 90 and 72),
and this is confirmed by his letter to Cowell of March 1857: 'I am sure
what Tennyson said to you is true: that Háfiz is the most Eastern—or, he
should have said, most *Persian*—of the Persians. He is the best repre-
sentative of their *Character*, whether his Saki and Wine be real or mysti-
cal . . . Háfiz, and old Omar Khayyám ring like true Metal' (*Letters*,
ii. 261–2).

Firdúsi: also Firdausi, Firdowsi (*c*.940–1020), author of the *Shah Namah*
(Book of Kings), the Persian historical and mythological epic whose pres-
tige (equivalent to that of Homer in Western culture) survived accus-
ations that its author was sympathetic to Zoroastrianism, the older,
pre-Islamic religion of Persia (see below); the *Shah Namah* and the 'old
Fire-worshipping Sovereigns' are mentioned again in FitzGerald's note
11 on Persepolis (pp. 56–7).

10 *Sáki*: cupbearer; the term occurs frequently in the Persian text, and can
apply either to a male or female figure; FitzGerald does not use it in the
first edition of the poem, but it does appear in a stanza added in the
second edition (see Variants, p. 78).

11 *Fansy*: this spelling was already archaic in the period; *OED*'s last citations
are from the mid-eighteenth century.

the Greeks were Children in Gossip: Acts 17: 21: 'For all the Athenians and
strangers which were there spent their time in nothing else, but either to
tell, or to hear some new thing.'

what does Persian Literature imply but a Second Childishness of Garrulity?:
FitzGerald makes the same point in the preface to *Salámán and Absál*, in
the form of a letter addressed to Cowell, explaining the need for selection:
'Jámí, you know, like his Countrymen generally, is very diffuse in what
he tells and his way of telling it.' Cowell himself makes the point in his
article in the *Calcutta Review*: 'Every other poet of Persia has written too

much,—even her noblest sons of genius weary with their prolixity. The language has a fatal facility of rhyme, which makes it easier to write in verse than in prose, and every author heaps volumes on volumes, until he buries himself and his reader beneath their weight. Our mathematician is the one solitary exception. He has left fewer lines than Gray' (p. 154). For the phrase 'fatal facility', see below.

no ungeometric Greek was to enter Plato's School of Philosophy: according to legend the inscription above Plato's door at the Academy in Athens read 'ἀγεωμέτρητος μηδεὶς εἰσίτω' ('Let no one enter who does not know geometry').

"fatal Facility": a double quotation; used by Cowell in his *Calcutta Review* article, but originally from Byron's preface to *The Corsair* (1814): 'Scott alone, of the present generation, has triumphed over the fatal facility of the octo-syllabic verse.'

before the native Soul . . . foreign Conquest: FitzGerald would have found this common view of Persian history in Binning, among other sources. Binning describes the fall, in the seventh century AD, of the 'last of the genuine Persian monarchs' to 'the ferocious Arabs, brimfull of zeal in their new religion . . . Islâm was established upon the ruins of the fire-temples' (Binning, ii. 246).

who scorned . . . came clothed: Firdusi boasted in the *Shah Namah* that his thirty years' work on the poem revived the old Persian language; as he put it, he 'gave life to the Ajam' (meaning 'the illiterate', a term applied by the Arabs to their Persian subjects). But he did not, as FitzGerald implies, use Persian in order to turn his back on Islam. In a letter to Elizabeth Cowell of 24 January 1854, FitzGerald wrote: 'I have bought the Firdusí from Quaritch: and shall have some desire to read some pure Persian. For the Arabic words seem to me the ugly ones, though perhaps needed to give muscle to the Persian' (*Letters*, ii. 119).

Zerdusht: alternative form of Zoroaster.

The MSS. of his Poems . . . Oriental Transcription: for the manuscripts on which FitzGerald based his translation, see Introduction (pp. xx, xxiii), and note the expansion of this portion of the Preface in subsequent editions. FitzGerald's information about the 'average Casualties of Oriental Transcription' derives from authorities such as Ousely: 'Before the true sense of a single passage can be ascertained, it is often necessary to examine most attentively, several copies of the same work; each perhaps, furnishing a variety of readings; some half corroded by time, or nearly illegible through accidental injury; others written in a difficult or uncouth hand; or deficient in those diacritical points which so essentially regulate the orthography of proper names; and on which, indeed, the meaning of a whole passage frequently depends' (preface to vol. i, pp. viii–ix). Binning (i. 311–12) distinguishes between MSS transcribed in Persia and India, the former being 'always far more accurate'; this is certainly the case with the two MSS on which FitzGerald relied, the (Persian)

Ouseley MS and the Calcutta MS. Indian scribes, according to Binning, are ignorant of Persian and alter the text at will: 'When a work thus garbled, is put into the hands of an ignorant copyist, one may imagine what a mutilated production will be the result of his labours.' Later in the book he speaks of 'the carelessness of copyists' in relation to the text of Firdusi's *Shah Namah*, which has become 'much corrupted by errors, interpolations, and omissions' (ii. 387).

12 *the India House*: East India House, in Leadenhall Street in the City; headquarters of the East India Company, which had a large collection of Oriental MSS. Cowell had studied there and knew the Librarian personally (*Life of Cowell*, p. 58). By the time the poem was published the Company had lost its political power in the aftermath of the Indian Mutiny of 1857, and East India House itself was pulled down in 1862; however, this reference remained unchanged in successive editions.

One in the Asiatic Society's Library of Calcutta: FitzGerald learned of the existence of this MS from Cowell soon after Cowell's arrival in Calcutta in November 1856: 'Yesterday I went to the Kiblah—the library of the Royal Asiatic Society & hunted up Omar Khayyam. They have only *one* MS, & that an imperfect one, so you may judge how rare the book is' (Arberry, p. 48).

We know but of one in England . . . double that Number: paraphrasing Cowell's note in his *Calcutta Review* article, which FitzGerald cites in his own footnote (see below) as though he had not taken this information from it as well. The printed edition to which Cowell refers does not in fact constitute an independent source, but was based on the Calcutta MS.

a Tetrastich . . . taken out of its alphabetic order: a 'tetrastich' is a four-line stanza. Only later in the Preface does FitzGerald explain the prosodic form of the *ruba'i* and the mode of arrangement in the Persian manuscripts.

The Scribes, too . . . execrate himself: FitzGerald expanded this comment (and moderated its tone) in *1868*, including translations of the two opening quatrains to which he alludes here: see Variants, p. 67.

13 *Both indeed men*: with 'were' understood; an elision, not a misprint (unchanged in all editions).

who yet fell . . . a Law to themselves: FitzGerald refers to pre-Christian philosophers and poets whose spiritual and moral code was founded on a 'better Hope' for human life than sceptics such as Lucretius and Omar, even though they could not base this hope on the 'better Faith' of Christianity. Socrates was often cited as a precursor of Christian thought, a parallel strengthened by the sacrificial manner of his death; and the traditional reading of Virgil's Fourth Eclogue as a prophetic intimation of Christ, though under increasing attack from classicists, was still widespread. FitzGerald's concession to the superiority of Christianity may be a placatory gesture towards Cowell, to whom he had written on 8 December 1857: 'I think these free opinions are less dangerous in an old

Mahometan, or an old Roman (like Lucretius) than when they are returned to by those who have lived on happier Food' (*Letters*, ii. 305). In his *Calcutta Review* article, Cowell wrote of Omar: 'Like the Roman Lucretius, his very science leads him astray; he has learned enough to unsettle his ancient instincts, but not enough to rebuild them on a surer basis . . . he proceeded from the gods of mythology to demolish the very idea of a Providence at all' (p. 158).

Lucretius, indeed . . . mechanical Drama of the Universe: in *De Rerum Natura* Lucretius argues that the universe was not created, but came into being through the random collision of atoms, and that natural laws accounted for all phenomena. FitzGerald's phrasing paraphrases Cowell's censure of Lucretius' 'self-acting system' in his *Calcutta Review* article (p. 159).

himself and all about him . . . the outer Sun: the sense is that Lucretius was blinded by the contemplation of material phenomena to the existence of a transcendent divine principle. The description of the Roman theatre is in Bk. 4 of *De Rerum Natura*, in a passage describing how the surfaces of things 'throw off' thin films of matter: 'Awnings do this, yellow and red and purple | Spread over a great theatre, for all to see, | On posts and beams, flapping and billowing; | For then the great assembly massed below, | The scenes on the stage, the grandees in their boxes, | They dye, and make to glow and flow with colour' (ll. 74–80). In a letter to Elizabeth Cowell of 24 March 1851, FitzGerald wrote: 'I am reading Lucretius again, tell Cowell: who steeps my soul in a sort of gloomy colour, as that Veil he tells of coloured the pit of the Roman Theatre' (*Letters*, ii. 25).

nothing more than hopeless Necessity: FitzGerald claims that Lucretius was a determinist, whose system disallowed free will.

their insufficient glimpses: i.e. the 'glimpses' (insights) afforded by Omar's 'Genius and Learning'; the sense is that his intelligence enabled him to demolish the illusions and false consolations of religious belief in his own day, but not to replace them with Christian truth.

only diverted his thoughts . . . Annihilation: echoing Cowell, again, in the *Calcutta Review* (pp. 159–60): 'Fate and free will, with all their infinite ramifications and practical consequences,—the origin of evil,—the difficulties of evidence—the immortality of the soul—future retribution,—all these questions recur again and again. Not that he throws any new light upon these world-old problems, he only puts them in tangible form, condensing all the bitterness in an epigram.' But FitzGerald's term 'divert' may also recall the attempt by Milton's fallen angels to distract themselves in hell: 'Others apart sat on a hill retired, | In thoughts more elevate, and reasoned high | Of providence, foreknowledge, will, and fate, | Fixed fate, free will, foreknowledge absolute, | And found no end, in wandering mazes lost' (*Paradise Lost*, ii. 557–61).

14 *such Stanzas as the following*: transferred to the main text of the poem in subsequent editions: see Variants (p. 68). The Persian original of this

stanza was one of those translated by Cowell in the *Calcutta Review*, and Cowell remarks that it is one of 'a few rare tetrastichs' in which Omar's 'own genius . . . overmastered his habits, and wrung unwonted aspirations perforce from his lips' (p. 156).

14 *in this Clay Suburb*: as Arberry (p. 191) suggests, Tennyson may have recalled this phrase when he described FitzGerald's house, Little Grange, as a 'suburb grange' ('To E. FitzGerald', l. 1; see Appendix II, p. 134).

With regard to the present Translation: the explanation that follows of the metre of the original Persian poems is correct, but not easy to follow. Peter Avery offers this definition: 'The ruba'i, pronounced *rubā´ī*, plural *rubā´īyāt*, is a two-lined stanza of Persian poetry, each line of which is divided into two hemistichs making up four altogether, hence the name ruba'i, an Arabic word meaning foursome . . . The first, second, and last of the four hemistichs must rhyme. The third need not rhyme with the other three' (Avery and Heath-Stubbs, p. 7). FitzGerald did not invent the arrangement of the lines in quatrains; this was already a feature of European transcriptions of Omar.

Rubáiyát . . . musically called: the 'y' in FitzGerald's spelling replaces the Arabic letter ﻉ (ain), indicating a glottal stop (as in Cockney 'be'er' for 'better', etc.); the pronunciation should therefore be 'rubai´at'. (Information kindly supplied by Dick Davis.) Heron-Allen (1898, pp. xl–xli) objected to FitzGerald's transliteration, whose sound he thought 'spiritless and thin', and argued for 'rubaghyat', which 'conveys an idea of the rich sonority of the original'; he also disliked the use of the word in the title, which he claimed was the equivalent 'The Gedichte of Henry Heine'.

the Greek Alcaic: a strophe consisting of two 11-syllable lines and a third line, itself often divided into two so as to create, in effect, a quatrain; Roman poets who adopted this form, such as Horace, seem to have thought of it as a four-line stanza.

Grave and Gay: the pairing was proverbial; compare Browning's 'A Toccata of Galuppi's' (*Men and Women*, 1855), a poem which like the *Rubáiyát* evokes the intensity, and transience, of earthly pleasure: 'Brave Galuppi! that was music! good alike at grave and gay!' (l. 26).

something of an Eclogue: in his letter to Cowell of 2 November 1858 FitzGerald called the selection of quatrains he had sent to *Fraser's Magazine* 'a sort of Epicurean Eclogue in a Persian Garden'. The term connects the Persian landscapes of the *Rubáiyát* (e.g. sts. x–xi) with classical pastoral poetry of the Western tradition (Theocritus in Greek, Virgil in Latin). The classical eclogue has a dramatic form, either dialogue or soliloquy, and though spoken by 'low' or rustic characters, was a vehicle for sophisticated criticism of art and society. FitzGerald may have known the etymology of the word, which comes from a Greek word meaning 'to choose' and originally designated a selection from a larger work, which would also fit the sense here. (Information from Alex Preminger and T. V. F. Brogan (eds.), *New Princeton Encyclopedia of Poetry and Poetics* (Princeton: Princeton University Press, 1993), 317.

15 *"Drink and make-merry,"*: see note to st. XXXIX.3.

Oliver de Basselin: more correctly Olivier Basselin; 'a 15th-century fuller of Vire in Normandy, reputed author of drinking-songs, which were current in the *vau* or valley of the river Vire. They were known in consequence as *vaux-de-vire*, a name which was corrupted into *vaudeville*' (Harvey and Heseltine (eds.), *Oxford Companion to French Literature*). In a letter to Cowell of 9 November 1849 FitzGerald wrote: 'Have you got the Poems of Oliver de Basselin, the old Norman Anacreon and Vaudeville-ist? I have been reading some of his songs' (*Letters*, i. 655). He copied out one of these songs in his letter to Cowell of 10 May 1850, whose first stanza anticipates the 'philosophy' of the *Rubáiyát*: 'On plante des pommiers ès bords | Des cimetieres, près des morts, | Pour nous remettre en la memoire | Que ceux dont là gisent les corps | Ont aimé comme nous à boire' [We plant apple trees by the side of graveyards, near to the dead, to remind us that those whose bodies lie there liked, as we do, to drink] (*Letters*, i. 670). In April 1853 he ordered a copy of Basselin's works from Quaritch (*Letters*, ii. 87), and in the letter to Cowell of May–June 1857 in which he first mentioned his 'Monkish Latin' versions of Omar (see Introduction, p. xxxiv), he wrote: 'Poor Fellow; I think of him, and Olivier Basselin, and Anacreon; lighter Shadows among the Shades, perhaps, over which Lucretius presides so grimly' (*Letters*, ii. 273). The lyrics of the Greek poet Anacreon (6th century BC) were models of the poetry of love, wine, and the brevity of life. See also the note on 'Anacreon Moore' in the Preface to *1868* (Variants, pp. 73–4). FitzGerald dropped this allusion to Basselin in subsequent editions.

fell back upon TODAY . . . under his Feet: the metaphor responds to Cowell in the *Calcutta Review*: 'he plants his foot on the *terra firma* of to-day, and builds on it as if it were rock, and not a quick sand' (p. 155).

[*The Poem*]

Title: the form of the title here, identifying Omar Khayyám as 'of Naishápúr', differs from that on the original title page, where he is 'the Astronomer-Poet of Persia'.

I–III. Referring to the page layout of the fourth edition, FitzGerald wrote to Quaritch: 'Omar's first three Stanzas should contrive to go on his first page: they are the "Lever de Rideau" [curtain-raiser] as it were' (21 January 1879, *Letters*, iv. 176). This had been the case in *1859* and *1868*, but *1872* (from a copy of which *1879* was set) has only sts. I–II on its first page. FitzGerald's instruction was followed.

I. An early version of this stanza, translated from no. 134 of the Calcutta MS (Heron-Allen 1899, pp. 4–5), appears in FitzGerald's letter to Cowell of 23 June–2 July 1857: 'The Sun has thrown the Noose of

Morning over the House-top; the *Rouge-faced* Day . . . has thrown the Pebble into the Cup.' FitzGerald expressed his delight in the latter image, which 'so smacks of the Desert Life' (*Letters*, ii. 280).

1.1 *Awake!* Decker ('Other Men's Flowers', pp. 219–20) cites a number of biblical texts beginning with this word, though none in the absolute grammatical form that FitzGerald uses here; some may have appealed to his sense of mischief, e.g. Joel 1: 5: 'Awake, ye drunkards, and weep; and howl, all ye drinkers of wine, because of the new wine; for it is cut off from your mouth.' The trope is common in poetry from the sixteenth century onwards but, again, almost always with a named object ('Awake my soul', 'my Muse', 'thou sluggard' etc.); a rare exception is 'Expostulation', a poem by FitzGerald's friend Bernard Barton, the 'Quaker Poet': 'Awake! arise! if not for love | Of duty's call, at least for shame' (pub. in *A Widow's Tale, and Other Poems*, 1827).

II.1 and endnote 2. The image of 'Dawn's Left Hand', and indeed the whole concept of the 'false dawn', are not present in FitzGerald's Persian sources; Arberry (p. 193) suggests that he derived it from an entry in his dictionary, but the endnote suggests a specific piece of information which I have not been able to pinpoint. The quotation in the endnote is from *Macbeth*, III. iv. 125–6: '[Macbeth] What is the night? [Lady Macbeth] Almost at odds with morning, which is which.'

IV.1 [endnote 3] New Year . . . helped to rectify: for Omar's role in the reform of the solar calendar under the Seljuk ruler Malik Shah, see Preface, p. 7. The Muslim calendar which eventually superseded the solar calendar in Persia (as in other cultures which were conquered by the Arabs, or whose conquerors converted to Islam) is a pure lunar calendar, of twelve months to the year, without intercalated days (which were forbidden by the Prophet); as a result, thirty-three Muslim years are roughly equivalent to thirty-two Christian ones. The festival of Nouruz is celebrated to this day in Iran on the first four days of the month of Färvärdin (= 21–4 March). (Information from Bonnie Blackburn and Leofranc Holford-Strevens, *Oxford Companion to the Year* (Oxford: Oxford University Press, 1999).) FitzGerald's adjective 'clumsy' was probably influenced by Binning: 'A more clumsy and ill-contrived mode of reckoning could scarcely be devised' (ii. 208).

IV.1 [endnote 3] a late Traveller in Persia: named in endnote 11 as Robert Binning, whose *Journal of Two Years' Travel in Persia* was one of FitzGerald's main sources of information; see Introduction, pp. xxxi–xxxii. FitzGerald characteristically 'edits' the passage (ch. xxvii, ii. 165–6) by omission (one sentence after the Shakespeare quotation, another after 'Watercourses') and paraphrase (the sentence 'The Nightingale . . . a North-country Spring' reworks Binning's material); he also introduces his own preferred initial capitals for nouns, something he did not do to Cowell's text from the *Calcutta Review*. Earlier in the chapter Binning describes the origin of Now Rooz as 'the beginning of the solar year of the old fire-adoring Persians' and says that the festival 'is still kept up, although the people have changed their calendar along with their religion' (ii. 160–1); in ch. xviii, in a discussion of the Persian calendar, he mentions the legend that the festival was instituted by Jamshyd (ii. 207). The Shakespeare quotation is from *Midsummer Night's Dream*, II. i. 109–11.

IV.3–4 and endnote 4. In Exodus 4: 6, God commands Moses: 'Put now thine hand into thy bosom. And he put his hand into his bosom: and when he took it out, behold, his hand was leprous as snow.' D'Herbelot's entry for 'Moussa' (i.e. Moses) was probably FitzGerald's source: Moses takes out his right hand 'aussi blanche que la neige & aussi claire qu'un astre, dont l'éclat faisoit impression dans l'air & sur la terre' [as white as snow and shining like a star whose radiance appeared in the sky and on the earth] (p. 648). Jesus breathes life into a bird of clay in the Koran (ch. 3), a miracle linked by one commentator to his resurrection of Lazarus (Heron-Allen 1898, p. 130). The image of Jesus' breath 'suspiring' (i.e. exhaling) 'from the ground', which derives from a mistranslation of the Ouseley MS (Arberry, p. 109), anticipates Omar's wish that his own corpse should exude an aroma of wine (sts. LXXVII–LXXVIII). A version of these lines appears in FitzGerald's first recorded attempt at translating Omar into 'Monkish Latin'.

V. Only detached phrases from this stanza appear in the Persian sources, and Iram is not mentioned in any of them (Heron-Allen 1899, p. 13). Arberry (p. 194) points out that FitzGerald borrowed from his own translation of *Salámán and Absál* (1856); see following notes.

V.1–2 and endnote 5 Irám . . . Sev'n-ring'd Cup: Iram is mentioned in *Salámán and Absál* (p. 49): 'Here Iram Garden seem'd in Secresy | Blowing the Rosebud of its Revelation'; FitzGerald's gloss (in appendix, p. 84) cites Sir William Jones as authority and is slightly fuller than the one he gives here. Jamshýd's cup is mentioned in a footnote on page 51, where it is also associated with divination.

V.1 gone with all its Rose: on 1 July 1857 (while he was working on Omar Khayyám) FitzGerald wrote to Cowell: 'June over! A thing I think of with Omar-like sorrow! And the Roses here are blowing—and going—as abundantly as even in Persia' (*Letters*, ii. 281).

VI.1 David's Lips: King David, as singer and author of the Psalms, is celebrated in the Islamic as well as Judaeo-Christian tradition. FitzGerald imported him from one of the quatrains of the Calcutta MS into the Ouseley MS quatrain which was the source for the nightingale's 'high-piping Péhlevi' (Arberry, p. 197).

VI.2 and endnote 6 Péhlevi: or Pahlavi, 'any of the pre-Islamic Iranian languages, *spec.* Middle Persian, the language used under the Parthians and Sassanians' (*OED*); here a metaphor for the nightingale's unchanging song. FitzGerald attributes the thought to Háfiz in his note, but he may also have had in mind the 'self-same song' of Keats's nightingale (l. 65). See also endnote 11. FitzGerald's accentuation here does not indicate a long vowel, but that the word should be stressed on the first syllable.

VI.4. Decker ('Other Men's Flowers', p. 231) suggests that 'the word "incarnadine" inescapably calls to mind its unique appearance in Shakespeare', alluding to Macbeth's fear that his bloody hand would 'The multitudinous seas incarnadine' (II. ii. 59); however, the word may have caught FitzGerald's eye in a phrase, and context, closer to those of the poem, Thomas Carew's 'Obsequies to the Lady Anne Hay' (*Poems*, 1640), in which 'Virgins of equal birth' are imagined as forming a composite picture of the lady's lost beauty: one of them will 'incarnadine | Thy rosie cheeke' (ll. 53–4).

VII. The first two lines are based on the same Persian source which FitzGerald adapted for st. LXX, also about repentance; the image of the 'Bird of Time' derives from a source outside Omar, Attar's *Mantic ut-tair* [Parliament of Birds]: 'The bird of the sky flutters along its appointed path' (Heron-Allen 1899, p. 17). Note also the 'Bird of Youth' which FitzGerald would have found in his source for st. LXXII, but did not use.

VIII.3. This line appears in FitzGerald's first recorded English verse translation of a quatrain by Omar Khayyám: see Introduction, p. xxxv.

VIII.4 Kaikobád: in Persian historical myth, the founder of the 'Keiyânee' dynasty (the spelling is Binning's, ii. 242), the second Persian dynasty, who followed the 'Peeshdâdee' dynasty; see below, note to XVII.2 and endote 11. D'Herbelot has an entry for him (under 'Caicobad', pp. 239–40). As with Kaikhosrú and Rustum, he is a figure of Persia's heroic legendary past, whose exploits feature in Firdusi's *Shah Namah*.

IX.1 old Khayyám: one of three occasions on which this phrase occurs in *1859* (see XXVI.1, XLVIII.2); all were eliminated in *1868*, though other indications that the speaker is an old man (e.g. st. XXVII) were retained. None of the Persian source(s) for these stanzas has Khayyám's name, though there are several quatrains in which he does name himself in both the Ouseley and Calcutta MSS; Cowell cites one of these in the *Calcutta Review* article which FitzGerald reprinted in his Preface (p. 8).

IX.2 Kaikhosrú: third king of the 'Keiyânee' dynasty; d'Herbelot's entry for him (under 'Cai Khosrau') is on pp. 237–9.

IX.3–4 and endnote 8 Rustum . . . Hátim Tai: the parallel between Rustum (or Rustam, or Rostam), the greatest warrior-hero of Persian legend, and Hercules, was well established; it occurs concisely in Binning (ii. 36–7) and at length in Ouseley (ii. 504–27). D'Herbelot (p. 438) remarks of Hátim Tai (Abou Adi Hatem Ben Abdallah Ben Sâad Al Thai): 'Ce personnage . . . s'est tellement rendu celebre par sa liberalité, qu'il a fait, pour ainsi dire, perdre le nom à cette vertu; car lorsque l'on veut loüer un homme de sa liberalité, on le qualifie toûjours du nom de Hatem Thai' [This person . . . has made himself so famous for his generosity that he has, so to speak, caused that virtue to lose its name; for when one wishes to praise a man for his generosity, one always calls him by the name of Hatem Thai]. D'Herbelot also states that Hatem lived before the Mahometan era and was not a Muslim, and neither of course was the (mythical) Rustum. Heron-Allen (1899, p. 18) prints the third line as 'And this first Summer month that brings the Prose', a misprint FitzGerald would have relished.

X.   Decker ('Other Men's Flowers', p. 238) compares Byron, *Childe Harold's Pilgrimage*, IV. clxxvii: 'Oh! that the Desert were my dwelling-place, | With one fair Spirit for my minister, | That I might all forget the human race, | And, hating no one, love but only her!' For a different kind of 'Byronic' allusion, see note to stanza LXX.

X.1–2. FitzGerald identified this marginal location as a favourite of Omar's; see Preface, p. 7.

X.1 Strip of Herbage strown: 'a strip of land sprinkled with greenery'; 'strown' as a variant of 'strewn' was still current in the period, e.g. Tennyson's *Geraint and Enid* (pub. in 1859 as part II of *Enid*): 'the marble threshold flashing, strown | With gold and scattered coinage' (ll. 25–6).

X.3 Slave and Sultán: Arberry (p. 200) points to the mention of 'Máhmúd' in the next line and suggests that FitzGerald had in mind 'the celebrated passion of Mahmūd for his slave-boy Ayāz, frequently cited by the Persian poets as an instance of the unpredictable vagaries of human love'. But the phrase may simply denote the whole social hierarchy, FitzGerald's Oriental equivalent for Keats's 'emperor and clown' in 'Ode to a Nightingale' (l. 64).

X.4 Sultán Máhmúd: Mahmud of Ghazni (971–1030); of Turkish descent, he succeeded his father as ruler of Ghazni (Afghanistan) in 997. For his legendary prowess as conqueror of India, see st. XLIV and endnote 18. The accent on the first *a* in *Máhmúd* indicates that the stress falls on the first syllable, not that the *a* is long; see XLIV.1.

XI.   The Persian original of this stanza was translated by Cowell in the *Calcutta Review* (p. 157), and by FitzGerald into Latin (Arberry, pp. 61, 121). Cowell uses the term 'díwán' for 'Book of Verse' (see above, Preface, 7). Decker ('Other Men's Flowers', p. 234) points out the parallel with the exiled Suffolk's words to Queen Margaret in Shakespeare's *2 Henry VI*: ''Tis not the land I care for, wert thou thence; | A wilderness is populous enough, | So Suffolk had thy heavenly company' (III. ii. 359–61).

XI.2–4 and Thou . . . enow: FitzGerald had introduced the image of the singer in his Latin version of this quatrain.

XI.4 enow: variant form of 'enough', already obsolete in the period except as here in poetic or deliberately archaic usage.

XII. The Persian original of this stanza was one of those FitzGerald translated into Latin (Arberry, pp. 59, 114–15).

XII.1 Sovranty: variant form of 'sovereignty', already archaic in the period.

XII.3 wave: waive, forgo; the spelling also suggests 'wave away'.

XII.4 and endnote 9. Arberry (pp. 114–15) points out that FitzGerald's Latin version inexplicably renders the Persian word for 'drum' as 'Tuba regalis' [royal trumpet], and that though the word is correctly translated in the English poem the 'royal' connection survives in the endnote with its reference to a 'Palace'.

XIII. FitzGerald's version is strikingly close to the Persian original (Arberry, pp. 201–2), but the idiom of line 3, which in the original reads 'I took the cord off the mouth of my purse', is enriched from an English source, Chaucer's description of the finery worn by the young and attractive Alisoun in *The Miller's Tale*: 'And by hir girdle heeng a purs of lether, | Tasseled with silk' (ll. 64–5). Gray (p. 106) argues that the stanza 'contains one of the most original misreadings of the final lines of Wordsworth's Intimations Ode: "To me the meanest flower that blows can give | Thoughts that do often lie too deep for tears"'.

XV. 'Those who hoarded their wealth, and those who spent it freely, have both been turned to earth, and not the kind of gold-yielding earth that men want to dig up again.' The implication is that you may as well be a spendthrift as a miser. The Persian original of this stanza was one of those FitzGerald translated into Latin (Arberry, pp. 60, 118).

*XVI.*1 *Caravanserai*: a halting-place for caravans, with buildings surrounding a large open space. There is a description in Binning (i. 171). *OED* cites Addison (*Spectator* no. 289, 1712) in a context close to FitzGerald: 'A house that changes its inhabitants so often, and receives such a perpetual succession of guests, is not a Palace but a Caravansery.'

XVII. The trope of wild beasts inhabiting the ruins of a king's palace is present in the original Persian (lion and fox), and is a recurring image of the destruction of earthly power in the prophetic books of the Bible, e.g. Isaiah 13: 19–21 on the fate of Babylon, 'the glory of kingdoms, the beauty of the Chaldees' excellency': 'wild beasts of the desert shall lie there; and their houses shall be full of doleful creatures'.

*XVII.*2 *and endnote 11.* As FitzGerald acknowledges, the account of Persepolis in the endnote is based on Binning's description in ch. xxii, the opening chapter of the second volume; this was both more recent, more colloquial, and shorter than Ouseley's dissertation-length chapter (vol ii, ch. xi, pp. 224–420), though FitzGerald certainly knew and liked it; he would also have been able to consult D'Herbelot, his standard reference work. Binning has slightly different spellings (e.g. *chihl minar* for *Chehl-minar*, *Shah Nameh* for *Shah-náma*) but in other respects FitzGerald sticks closely to his source, given that he is packing twenty pages into a paragraph; I have recorded only a few significant variations.

Jamshyd: see note to v.1–2 above.

the mythical Peeshdádian Dynasty: 'The first dynasty of Persian kings, according to their own chronicles . . . the founder of which was Kayoomers, supposed to have been great-grandson to Noah' (Binning, ii. 240).

(*doubtful if any where a Woman*): Binning is more positive: 'Among all of the many hundreds of figures . . . I did not observe a single one representing a female' (ii. 19), and he is backed up by Ouseley (ii. 277).

Arrow-head Characters: Binning speaks of 'the mysterious cuneiform or arrow-head character' (ii. 6). Cowell had published an article on 'Persian Cuneiform Inscriptions and Persian Ballads' in the *Westminster Review* in 1850.

the Ferooher—Symbol of Existence—with his wing'd Globe: FitzGerald's 'his' is obscure without Binning's gloss of *ferooher*: 'a winged man, without legs, encompassed with a circle' (ii. 15).

a double Flight of Stairs that may be gallop'd up: Binning's phrasing is (so to speak) more pedestrian: 'The steps are more than seven yards in breadth; and only three inches and a half in height; rendering the ascent so gradual and easy, that one may go up stairs on horseback, without difficulty' (ii. 5). FitzGerald had told Cowell in February 1857 of his admiration for Ouseley's account of 'the great Marble Staircase which was for Horsemen to ride up!' (*Letters*, ii. 254).

the Koh'i Ráhmet, Mountain of Mercy: Binning has 'hill of mercy' (ii. 4).

The substance of the comment on the quatrain found by Binning, including the remark about 'the Persian Tourists having the same propensity as English to write their Names and Sentiments on their National Monuments', is found in a letter to Cowell of 13 January 1859 (*Letters*, ii. 325). The mysterious second line is glossed by Binning's more literal version: 'Kings and princes came hither to rub their foreheads on its threshold' (ii. 20), i.e. to pay obeisance to its rulers. FitzGerald subsequently incorporated this quatrain into the main text of the poem, then changed his mind again: see Variants, p. 89.

XVII.3–4 and endnote 11. Ouseley mentions 'the vestiges of an edifice . . . supposed one of the seven villas erected by order of BAHRA´M GUR, to serve as places of residence for so many princesses' (ii. 422). In October 1858 FitzGerald told George Borrow that Cowell had sent him 'an MS. of Bahrám and his Seven Castles' which he had 'not yet cared to look far into' (*Letters*, ii. 321). The poem by Amir Khosrow of Dehli (d. 1325) is the *Khamshah* [Quintet], though FitzGerald's phrase 'one of the most famous Poems of Persia' is more applicable to the poem of the same name by Nizami (d. 1209), which Khosrow imitated and adapted. Bahram's seven princesses come from seven regions of the earth and are housed not in separate castles but in pavilions within his castle. 'The King of Bohemia and his seven castles' are the subject of Trim's much-interrupted story in Sterne's *Tristram Shandy* (vol. VIII, ch. 19). Binning describes being shown 'a remarkable spot called Bahram's grave—a part of the swamp which occupies the greater portion of the plain—for, according to tradition, this monarch, who was an inveterate sportsman, while hotly pursuing a wild ass, plunged into the morass, and met with the fate of the Master of Ravenswood' (ii. 357). The final chapter of Walter Scott's novel *The Bride of Lammermoor* (1819) relates the death of the Master of Ravenswood in the quicksand of 'Kelpie's Flow'. Scott was FitzGerald's favourite novelist; he 'borrows' the allusion without scruple. The phrase 'that great hunter' also recalls Nimrod, 'the mighty hunter before the Lord' (Genesis 10: 9).

XVIII. The Persian original of this stanza is one of those translated by Cowell in the *Calcutta Review* (p. 155) and by FitzGerald into Latin (Arberry, pp. 63, 127). The image of the hyacinth as a lock of hair was introduced in the Latin version; in the Persian, a violet represents 'a mole that was once on the cheek of some beauty'. The change from 'violet' to 'Hyacinth' may have been motivated by the difference in gender; but FitzGerald may also have wanted to make less obvious his own echo of *In Memoriam* XVIII, in which the speaker depicts Arthur Hallam's funeral: ' ''Tis well; 'tis something; we may stand | Where he in English earth is laid, | And from his ashes may be made | The violets of his native land' (ll. 1–4), itself recalling Laertes at Ophelia's graveside: 'Lay her i' th' earth, | And from her fair and unpolluted flesh | May violets spring!' (*Hamlet*, V. i. 238–40). The allusion to *Hamlet* is significant because FitzGerald's 'buried Caesar' in line 2 comes from the same scene: see next note.

XVIII.2 some buried Cæsar bled: the Persian original is less specific: Cowell has 'the blood of kings', as does FitzGerald's Latin version; Arberry's own translation (p. 204) has 'some prince's blood'. Nor does Omar refer to burial. FitzGerald's phrasing recalls the fate that Hamlet imagines for 'the noble dust of Alexander', which might be found 'stopping a bunghole': 'Imperious Caesar, dead and turned to clay, | Might stop a hole to keep the wind away' (V. i. 203–4, 213–14), and note that FitzGerald rhymes 'clay' with 'away' in st. VIII. This is one of a number of Shakespearean echoes in the poem; for another nearby example, see st. XXIII.4.

XVIII.3 Hyacinth: in Greek myth, the flower springs from the blood of the eponymous youth accidentally killed by Apollo.

XXII.2 and Summer: with 'whom' understood: 'and whom Summer'.

XXII.3 Ourselves must we: 'Must we ourselves'; a rare example of FitzGerald resorting to syntactical inversion for the sake of the metre.

XXIII.3 Dust into Dust: the change from 'to' to 'into' makes a small deviation from the Burial Service in the Book of Common Prayer: 'Ashes to ashes, dust to dust', in turn deriving from Genesis 3: 19: 'dust thou art, and unto dust shalt thou return'.

XXIII.4. The Persian source for this line reads 'without companion, without comrade, without partner and mate' (Arberry, p. 207); FitzGerald's use of 'sans', however, irresistibly summons the climax (or nadir) of the 'Seven Ages of Man' in *As You Like It*: 'Sans teeth, sans eyes, sans taste, sans every thing' (II. vii. 166).

XXIV.3. The 'muezzin' calls the faithful to prayer in Islamic ritual, traditionally from a high place such as the minaret of a mosque. Heron-Allen (1899, p. 43) has 'muezzin', but Arberry (p. 207) declares this reading 'quite fanciful' and translates 'suddenly a proclamation emerges from a hiding-place'; Avery and Heath-Stubbs (p. 108) have 'But I fear one day the cry will go up'.

XXV. The Persian original of this stanza was one of those FitzGerald translated into Latin (Arberry, pp. 59, 111–12).

XXV.2. the Two Worlds: this world and the next (the afterlife).

XXV.3–4. The vocabulary of these lines is strongly marked by biblical associations. 'Foolish prophets' are found in Ezekiel 13: 'Woe unto the foolish prophets ... They have seen vanity and lying divination ... they shall not be in the assembly of my people, neither shall they be written in the writing of the house of Israel' (vv. 3, 6, 9). The Lord 'overthroweth the words of the transgressor' (Proverbs 22: 12). 'Scatter' and 'scorn' are frequently used of God's retribution, as in Psalm 44: 'Thou ... hast scattered us among the heathen ... Thou makest us a reproach to our neighbours, a scorn and a derision to them that are round about us' (vv. 11, 13). The image of a mouth 'stopt with Dust' is one of death; but the context also suggests Proverbs 20: 17: 'Bread of deceit is sweet to a man; but afterwards his mouth shall be filled with gravel.' FitzGerald's Latin version says of the 'sapientes' [wise ones] that 'Pulvis illi sunt, et Ventus illud quod edocuêre' [they are dust, and wind is that which they taught].

XXVI. Only line 4 has a specific source; 'FitzGerald supplied the greater part of this stanza out of the general context of Omar's poems' (Arberry, p. 208).

XXVII–XXVIII. The (single) Persian original of these stanzas was one of those FitzGerald translated into Latin (Arberry, pp. 62, 125). Arberry points out that the metaphor of sowing and harvest, which is not in the original, was introduced into the Latin version, 'remarkable evidence of the extent to which [FitzGerald's] English version depended upon his Latin'. The metaphor of the 'Seed of Wisdom' recalls the New Testament parable of the sower (Matthew 13); see also below, LIII.2 and note.

XXVII.2 Doctor: in the sense of 'sage', as in XXV.1, 'Saints and Sages'.

XXVII. 3 About it and about: Decker ('Other Men's Flowers', p. 226) suggests a memory of Pope, *The Dunciad*, iv. 251–2, in which Richard Bentley, representing scholarly pedantry and futile metaphysical debate, addresses Dulness and claims that he and his kind 'For thee explain a thing till all men doubt it, | And write about it, Goddess, and about it'.

XXX. The Persian original of this stanza is one of those translated by Cowell in the *Calcutta Review* (p. 157) and by FitzGerald into Latin (Arberry, pp. 63, 128–9).

XXX.4. Neither 'Impertinence' nor the revised term 'Insolence' (see Variants, p. 70) features in the Persian original; 'insolence' was introduced into the Latin version as a result of FitzGerald's misunderstanding of the Persian, an error which, as Arberry points out, he chose not to correct even after seeing Cowell's more accurate rendering.

XXXI. These lines may be read as the account of a spiritual vision, or as an elaborate metaphor for Omar's astronomical observations.

XXXII.2. Echoing the conclusion of *In Memoriam* LVI: 'What hope of answer or redress? | Behind the veil, behind the veil.'

XXXII.4 endnote 14. In *1859* the endnote numerals 14, 15 (st. XXVIII), 16 (st. XLI) are out of sequence, running 15, 16, 14. Decker (pp. li–lii) suggests that st. XLI originally came between sts. XXXI and XXXII, and that the printer moved the stanza without thinking to adjust the numerals; the survival of the error into the published text indicates either that FitzGerald missed it, or that he made the change at a very late stage in proof, and did not see a revise before the edition went to press.

XXXIII. This stanza bears only an approximate relation to that cited by Arberry (p. 212) as its Persian source; Heron-Allen (1899, p. 57) does not comment on the *1859* text, which was radically revised in later editions (see Variants, p. 77). I think it more likely that FitzGerald was recalling Lucretius, *De Rerum Natura*, 2. 14–16: 'O wretched minds of men! O hearts so blind! | How dark the life, how great the perils are | In which whatever time is given is passed!' (The phrase 'blind hearts', which translates 'pectora caeca', can also be rendered 'blind intelligences'.) FitzGerald's 'blind Understanding' resonates with biblical texts such as 2 Esdras 25: 'I shall light a candle of understanding in thine heart' or Matthew 15: 14: 'blind leaders of the blind'. Note also *In Memoriam* cxxiv, where the heart's 'blind clamour' is paradoxically comforting: 'Then was I as a child that cries, | But, crying, knows his father near' (ll. 18–20).

XXXIV. The Persian original of this stanza is one of those translated by Cowell in the *Calcutta Review* (p. 161) and by FitzGerald into Latin (Arberry, pp. 62, 126).

XXXIV.2 (and XXXVIII.2) Well of Life: in the Authorized Version, Psalms 36: 9 has 'For with thee is the fountain of life', often cited or paraphrased as 'Well of Life'. In *Paradise Lost*, the archangel Michael prepares Adam's eyes for his prophetic vision: 'And from the well of life three drops instilled' (xi. 416). The strength of the Christian current in the phrase (and of FitzGerald's resistance to it) may be gauged by lines from Cowper's *Conversation*: 'Hearts may be found that harbour at this hour | That love of Christ in all its quickening power, | And lips unstain'd by folly or by strife, | Whose wisdom, drawn from the deep well of life, | Tastes of its healthful origin, and flows | A Jordan for the ablution of our woes' (ll. 551–6). This is the consolation that the *Rubáiyát* rejects.

XXXV. The Persian original of this stanza is one of those translated by Cowell in the *Calcutta Review* (p. 155), and one of those FitzGerald translated into Latin. The 'kisses' of lines 3–4 do not feature in the original; FitzGerald introduced them into the Latin version in order to emulate a pun in the Persian (Arberry, pp. 60, 119–20).

XXXV.4 take—and give!: FitzGerald reverses this phrase in st. LVIII.4.

XXXVI. The Persian original of this stanza was one of those FitzGerald translated into Latin (Arberry, pp. 60, 117). The potter here is a literal figure;

only in the 'Kúza-Náma' section (sts. LIX–LXVI) does he become a metaphor for a divine Creator.

XXXVII. This stanza, and st. XLV, were the only two that FitzGerald cut out of the poem in their entirety from *1868* onwards. The Persian original of line 4 occurs in one of the quatrains translated by Cowell in the *Calcutta Review* (p. 155), and by FitzGerald into Latin (Arberry, pp. 63, 129).

XXXVIII.4 and endnote 15. FitzGerald revised this line in the third edition after Tennyson suggested he had borrowed the image from one of his poems; see Variants, pp. 80–1, and Introduction, pp. xlvi–xlvii. Binning observes that 'Journies are made at night after Now Rooz; for although the nights are still cold, the weather is getting hot during the day' (ii. 165) but does not attribute this to Muhammad's command.

XXXIX.1 How long, how long: the phrase 'How long' does not occur in the Persian original of this stanza (Arberry, p. 216), though it does occur in other quatrains attributed to Omar; it is frequent in the Bible, especially as an address to God, e.g. Psalms 6: 3: 'My soul is also sore vexed: but thou, O Lord, how long?' But FitzGerald may also have intended a riposte to Wisdom's complaint of neglect in Proverbs 1: 22: 'How long, ye simple ones, will ye love simplicity? and the scorners delight in their scorning, and fools hate knowledge?'

XXXIX.3 merry: a traditional, and biblical, euphemism for 'drunk' (Genesis 43: 34 and other texts); the injunction to 'be merry' has ominous antecedents in Luke 12: 19–20, where the rich man says to his soul: 'eat, drink, and be merry', unaware of his impending death; Luke is citing an Old Testament text, Ecclesiastes 8: 15: 'Then I commended mirth, because a man hath no better thing under the sun, than to eat, and to drink, and to be merry: for that shall abide with him of his labour the days of his life, which God giveth him under the sun.'

fruitful Grape: in view of the stanza that follows, compare Psalms 128: 3: 'Thy wife shall be as a fruitful vine by the sides of thy house.'

XXXIX.4 sadden after: 'become sad after obtaining'; but there may also be a suggestion of 'become sad through longing for', as in the idiom 'hanker after'.

bitter, Fruit: the phrase 'bitter fruit' was a poetic commonplace by FitzGerald's time, but the context recalls Tennyson's 'Locksley Hall': 'Am I mad, that I should cherish that which bears but bitter fruit? | I will pluck it from my bosom, though my heart be at the root' (ll. 65–6).

XL. Biographical readings should be treated with caution, but it is hard not to associate FitzGerald's decision to translate this particular *ruba'i* with the failure of his own marriage. Barrenness is not mentioned in the Persian source, where the divorce is from both reason and faith (Arberry, p. 217).

XLI.1–2 and endnote 16. Note the changes to the text, and the expansion of the endnote, in the second and subsequent editions (Variants, pp. 82, 91).

In fact Omar is not alluding to mathematics here, but to philosophical concepts such as being and non-being (Arberry, p. 217, and see Avery and Heath-Stubbs, p. 65 n. 16).

XLII.2 an Angel Shape: the Persian original reads simply 'old man'; Arberry (pp. 21–2) suggests that FitzGerald did not intend to embellish the text, but had misread 'pīrī' (old man) as 'pirī' (a fairy).

XLIII.2 and endnote 17 The Two-and-Seventy jarring Sects: as it stands this phrase refers to divisions within Islam; FitzGerald modified the endnote after consulting Cowell as to the bearing of this phrase (see Variants, p. 92).

XLIII.3 that in a Trice: with 'can' understood: 'that can in a Trice'.

XLIV and endnote 18. Mahmud of Ghazni (see note to x.4) invaded India in 1001—the first of twelve expeditions, according to Gibbon, which established an empire that 'surpassed the limits of the conquests of Alexander' and culminated in the killing of 50,000 idolaters and the destruction of their idol at Sumnat (this account occurs in the same chapter as the one cited by FitzGerald in relation to the reform of the calendar: see note on p. 139). The Muslim conquest of India is represented here in terms of both religious and racial superiority; FitzGerald would have found this view in both Muslim and Western historiography, and Arberry (p. 219, following Heron-Allen) suggests a specific source in Attar's *Mantic ut-Tair* [Parliament of Birds].

XLV. This stanza has no original in the Persian sources (Arberry, p. 220). Along with st. XXXVII it was dropped completely from the poem in *1868*.

XLV.3 the Hubbub: as Satan approaches the throne of Chaos, he hears 'a universal hubbub wild / Of stunning sounds and voices all confused' (*Paradise Lost* II 951–2). In Tennyson's *Maud*, the hero longs for a 'passionless peace . . . Far-off from the clamour of liars belied in the hubbub of lies' (ll. 150–2).

XLVI and endnote 19. The Persian original of this stanza is one of those translated by Cowell in the *Calcutta Review* (p. 162); it has the spelling 'lanthorn' which was still current in the period and was retained in the endnote in all editions; however, in his revision of the stanza itself FitzGerald used the more modern 'lantern' (see Variants, p. 83). The endnote is an abbreviated paraphrase of a note added at the end of Cowell's *Calcutta Review* article by the journal's editor, hence the allusion to India. In a letter to Cowell of 29 January 1868, FitzGerald wrote that he was 'trying to get an old Woodbridge Artist (now in London) to make a sort of rough etching [of the 'Magic-lanthorn'] . . . which I would stick at the beginning by way of Vignette Title. But I don't know if he can manage it' (*Letters*, iii. 78). The artist was G. J. Rowe, and he couldn't. A further attempt was made by Edwin Edwards in 1871, with a view to the third edition, but this too was not adopted (*Letters*, iii. 79 n. 4).

XLVII. The Persian original of this stanza, which FitzGerald described to Cowell as 'remarkable for its terseness' (*Letters*, ii. 279), was one of those he translated into Latin; this version has what Arberry (pp. 61, 122–3) calls an 'intrusive reference to roses' in line 1, which was omitted in the English version 'or rather transferred to the following stanza'.

XLVIII.3 the Angel with his darker Draught: Azräel, the Angel of Death in Islamic tradition; he is named in an addition to the endnotes which FitzGerald made in *1868* (see Variants, p. 90).

XLIX. The Persian original of this stanza is one of those translated by Cowell in the *Calcutta Review* (p. 161). The use of chess as a metaphor of human life or behaviour has roots in English as well as Persian literature; examples in the half-century before the publication of the poem include poems or plays by Byron (*Don Juan* XIII, st. 89), Coleridge (*Wallenstein*, III. viii. 22–30), Browning (*Luria* [1846], IV. i. 6–11), Kingsley (*The Saint's Tragedy* [1848], IV. ii. 32), and Macaulay ('Sermon in a Churchyard' [1825] 45–60). FitzGerald almost certainly knew his Cambridge contemporary Richard Chenevix Trench's 'The Pantheist', published in *Poems from Eastern Sources* (1842): 'If evil, then, be not against God's will, | 'Tis wrongly named, it is not truly ill: | Rather the world a chess-board we should name, | And God both sides is playing of the game' (ll. 7–10). But the closest parallel is found in section III of a poem in 'Negro' dialect by Charles Dibden, published in 1814 in a two-volume *Collection of Songs* which FitzGerald owned (*Letters*, i. 244): 'One game me see massa him play, him call chess, | King, queen, bishop, knight, castle, all in a mess; | King kill knight, queen bishop, men castle throw down, | Like card-soldier him scatter, all lie on a ground: | And when the game over, king, bishop, tag, rag, | Queen, knight, all together him go in a bag:— | So in life's game at chess, when no more we can do, | Massa Death bring one bag, and we Kickaraboo.'

L. The allusion is to the game of *chúgán*, or polo; when FitzGerald wrote the poem it had not yet been adopted by the British, and FitzGerald's knowledge of it was purely literary. In a letter to Cowell of mid-September 1854 (*Letters*, ii. 140), FitzGerald mentioned a long account of the game in Ouseley (appendix VI, i. 345–55) and in a subsequent letter of 17 September (ibid. 143–4) he paraphrased this account and enclosed his own copy of an engraving reproduced by Ouseley (vol. i, plate XXII) depicting a polo match; this engraving was used as the frontispiece to his first Persian translation, *Salámán and Absál* (1856), and Ouseley's account is reprinted in the appendix to that work (pp. 77–9). On 22 August 1857 he wrote to Cowell about No. 427 of the Calcutta MS of Omar Khayyám, quoting the line گو ای رفته بچو گان قضاهم چرن [Oh you who are driven by the mallet of Fate] and commenting that it 'brings us to our old game which I had not remembered to have yet seen in Omar: but I can't quite construe him here—Something to the effect, I suppose, of "Whither Destiny strikes the Ball must go—no use Grumbling: for he who strikes as he runs او داند او داند او داند او داند [He knows—He knows—He knows—He—] Which sounds rather awful though I am not sure of scanning or meaning—"He knows what he is about etc." Can it be that, leaving off with the nominative as the Wood Pigeon leaves off so often with the first phrase of her Song? Do you not remember it up in the trees of old England, and how the Boys construe her?

My Toe's so cold—my Toe's so cold—
My Toe's—

But I can't help fancying this او داند [He knows] may be some technical call at the چرگان [Polo] Game' (*Letters*, ii. 297–8). This latter speculation was probably ruled out by Cowell, since it does not appear in endnote 20 where FitzGerald glosses the line. It continued to trouble him, however; in February 1868, while revising the poem for the second edition, he asked Cowell about it again, saying that he had lost track of the original in the Calcutta MS: 'I can't find it in any Copy now: and I can scarce believe that the Line as I give it can be made to scan' (*Letters*, iii. 79–80).

LI. Two Persian quatrains contributed to this stanza, one of them translated by Cowell in the *Calcutta Review* (p. 158), and both translated by FitzGerald into Latin (Arberry, pp. 58, 110 for the first, pp. 62, 125–6 for the second).

LI.2 *Piety nor Wit*: Decker ('Other Men's Flowers', p. 228) points out the echo of Dryden's elegy 'To the Pious Memory of . . . Mrs Anne Killigrew', l. 153: 'Not wit, nor piety could fate prevent'.

LII.1–2 Echoing Hamlet: 'What should such fellows as I do crawling betwixt earth and heaven?' (III. i. 126–8).

LIII. The Persian original of this stanza was one of those translated by FitzGerald into Latin (Arberry, pp. 63, 129–30); the Latin version, especially line 4 ('Quare me Peccati pudet quod peccare designatum?' [Why should I be ashamed of a sin which was predestined to be sinned?]), strengthens the association of 'Oriental' fatalism with Western religious and philosophical ideas. The English stanza alludes both to the Calvinist doctrine of predestination (more explicitly treated in sts. LVII–LVIII) and to the materialist idea of determinism, the 'hopeless Necessity' which FitzGerald associated with Lucretius: see Preface, pp. 12–13, and notes, p. 145. For the 'Last Harvest' as an image of the Last Judgement, see among other biblical texts Matthew 13: 37, 39: 'He that soweth the good seed is the Son of man . . . the harvest is the end of the world.'

LIV–LV. The only instance in *1859* where a sentence runs over two stanzas, though strictly speaking sts. XLIII–XLIV ought to be syntactically connected, as they are in *1868* (see Variants, p. 82); the same may hold for sts. LXVII–LXVIII. *1868* has several other examples, including one of a sentence running over three stanzas (p. 81).

LIV *and endnote 21*. At the Creation, a stallion (the 'flaming Foal') is harnessed to the sun; the starry heavens are flung over his shoulders like cloths. He starts *from*, not *for*, 'the Goal'; the whole course of time, like that of the sun, is circular and will eventually return to its point of origin. The astronomical reference is appropriate to Omar as 'Astronomer-Poet';

'Parwín and Mushtara' are also emblems of male and female principles. FitzGerald altered the Persian original in order to make the second line continue the metaphor in the first; Heron-Allen (1899, p. 111) translates 'And settled the laws of Parwīn and Mushtarī'.

LIV.4–LV.1 In my predestin'd Plot of Dust and Soul | The Vine had struck a Fibre: i.e. 'I was fated to become a drunkard'. 'Plot' has the double sense of 'a piece of ground' and 'a narrative design'.

LV.1–2 The Vine had struck a Fibre; which about | If clings my Being—let the Súfi flout: the syntax elides a statement ('The Vine had struck a Fibre about which my Being clings') with a conditional ('suppose my Being does cling to this Fibre'), followed by the defiant challenge to the 'Súfi'. 'Flout' is intransitive here: 'to mock, jeer, scoff; to express contempt either by action or speech' (*OED*).

LV.4 the Door he howls without: 'the Door outside which he howls'; but 'without' also punningly suggests that the Sufi is 'without' the key.

LVI–LVIII. FitzGerald's version of Omar's challenge to God's justice is heavily inflected with the vocabulary of the Bible and of Christian theology: terms such as 'True Light', 'Wrathconsume', 'Temple', 'Pitfall', 'Gin', 'Predestination', 'Fall', and 'Sin' may be more or less accurate as renderings of Persian words, but together they would impel most English readers of the time towards a familiar, and specifically Christian debate; the impression would have been sealed by the mention of 'Eden' and 'the snake'.

LVI.1 the one True Light: Christ is so described in John 1: 9: 'That was the true Light, which lighteth every man that cometh into the world.'

LVI.2 Wrathconsume: 'destroy in anger'; the hyphen supplied in *1868* confirms that this is not a misprint (two words printed as one, with 'Wrath' as a noun) but that FitzGerald intended a compound verb. Both 'wrath' and 'consume' carry strong biblical echoes, and are joined in Psalm 59: 13: 'Consume them in wrath, consume them, that they may not be.'

LVI.4 Better: with 'is' understood: 'Is better'.

LVII. The accusation that God entraps mankind is present in the Persian source (Arberry, p. 227) but FitzGerald's English vocabulary, again, takes his readers to the Bible, especially the Old Testament. The wicked 'set gins' for the righteous (Psalms 140: 5), and fall into their own pit (Proverbs 28: 10); Isaiah not only laments that 'Fear, and the pit, and the snare, are upon thee, O inhabitant of the earth' (24: 17), but warns that God himself can be such a trap: 'Sanctify the Lord of hosts himself; and let him be your fear, and let him be your dread. And he shall be for a sanctuary; but for a stone of stumbling and for a rock of offence to both the houses of Israel, for a gin and for a snare to the inhabitants of Jerusalem. And many among them shall stumble, and fall, and be broken, and be snared, and be taken' (8: 13–15). Cp. also Job 18: 8–10. FitzGerald made his theological point (that God, not mankind, is to blame) more explicit, though at considerable poetic cost, in the stanzas he added in *1868*: see Variants, p. 85.

LVIII.2. The Persian original does not have anything about Eden and the snake; Heron-Allen (1899, p. 119) suggests the influence of a passage in Attar's *Mantic ut-tair* [Parliament of Birds] 'in which we read of the presence of the Snake (Iblis) in Paradise, at the moment of the creation of Adam'.

LVIII.3–4. The Persian original has nothing resembling the offer of forgiveness *to* God, the boldest moment of heterodoxy in the poem. The original reads: 'O Lord, grant me excuse and accept (my) repentance, | O You who give repentance and accept every man's excuse' (Arberry, p. 228). Arberry claims that FitzGerald 'was the victim of a simple misunderstanding of the original and not, as has sometimes been suggested, the wilful inventor of a blasphemy' (p. 140). This is probably true in the first instance, but when Cowell later objected to the reading FitzGerald refused to alter it. He wrote to Cowell on 17 December 1867, while he was revising the poem for the second edition: 'As to my making Omar worse than he is in that Stanza about Forgiveness—you know I have translated none literally, and have generally mashed up two—or more—into one. Now, when you look at such Stanzas as 356, 436, and many besides, where "La Divinité" is accused of the Sins we commit, I do not think it is going far beyond by way of Corollary to say—"Let us forgive one another." I have certainly an idea that this *is* said somewhere in the Calcutta MS. But it is very likely I may have construed, or remembered, erroneously. But I do not *add* dirt to Omar's face' (*Letters*, iii. 68–9). The stanza numbers '356' and '436' are those of Nicolas's edition (see Publication History, pp. xlix–l); both quatrains dispute the justice of God's judgements. The last two lines of No. 436, for example, read (in E. H. Whinfield's translation): 'Though we are sinful slaves, is it for Thee | To blame us? Who created us but Thou?' (cited *Letters*, iii. 70 n. 3). 'La Divinité' ('The Deity') is the standard phrase used by Nicolas in allegorical readings of Omar, to which FitzGerald objected in the long polemical passage he added to the Preface in *1868*: see Variants, p. 69. In her article critical of FitzGerald's translation, Jessie Cadell singled out this stanza (no. LXXXI in the third edition): see Appendix I, pp. 131–3.

LVIII.1. The creation of mankind from the 'dust of the ground' (Genesis 2: 7) is common to both Judaeo-Christian and Islamic belief, but neither implies that the material was 'baser' and so more liable to sin.

LVIII.2. Devout Christians such as Cowell might accept that God was responsible for the existence of evil, but only as a necessary consequence of free will; to say that God 'devise[d] the snake' would imply that God created evil itself. This question is addressed in the following section of the poem.

After LVIII KÚZA-NÁMA: 'Book of Pots', a made-up phrase which FitzGerald put in 'for fun' and dropped in later editions; in *1872* he added an endnote pointing out biblical and classical antecedents for the 'Relation of Pot and Potter to Man and his Maker' which preoccupies this section (see Variants, pp. 92–3). Biblical sources include both Old and New Testament texts. Isaiah 45: 9 offers a challenge which the poem takes up: 'Woe unto him that striveth with his Maker! Let the potsherd strive with the potsherds of the earth. Shall the clay say to him that fashioneth it, What makest thou? or thy work, He hath no hands?' Jeremiah 18: 3–6 has the 'potter's house' and the concept that the potter could spoil his work: 'Then I went down to the potter's house, and, behold, he wrought a work on the wheels. And the vessel that he made of clay was marred in the hand of the potter: so he made it again another vessel, as seemed good to the potter to make it. Then the word of the Lord came to me, saying, O house of Israel, cannot I do with you as this potter?' Romans 9: 18–21 also bears on the poem's quarrel with God; St Paul, citing the Old Testament texts, justifies God's power to create 'vessels of wrath' doomed to destruction: 'Therefore hath he mercy on whom he will have mercy, and whom he will harden. Thou wilt say then unto me, Why doth he yet find fault? For who hath resisted his will? Nay but, O man, who art thou that repliest against God? Shall the thing formed say to him that formed it, Why hast thou made me thus? Hath not the potter power over the clay, of the same lump to make one vessel unto honour, and another unto dishonour?' Besides questioning God's justice, FitzGerald's pots allude to contemporary philosophical and religious debates about the existence of the soul and the afterlife (see below).

In his 'reply' to FitzGerald, 'Rabbi Ben Ezra' (*Dramatis Personae*, 1864), Robert Browning took up the metaphor of the divine potter, but ignored the issue of God's responsibility for evil; instead, he used it to justify God's purpose in the creating the conditions of time and mortality, and to engage with the larger theme of FitzGerald's poem:

> Ay, note that Potter's wheel,
> That metaphor! and feel
> Why time spins fast, why passive lies our clay,—
> Thou, to whom fools propound,
> When the wine makes its round,
> 'Since life fleets, all is change; the Past gone, seize to-day!'
>
> Fool! All that is, at all,
> Lasts ever, past recall;
> Earth changes, but thy soul and God stand sure:
> What entered into thee,
> *That* was, is, and shall be:
> Time's wheel runs back or stops; Potter and clay endure.
> (sts. 26–7).

LIX–LX. The Persian original from which FitzGerald adapted these two stanzas is one of those translated by Cowell in the *Calcutta Review* (p. 161), and is one of those FitzGerald translated into Latin (Arberry, pp. 58, 111).

LIX.1–2 One Evening . . . arose: see endnote 22. The form 'Ramazan' (for 'Ramadan') was current in the period, e.g. Walter Scott's burlesque poem. 'The Search after Happiness; or, the Quest of Sultaun Solimaun': 'They drink good wine and keep no Ramazan' (xii 6). The second line of this stanza, most unusually for FitzGerald, is unmetrical, with an extra syllable that cannot be accommodated except by elision of 'Ramazán' to 'Ram'zán'; the jarring note may have been intentional, but FitzGerald removed it in subsequent editions: see Variants, p. 86.

LX.3–4. The wording and placing of this intervention gave FitzGerald trouble: see Variants, p. 86. The question in line 4 represents the kind of fruitless philosophical speculation criticized earlier in the poem (e.g. sts. XXVI – XXVII).

LXI–LXII. These two stanzas are arguments for the afterlife; FitzGerald may have had in mind Tennyson's *In Memoriam*, e.g. st. XXXV: 'My own dim life should teach me this, | That life shall live for evermore, | Else earth is darkness at the core, | And dust and ashes all that is' (ll. 1–4), or LIV, in which the speaker (tentatively) trusts 'That nothing walks with aimless feet; | That not one life shall be destroyed, | Or cast as rubbish to the void, | When God hath made the pile complete' (ll. 5–8). Tennyson's argument reaches an anguished climax in st. LVI, where the speaker confronts the idea that 'Nature' cares nothing for the survival of the human species, and that 'Man, her last work, who seemed so fair, | Such splendid purpose in his eyes' may be doomed to extinction, making 'life as futile, then, as frail!' (ll. 9–10, 25).

LXI. Decker ('Other Men's Flowers', p. 218) points out the parallel with the concluding lines of Tennyson's 'To ——. With the Following Poem' (i.e. *The Palace of Art*, 1832): 'Not for this | Was common clay ta'en from the common earth | Moulded by God, and tempered with the tears | Of Angels, to the perfect shape of man.'

LXIV.1 a surly Tapster: the metaphor here shifts from God as a potter to God as an innkeeper who draws his ale or wine from the assembled vessels, and 'tests' the quality either of the container or its contents; the theological issue is to do with God's willingness to condemn sinners to damnation. 'Tapster' is the kind of blunt old English word that FitzGerald relished, but no one had ever applied it to God; the Persian original has 'that dear Friend' (Arberry, p. 232). Tapsters were bywords for cheats: 'the oath of a lover is no stronger than the word of a tapster; they are both the confirmer of false reckonings' (*As You Like It*, III. iv. 30–2). Perhaps even FitzGerald thought this too strong; he eliminated the term in *1868* in favour of 'Master', and the final reading is the blandest of all (see Variants, p. 87).

LXVI and endnote 22. Ramadan is the ninth month in the Muslim calendar, during which believers must fast from first light to nightfall. FitzGerald had no personal experience of Muslims becoming 'unhealthy and unamiable' during Ramadan; he derived this observation from Binning's account of his sojourn in Ispahan. Binning states that 'During the day they are dull and stupid, like logs', and that he had 'seen several stout portly individuals, who, towards the end of the month, had become lank and emaciated' (ii. 323). The Persian original of this stanza is one of those translated by Cowell in the *Calcutta Review* (p. 161).

LXVI.4 Shoulder-knot: the padded cloth on which a porter rested his load.

LXVII.4. This detail, which is not in the Persian source, probably derives, as Arberry (p. 234) suggests, from the anecdote about Omar's prophecy of his burial-place which FitzGerald relates in his Preface (pp. 8–9).

LXVIII. In the Persian source, it is not a 'True Believer' that Omar imagines passing by his grave; Arberry (p. 234) gives 'a crop-sick man', Avery and Heath-Stubbs (p. 63) 'a toper'.

LXIX–LXX. Arberry (p. 235) traces these two stanzas to sources in the Calcutta MS which seem of doubtful relevance, and ignores two stanzas in the Ouseley MS, nos. 61 and 65, which supplied the themes of lost reputation and short-lived repentance, and the image of the torn garment. Heron-Allen translates ll. 3–4 of no. 61: 'My sweetheart has destroyed the penitence born of reason, | and the passing seasons have torn the garment that patience sewed', and the whole of no. 65: 'In the tavern thou canst not perform the Ablution save with wine, | and thou canst not purify a tarnished reputation; | be happy, for this veil of temperance of ours | is so torn that it cannot be repaired.'

LXIX.1 the Idols: the false gods denounced by all branches of monotheistic religion (Judaism, Christianity, and Islam) are a metaphor here for the love of earthly pleasures; but FitzGerald's choice of the term, which does not form part of the Persian quatrain he adapted, may also have been influenced by Francis Bacon's theory of human knowledge, in which true understanding is thwarted by 'idols of the mind'; James Spedding, the great nineteenth-century Baconian scholar, was a friend, and his work on Bacon is frequently mentioned in FitzGerald's letters.

LXX. Compare Byron, *Don Juan* i. cxix: 'I make a resolution every spring | Of reformation, ere the year run out, | But somehow, this my vestal vow takes wing, | Yet still, I trust it may be kept throughout: | I'm very sorry, very much ashamed, | And mean, next winter, to be quite reclaim'd.' This self-satire represents one aspect of the 'Byronic'; for the more emotive aspect, see note to stanza x.

LXXI. The Persian original of this stanza is one of those translated by Cowell in the *Calcutta Review* (p. 157).

LXXII. The Persian original of this stanza is one of those translated by Cowell in the *Calcutta Review* (p. 161).

LXXII.2 Youth's sweet-scented Manuscript: 'sweet-scented' is not in the Persian source. Decker (p. xxx) points out the connection with FitzGerald's letter to Cowell on 15 June 1857, in which he described how the Calcutta MS he had just received had been 'perfumed' by an accompanying present to his wife, a box made from aromatic wood (*Letters*, ii. 274). See also Introduction, pp. xxiii–xxiv.

LXXII.3–4. In the Persian source for this stanza, these lines repeat the lament for lost youth in ll. 1–2: 'that bird of joy whose name was Youth— | alas, I know not when it came, when it went' (Arberry, p. 236). FitzGerald disliked the repetitiousness of Persian poetry, see Preface, p. 11, and notes, pp. 142–3.

LXXIII.2 this sorry Scheme of Things: the phrase 'scheme of things' had been in use for over a century as a way of denoting the providential design of the universe; as might be expected, FitzGerald's epithet 'sorry' goes against the current. Compare, for example, James Thomson's *The Seasons* (1726–30), often cited as a textbook of natural theology, which praises 'Inspiring God!' for the 'complex stupendous scheme of things' ('Spring', ll. 850–5), and attacks those who doubt God's wisdom and beneficence: 'Let no presuming impious railer tax | Creative Wisdom, as if ought was form'd | In vain, or not for admirable ends. | Shall little haughty Ignorance pronounce | His works unwise, of which the smallest part | Exceeds the narrow vision of her mind? . . . And lives the man, whose universal eye | Has swept at once the unbounded scheme of things; | Mark'd their dependance so, and firm accord, | As with unfaltering accent to conclude | That this availeth nought?' ('Summer', ll. 318–23, 329–33).

LXXIV. The germ of this stanza is in a letter of 15 July 1856 to Tennyson: 'I have been the last Fortnight with the Cowells who sail for India the end of the month. We read some curious Infidel and Epicurean Tetrastichs by a Persian of the 11th. Century—as savage against Destiny, etc., as [Byron's] Manfred—but mostly of Epicurean Pathos of this kind—"Drink—for the Moon will often come round to look for us in this Garden and find us not"' (*Letters*, ii. 234). The same Persian original is translated by Cowell in the *Calcutta Review* (p. 157), and is one of those FitzGerald translated into Latin (Arberry, pp. 61, 120). He also transcribed it, in Persian and without a translation, in a letter of 24 May 1857 to George Borrow (*Letters*, ii. 277). In the poem, FitzGerald altered the Persian source by making a plural into a singular; in the original the moon 'will seek much . . . and will not find us', i.e. both the speaker and his companion will be dead; this is the reading in Cowell's version, in FitzGerald's letter to Tennyson, and in his Latin version; the poem's speaker, by contrast, singles out himself as the one who will be absent, a reading strengthened in successive editions (see Variants, p. 88). Arberry (p. 47) points out that in his letter to Tennyson FitzGerald had 'already introduced the romantic setting of a garden, which is wanting in the original'.

After LXXV *TAMÁM SHUD*: from *1868* simply 'Tamám', which means 'finished'; 'tamám shud' means something like 'it is finished' or 'it is accomplished', and FitzGerald may have made the change because this phrase too obviously cocks a snook at Jesus's dying words on the Cross (John 19: 30).

The Oxford World's Classics Website

www.worldsclassics.co.uk

- Browse the full range of Oxford World's Classics online
- Sign up for our monthly e-alert to receive information on new titles
- Read extracts from the Introductions
- Listen to our editors and translators talk about the world's greatest literature with our Oxford World's Classics audio guides
- Join the conversation, follow us on Twitter at OWC_Oxford
- Teachers and lecturers can order inspection copies quickly and simply via our website

www.worldsclassics.co.uk

American Literature

British and Irish Literature

Children's Literature

Classics and Ancient Literature

Colonial Literature

Eastern Literature

European Literature

Gothic Literature

History

Medieval Literature

Oxford English Drama

Poetry

Philosophy

Politics

Religion

The Oxford Shakespeare

A complete list of Oxford World's Classics, including Authors in Context, Oxford English Drama, and the Oxford Shakespeare, is available in the UK from the Marketing Services Department, Oxford University Press, Great Clarendon Street, Oxford OX2 6DP, or visit the website at www.oup.com/uk/worldsclassics.

In the USA, visit www.oup.com/us/owc for a complete title list.

Oxford World's Classics are available from all good bookshops. In case of difficulty, customers in the UK should contact Oxford University Press Bookshop, 116 High Street, Oxford OX1 4BR.